SOVEREIGNT

SOVEREIGNTY MATTERS

Locations of Contestation and Possibility in Indigenous Struggles for Self-Determination

EDITED BY

Joanne Barker

University of Nebraska Press • Lincoln and London

The following articles have been reproduced with permission of the author and publisher. The articles by Childs, Kauanui, and Perez were written originally for this volume but have since been published elsewhere.

Taiaiake Alfred, "Sovereignty." In *A Companion to American Indian History*, ed. Philip J. Deloria and Neal Salisbury (New York: Blackwell Publishers, 2002).

John Brown Childs, "Crossroads: Toward a Transcommunal Black History Month." In *Annales du Monde Anglophone: Écritures de l'Histoire Africaine Amèricaine*, ed. Hélène Le Dantec-Lowry and Arlette Frund (Paris: Institut du Monde Anglophone de la Sorbonne Nouvelle and Éditions L'Harmattan, 2003).

J. Kehaulani Kauanui, "The Politics of Blood and Sovereignty in *Rice v. Cayetano.*" *Political and Legal Anthropology Review* 25, no. 1 (2002): 110 28.

Michael P. Perez, "Contested Sites: Pacific Resistance in Guam to U.S. Empire." *Amerasia Journal* 27, no. 1 (2001): 97–115.

Library of Congress Cataloging-in-Publication Data
Sovereignty matters : locations of contestation and possibility in indigenous struggles for self-determination / edited by Joanne Barker.
p. cm.
Chiefly papers presented at a conference entitled "Sovereignty 2000: Locations of Contestation and Possibility" held May 2000 at the University of California, Santa Cruz.
Includes bibliographical references and index.
ISBN-13: 978-0-8032-6251-5 (pbk. : alk. paper)
ISBN-10: 0-8032-6251-5 (pbk. : alk. paper)
1. Indians—Politics and government. 2. Indians—Government relations. 3. Indigenous peoples—Pacific Area—Politics and government. 4. Indigenous peoples—Pacific Area—Government relations. 5. Self-determination, National. 6. Sovereignty. I. Barker, Joanne, 1962– . II. Series.
E59.P73S68 2005 320.1'5'089–dc22
2005016499

Contents

Acknowledgments

In many ways this anthology would not have come together if not for Alfreda Mitre (Southern Paiute). In May of 2000, she and I co-organized a conference at the University of California, Santa Cruz (UCSC) called "Sovereignty 2000: Locations of Contestation and Possibility." Working with the support of the staff of the Cultural Studies Institute and the students, faculty, and staff of the Native American Studies Research Cluster, we assembled a program that would include a culturally and politically diverse range of indigenous scholars, leaders, activists, and cultural producers. As former chair of the Las Vegas Paiute, Alfreda is respected among California Indian tribes, and this allowed us to secure their participation and sponsorship from the beginning. Their support, in turn, welcomed many other participants and attendees from around the world.

The two-day program included longer sessions with keynote speakers, to allow for dialogue, with a second day of breakout panels. The speakers we secured included Dore Beitz (Northern/Southern MeWuk), founder and director of the California Indian Lands Office, who was scheduled to speak about California Indian land rights issues but was unable to attend; Jack D. Forbes (Powhatan, Lenape), professor emeritus of Native American studies (NAS) at the University of California, Davis (UCD), who addressed the issue of sovereignty in the education system; Debra Harry (Northern Paiute), executive director of the Indigenous People's Council on Biocolonialism, who discussed the politics of the Human Genome Diversity Project; Inés Hernández-Aacutevila (Chicana/Nez Perce), professor of NAS at UCD, who examined language recovery projects in Mexico; Mark Macarro (Pechanga), tribal chairman of the Pechanga Band of Luiseño (Temecula, California), who reviewed California Indian gaming politics; Glenn T. Morris (Shawnee), associate professor of political science at the University of Colorado, Denver, who analyzed the discourse of colonialism in U.S. federal law; Anthony R. Pico (Kumeyaay), tribal chairman of the Viejas Band of the Kumeyaay Nation, who talked about the relationship between gaming and sovereignty; Mililani B. Trask (Native Hawaiian), then trustee-at-large for the Office of Hawaiian Affairs, who was scheduled to speak about international law but was unable to attend; Hulleah J. Tsinhnahjinnie (Seminole, Muskogee, Dine), photographer and writer, who analyzed the politics of representation; and Stefano

Varese, professor of NAS at UCD, who talked about local strategies for self-determination. Additionally, Pico organized the closing panel with Rick Hill (Oneida), then chair of the National Indian Gaming Association, and Ivan Makil, president of the Salt River Pima Maricopa, to participate. Clarence Atwell, tribal chair of the Santa Rosa Rancheria Tachi Yokut, gave the opening blessing.

Once we secured the keynote speakers, we put out a call for papers. Panel participants included Leonie Pihama, Fiona Cram, and Donna Gardiner (all Maori), who addressed their cultural views on biodiversity; Robert J. Miller (Eastern Shawnee Tribe of Oklahoma) and David Harrison (Athabascan, Chickaloon Village, Alaska), who spoke to the politics of cultural self-determination in whaling and fishing rights; Linda Rose Locklear (Lumbee) and Kathryn S. Clenney (Blackfoot), who discussed online strategies for representing sovereignty struggles; Monique Sonoquie (Chumash, Apache, Zapotec), who screened and discussed her documentary, *The Sovereignty Tour 1997*; Déborah Berman Santana (Puerto Rican/Boricua) and Michael Perez (Chamorro), who spoke about struggles in Puerto Rico and Guam; J. Kehaulani Kauanui (Native Hawaiian) and myself, who addressed the racialization of indigenous citizenship in federal law and tribal membership criteria; Brian Blancke and Bianca Wulff, who spoke about strategies for conflict resolution in land rights struggles; John Brown Childs (Massachuset/Brothertown-Oneida/Madagascan) and Guillermo Delgado-P. (Quechua), who addressed pedagogical issues; Mereana Taki (Ngaiterangi/Te Arawa, Maori), Helen Potter (Maniapoto, Maori), and Glenis Philip-Barbara (Ngati Porou, Maori), who examined Maori theories of self-determination; and Dan Taulapapa McMullin (Samoan), who discussed U.S. colonization of Samoa and read from his play, *The Shark in the Woods*.

The diverse geography of nations, debates, and cultural and political perspectives represented by the speakers and participants was never intended to be exhaustive (a colonial strategy that promises objective comprehension over subjects that can be mastered). Other geographies and conversations exist. The conference was one instance of the ongoing political and cultural alliances and conversations about what sovereignty means as a category of scholarship, activism, and cultural production among indigenous peoples in the Americas and the Pacific. It marked the existence of a particular set of debates and struggles and served as a forum for indigenous scholars, leaders, activists, and cultural producers to think with one another about concrete strategies for solidarity and change.

After the conference, participants were invited to contribute their essays to the anthology. We also invited additional contributors whose work has addressed sovereignty; Taiaiake Alfred (Mohawk) and Kilipaka Kawaihonu Nahili Pae Ontai (Native Hawaiian) responded with their important essays. The review and publishing process is a long one and unfortunately we lost some individual essays along the way to the demands of work and life. I detail the conference program to acknowledge the importance of those individuals to the discussions that took place there and that impacted the final configuration of the work here.

Special thanks to Karen Anton, graduate student in ethnic studies at San Francisco State University, for assistance with the index.

To all our relations, and the future we create in our writing, this work is dedicated.

SOVEREIGNTY MATTERS

Joanne Barker (Lenape)

For Whom Sovereignty Matters

As a category of scholarship, activism, governance, and cultural work, sovereignty matters in consequential ways to understanding the political agendas, strategies, and cultural perspectives of indigenous peoples in the Americas and the Pacific. This is not to suggest that all indigenous peoples within these diverse regions share the same understanding of what sovereignty is or how it matters, nor that all of their concerns and labor can be reduced to sovereignty as a kind of raison d'être. Rather, following World War II, sovereignty emerged not as a new but as a particularly valued term within indigenous discourses to signify a multiplicity of legal and social rights to political, economic, and cultural self-determination. It was a term around which social movements formed and political agendas for decolonization and social justice were articulated. It has come to mark the complexities of global indigenous efforts to reverse ongoing experiences of colonialism as well as to signify local efforts at the reclamation of specific territories, resources, governments, and cultural knowledge and practices.

At the same time and owing much to its proliferation, sovereignty has become notoriously generalized to stand in for all of the inherent rights of indigenous peoples. Certainly many take for granted what sovereignty means and how it is important. As a result sovereignty can be both confused and confusing, especially as its normalization masks its own ideological origins in colonial legal-religious discourses as well as the heterogeneity of its contemporary histories, meanings, and identities for indigenous peoples.

Origins

In "Self-Determination and the Concept of Sovereignty," Lakota scholar Vine Deloria, Jr., writes that sovereignty originated as a theological term within early east Asian and European discourses: "Sovereignty is an ancient idea, once used to describe both the power and arbitrary nature of the deity by peoples in the Near East. Although originally a theological term it was appropriated by European political thinkers in the centuries following the Reformation to characterize the person of the King as head of the state."[1] The king, or the sovereign, was thought to have inherited the authority to rule from God. This "divine right" was understood to be absolute, a power that was accountable only to the god from whom it originated.[2] The power was manifested specifically within the authority of the king to make war and govern domestic affairs (frequently in the name of God).[3]

The Protestant and Catholic churches, however, were also important governing powers during the early uses of sovereignty and consequently church doctrine impacted its meaning. The churches understood their roles as both the translators of the laws of God to the people and as governing the people's adherence to those laws, work sometimes interfered with or undermined by the king. Competing claims of legitimacy and sanction to speak for God and to rule over God's subjects between the church and the king, and between Protestants and Catholics, characterized the early politico-theological debates over sovereignty and who was sovereign. The church maintained that only God was the true sovereign and the church was the medium of God's will on earth, while the king claimed to be a sovereign who inherited from God the right to rule. While both understood sovereignty as an absolute power to govern, the views were diametrically opposed as to its revelation and exercise.

The powers of the church and the king slowly gave way through various political revolutions against the tyrannies of dogma and kingdoms to the ideologies and structures of the nation. The nation reorganized concepts of social status and responsibility from the obligations of subjects either of the church or of the kingdom to notions of citizenship, civil society, and democracy. In some of the early debates, it was argued that sovereignty emanated from individuals (citizens).[4] Individuals possessed rights to personal freedoms that informed their collective rights to rule themselves as nations. In other debates, sovereignty was linked to the "law of nations." Therein nations were based on the collective rights of individuals to civil society, life, happiness, property, justice, and defense; nations held rights to be free, independent, and respected as equals in the pursuit of securing the collective rights of their citizens.[5] In both kinds of debates, sovereignty was about figuring out the relationship between the rights and obligations of individuals (citizens) and the rights and obligations of nations (states). Sovereignty seemed to belong to nations but was then understood to originate either from the people who made up those nations or as a character of the nation itself (nationhood).[6] The former assertion has defined the work of contemporary indigenous scholars and activists, who have argued that sovereignty emanates from the unique identity and culture of peoples and is therefore an inherent and inalienable right of peoples to the qualities customarily associated with nations.[7] The latter assertion has dominated legal debates over how nations exercise their sovereignty in relation to one another.[8]

In time the nation would be characterized by rights to "exclusive jurisdiction, territorial integrity, and nonintervention in domestic affairs," and these rights would be correlated to concepts of sovereignty.[9] The rights to jurisdiction and territory were modeled on concepts of individual personal freedom and linked to both secular and Christian ideologies about civilization.[10] Unaffiliated individuals, or individuals in kin groups, were believed to live in baser states of nature according to the demands of survival and dictates of instinct. They merely roamed upon the lands to acquire the material goods needed to survive. Social groups emerged as individuals or kin groups recognized their need for help and took on the responsibilities of aiding one another toward achieving their mutual goals for survival. Nations formed when social groups developed higher aspirations for civil society and government. Depending on the theorist, civility was evidenced by the existence of reason, social contract, agriculture, property, technology, Christianity, monogamy, and/or the structures and operations of statehood. These aspects of society or civilization were associated with the possession of sovereignty. Nations possessed the full measure of sovereignty because they were the highest form of civilization; individuals roaming uncultivated lands did not possess either civilization or sovereignty.[11]

In Christian ideology the dichotomy was not between the uncivil and civil but between the unbelieving and believing, though it would be false to suggest that these terms were mutually exclusive. The uncivil was equated with the unbelieving, the civil with the believing.[12] These associations were grounded in the projects of colonization and the congruous objectives of the nation and the church to civilize/christianize the uncivil/nonbelieving world in the name of God and the manifest destiny of the nation. In fact missionaries often went before and worked within the processes of establishing trade routes and military bases with national militaries in the name of extending God's kingdom on earth.[13] While some individual missionaries were highly critical of the colonial project and the church's complicity with the genocide and enslavement of indigenous peoples, the church as a sociopolitical institution consistently advanced and acted upon the notion of the rights of believers over those of nonbelievers, both to lands and resources and to existence as peoples.

The church even helped to sort through rival national interests over the rights to "discover" specific territories and exploit indigenous labor located therein. In many instances it is impossible to talk about a difference between the interests of the church and of the nation.[14] Many have argued, in fact, that the claim to the separation of church and state is ideologically and politically hypocritical.[15]

Out of the political and theological debates about what constituted the nation, debates deeply embedded within the ideologies and activities of colonialism, modern international law was defined as such. The two primary vehicles that served for the articulation of international legal precepts about nationhood, and so of the sovereignty with which such a character was defined, were the national constitution and the treaty. The constitution functioned as a document of nation formation and was used by colonists, rebellions, and commonwealths to assert territorial boundaries and the authority and terms of the nation-so-formed to govern within them. Yet the declarative status of the constitution disguised the fact that the nation so defined was contingent upon it being recognized as legitimate by other already recognized nations. Therefore custom within international law emerged around the treaty as a mechanism for both the exercise of nationhood and the recognition of national sovereignty. Treaties required that they be honored as legally binding compacts or agreements between nations, as the terms would be understood by the signatories. Nations recognized each other's status as nations by entering into treaties with each other. Territorial boundaries and jurisdiction dominated the specific articles of treaties throughout the colonial period. So too did peace, rights of passage, alliance in instances when other nations breached boundaries or interfered with government operations (i.e., broken treaties), and the like. The integrity of the exercise of nationhood and the recognition of sovereignty by treaty depended, of course, on the nation's honoring of the treaties into which it entered. However, because nationhood and sovereignty were interlocked through the entire discursive apparatus of treaty making, the recognition of one implied the recognition of the other.[16]

Inflections

Nations certainly put sovereignty to work during the colonization of the Americas and the Pacific to justify—by explanation or denial—the dispossession, enslavement, and genocide of indigenous peoples. In Australia, it was inflected through the doctrine of discovery to justify the complete dispossession of Aborigines from their lands and the outright refusal by the colonists to enter into treaties with them. In Canada sovereignty was invoked to defend the use of military force, such as happened in the territories of Newfoundland and Nova Scotia, where most indigenous peoples were massacred by colonists during early conflicts over territorial rights.[17] In the southwestern region of the United States and northern parts of Mexico, it informed the efforts of the church to have the enslavement and conversion of nonbelievers supported by the military—first by Spain, then by Mexico, and later by an emergent immigrant class that would reform themselves as a state of the union.[18] In each instance the concept of sovereignty served the colonists in negating indigenous territorial rights and humanity while justifying the right of conquest by claims to national superiority.

The question that follows is whether the sovereignty of indigenous peoples was ever really recognized within international customary or documentary law. England, France, Canada, New Zealand, and the United States certainly negotiated, signed, and ratified treaties with indigenous peoples. Many have noted, however, that such efforts were less about the recognition and provision for the *sovereignty* of indigenous peoples than they were about the assertion of the respective nations' status as the more powerful sovereign within a given territory, against other European powers and over indigenous peoples.[19] Given the fact that every single treaty signed with indigenous peoples in the Americas and the Pacific was broken, it would seem to be so. England, France, Canada, New Zealand, and the United States used the treaty-making process to neutralize the political force of allied and individual indigenous groups and then deployed specific articles of signed treaties to secure the right over and against other European countries to relate with, trade, and govern with those groups as a matter of domestic policy. They understood perfectly well the precedence within international law that defined sovereignty through the attributes of territorial integrity and jurisdiction, and they were hardly likely ever to acquiesce these principles to indigenous peoples, by treaty or otherwise.

Yet the fact remains that indigenous peoples were recognized by England, France, Canada, New Zealand, and the United States as constituting nations that possessed rights to sovereignty—by treaty, by constitution, by legislative action, and by court ruling. Even U.S. Chief Justice John Marshall conceded that terms like *nation*, *sovereign*, and *treaty* had been used in colonial and U.S. law in reference to American Indian tribes and that the U.S. Supreme Court was therefore obligated to adhere to the internationally accepted definitions of those terms in relating to the tribes as independent sovereigns.[20] This is remarkable given the ideological force of theories of civilization and Christian theology that worked against the acknowledgment that indigenous peoples possessed any such rights on the grounds that they lacked proper civility or belief in God. Still, adherence to the tenets of international law and Christian theology demanded that particular steps be taken in securing desired territories and claiming jurisdiction therein. European nations were required to treat with indigenous peoples in order to secure lands by cession and purchase; treaties resulted.

The contradictions within recognition-by-treaty histories are not in the moments of alleged adherence to international law by the nations of Europe and North America, who had to follow customary practices by entering into treaties with indigenous peoples in order that their territorial claims in the colonies be respected by one another. The blatant contradictions are between the recognition of the sovereignty of indigenous peoples through the entire apparatus of treaty making and the unmitigated negation of indigenous peoples' status and rights by national legislation, military action, and judicial decision.

The "Marshall trilogy"—*Johnson v. McIntosh* (1823), *Cherokee Nation v. Georgia* (1831), and *Worcester v. Georgia* (1832)—is probably one of the most important instances of these incongruities.[21] The trilogy provided the first substantive definition of sovereignty for American Indians by the U.S. judiciary and subsequently served to establish precedence for the trust relationship between the U.S. federal government and American Indian tribes (and, since 1972, Alaskan Native villages and, since 1920, Native Hawaiians). The way that the trilogy was taken up by England's Colonial Office in directing relations with indigenous peoples in Canada, New Zealand, and Australia signifies much about the international exchange of ideas regarding the character and rights of sovereignty for the nations of Europe and North America as well as the attempt to justify the denial of that status and rights for indigenous peoples.[22] The subjugation of indigenous peoples to U.S. plenary power through Marshall's fictionalized accounting of the doctrine of discovery provided the Colonial Office with the legal precedence it needed to justify its colonization of North America and the Pacific.

Johnson v. McIntosh involved competing claims to a single parcel of land in the state of Illinois between Johnson, who had acquired a deed to the land from the Piankeshaw, and McIntosh, who had acquired a deed to the land from the United States. It was determined that the Piankeshaw were in possession of the land when they issued the deed, as evidenced by two treaties that had been signed with the Illinois and Piankeshaw tribes in 1773 and 1775 over the lands in question. It was also determined that the U.S. had acquired title to those lands by those same treaties and subsequently had sold the parcel to McIntosh (there was a dispute in the case over whether the parcel was located within the ceded area, but it was ruled that it had been).

The immediate question before the Supreme Court, as Marshall framed it in his opinion, was what kind of title the Piankeshaw had in the lands. Obviously it was a title that they could treat upon. Within the customs of international law, treaties implied nationhood and so sovereignty and so inherent territorial rights. While not missing the import of such links, Marshall sided with the defendant, whose argument he summarized as follows:

> The uniform understanding and practice of European nations, and the settled law, as laid down by the tribunals of civilized states, denied the right of the Indians to be considered as independent communities, having a permanent property in the soil, capable of alienation to private individuals. They remain in a state of nature, and have never been admitted into the general society of nations. All the treaties and negotiations between the civilized powers of Europe and of this continent, from the treaty of Utrecht, in 1713, to that of Ghent, in 1814, have uniformly disregarded their supposed right to the territory included within the jurisdictional limits of those powers. Not only has the practice of all civilized nations been in conformity with this doctrine, but the whole theory of their titles to lands in America, rests upon the hypothesis, that the Indians had no right of soil as sovereign, independent states.[23]

Effectively, Marshall rewrote treaty history by ruling that the treaties signed between American Indians and European powers functioned in a way contrary to the precepts of existing international law. Instead of recognizing the sovereignty of Indians, Marshall argued that the treaties had "disregarded" Indian land rights and so the status of Indians as "sovereign, independent states." Marshall's evidence for this "disregard" was not located within the fact or provision of the treaties but by the doctrine of discovery.

According to Marshall, the doctrine established that American Indians were not the full sovereigns of the lands that they possessed but were rather the users of the lands that they roamed and wandered over for purposes of shelter and sustenance. This distinction was informed by European worldviews, particularly the theories of English philosopher John Locke, who argued that hunter-gatherer societies "might have property in what they found or captured . . . but not in the land over which they traveled in its pursuit."[24]

While it was accepted that Indians maintained particular rights associated with their status as the original inhabitants of the land, the exclusive rights of property in the land belonged to the nation who discovered the lands. Discovery was demonstrated by the appropriation of the lands for agriculture, which in turn secured the rights of the discovering nation to claim full sovereignty within the lands and against all other claims:

> Discovery is the foundation of title, in European nations, and this overlooks all proprietary rights in the natives. The sovereignty and eminent domain thus acquired, necessarily precludes the idea of any other sovereignty existing within the same limits. The subjects of the discovering nation must necessarily be bound by the declared sense of their own government, as to the extent of this sovereignty, and the domain acquired with it. Even if it should be admitted that the Indians were originally an independent people, they have ceased to be so. A nation that has passed under the dominion of another, is no longer a sovereign state. The same treaties and negotiations, before referred to, show their dependent condition.[25]

From the Lockean hunter-gatherer/agriculturalist dichotomy, and with the correlation in international law between sovereignty, jurisdiction, and territorial rights in hand, it followed in Marshall's reasoning that by virtue of their relationship to the land as hunter-gatherers, Indians had been made "subject to the sovereignty of the United States."[26] These were well-established facts, Marshall contended, of colonial law, which had treated Indians "as an inferior race of people, without the privileges of citizens, and under the perpetual protection and pupilage of the government" on the basis that they were not in full possession of the lands upon which they roamed and wandered.[27]

In lieu of full title to or property in the lands, Marshall offered "aboriginal title" as the legal definition for the kinds of rights that Indians had in the lands. This title presupposed their relationship to the lands as hunters-gatherers. It was "a mere right of usufruct and habitation, without power of alienation."[28] All "civilized nations" were "founded on this principle" and distinction.[29] No civilized person, Marshall went on, would expect those who had appropriated the lands for agriculture, and thereby acquired full title to the lands by right of discovery, to give up the lands to "natives" who merely wandered over them in search of materials to satisfy their immediate needs for clothing, shelter, and sustenance:

> By the law of nature, [Indians] had not acquired a fixed property capable of being transferred. The measure of property acquired by occupancy is determined, according to the law of nature, by the extent

> of men's wants, and their capacity of using it to supply them. It is a violation of the rights of others to exclude them from the use of what we do not want, and they have an occasion for. Upon this principle the North American Indians could have acquired no proprietary interest in the vast tracts of territory which they wandered over; and their right to the lands on which they hunted, could not be considered as superior to that which is acquired to the sea by fishing in it. The use in the one case, as well as the other, is not exclusive. According to every theory of property, the Indians had no individual rights to land; nor had they any collectively, or in their national capacity; for the lands occupied by each tribe were not used by them in such a manner as to prevent their being appropriated by a people of cultivators. All the proprietary rights of civilized nations on this continent are founded on this principle. The right derived from discovery and conquest, can rest on no other basis; and all existing titles depend on the fundamental title of the crown by discovery.[30]

Marshall's "aboriginal title" was directly at odds with the treaty-making efforts of the United States at the time. The treaty most certainly did recognize a title in the land that could be negotiated as well as the authority of the signatories to function as representatives of their governments. Under the precepts of international law, the 371 treaties ratified between the United States and indigenous peoples between 1778 and 1871 provided for the clear recognition of indigenous peoples as nations who could enter into treaties and, therefore, as nations who possessed jurisdiction and territorial rights. Yet Marshall's ruling in *Johnson v. McIntosh* maintained that indigenous peoples did not possess the kind of title in the lands that they could be and were negotiating by treaty.[31]

In 1830 the state of Georgia passed "an act to prevent the exercise of assumed and arbitrary power by all persons under pretext of authority from the Cherokee Indians, &c." The act sectioned Indian lands into state county districts, set up a process for state citizens to acquire individual parcels by lottery, required non-Indians to possess state permits to reside on Indian lands, declared all Indian laws null and void, outlawed public gatherings of Indians, and forbade the testimony of Indians against whites in court. The immediate impetus for the act was the discovery of gold on Cherokee lands in 1828, but the more foundational purpose was Georgia's aim, quickly followed by Alabama and Mississippi, to gain jurisdictional controls over Indian lands and to dissolve the political and economic clout of the powerful Cherokee.

With the support of their own multilingual lawyers educated in eastern U.S. universities, and diplomatic teams in Washington DC and London, the Cherokee sought an injunction against Georgia to stop it from applying laws that were obviously intended to "annihilate the Cherokee as a political society and to seize for the use of Georgia the lands of the nation which have been assured to them by the United States in solemn treaties."[32] The request for the injunction went before the Supreme Court.

In their arguments the lawyers for the Cherokee maintained that the Cherokee were a sovereign nation and that, as such, Georgia's laws could not be unilaterally enforced upon them. They based their arguments on the fact that the Cherokee had entered into treaty relations with the United States and so were a sovereign nation under the precepts of international law as well as according to the specific provisions of the treaties that provided for the protection of Cherokee rights by the U.S. government because of the Cherokee's demonstrated status as sovereigns.

The Supreme Court did not miss the implications of the Cherokee argument. Negating the significance of U.S. treaties signed with the Cherokee that suggested they possessed a sovereignty akin to that of the United States or European nations under the customs of international law, Marshall turned instead to article I, section 8, paragraph 3 of the U.S. Constitution to render his opinion. The article provides that the federal branch of the U.S. government has the sole right and responsibility "to regulate Commerce with foreign Nations, and among the several States, and with the Indian tribes." Marshall argued that the clause intended to show a legal distinction between the categories of sovereigns that it employed—foreign nations, state governments, and Indian tribes. The task before the Court was to enumerate the distinction of "Indians tribes."

Assuming that "Indian tribes" were not foreign nations or state governments, Marshall posited that they were instead "domestic dependent nations" whose relationship to the U.S. federal government, as the juridical power charged with regulating commerce and collateral issues with them, was like that "of a ward to a guardian." These two enumerations—domestic dependent nationhood and the ward/guardian analogy—would set the legal precedence for defining relations between the United States and indigenous peoples.

Translated in subsequent court decisions and legislative action as the plenary power doctrine and trust or protectorate relationship, Marshall's concepts sought to secure U.S. interests in controlling indigenous peoples and their lands by defining their relationship to the United States as wholly subjected and conquered. Removed from the realm of the "foreign," "Indian tribes" were likewise removed from the realm of international law, breaking any implied link between treaties, nationhood, sovereignty, territorial integrity, and jurisdiction that the United States would be obligated to recognize in Indians. Indian tribes were to be related to as "domestic" political entities whose specific rights to territorial integrity and jurisdiction were under the sole guardianship of the U.S. government. This allowed the United States to assume authority for representing tribal interests in matters of international law as well as to control the terms of the exercise of tribal sovereignty in the realm of domestic politics. Marshall effectively "passed [the Indian tribes] under" the governing authority of the United States and so made them "dependent" on U.S. protection from foreign and state interests.

Since under the U.S. Constitution only foreign nations can sue state governments before the Supreme Court, Marshall unsurprisingly denied the Cherokee request for an injunction against Georgia's laws on the basis that they were not a "foreign nation." Concerned about the legal implications of the decision, the Cherokee strategized a case that would force the Supreme Court to some accounting for the fact of U.S. treaty history with the Cherokee as a sovereign nation.

Missionaries Samuel A. Worcester, Elizur Butler, James Trott, Samuel Mays, Surry Eaton, Austin Copeland, and Edward D. Losure broke Georgia's newly passed law requiring that non-Indians possess a state license in order to reside on Indian lands. They were tried in state court and sentenced to four years of hard labor. Worcester appealed to the Supreme Court.

The same counsel from *Cherokee Nation v. Georgia* argued in *Worcester v. Georgia* that Worcester had entered Cherokee territory as a missionary under the authority of the U.S. president and with the approval of the Cherokee. They claimed that "the State of Georgia ought not to maintain the prosecution, as several treaties had been entered into by the United States with the Cherokee Nation by which that Nation was acknowledged to be a sovereign nation, and by which the territory occupied by them was guaranteed to them by the United States."[33] They further claimed that "the laws of Georgia under which the plaintiff in error was indicted are repugnant to the treaties, and unconstitutional and void, and also that they are repugnant to the Act of Congress of March, 1802, entitled 'An act to regulate trade and intercourse with the Indian Tribes.'"[34]

The Court recognized that the arguments made by the plaintiffs called into question not only the validity of Georgia's laws but "the validity of the treaties made by the United States with the Cherokee Indians."[35] The Court also acknowledged that the case raised questions about the jurisdictional authority of the Cherokee within their own territories and in relationship to Georgia as provided for by U.S. treaty and federal statute. Did states have jurisdiction over Indian tribes? Could states make laws regulating the status and rights of Indian tribes over and against federal law? The Cherokee argued that they could not. They contended that they enjoyed a special relationship to the U.S. federal government because they were a sovereign nation, proven by the fact that since 1785 they had entered into twelve treaties with the government that would constitute the United States.[36]

To render the Court's opinion, Marshall returned to the doctrine of discovery to establish that the United States possessed full title in the lands and, by implication, over the peoples residing within them. As in *Johnson v. McIntosh*, he traced the passage of title from the colonists to England to the United States in order to demonstrate U.S. property in the lands and commensurate plenary power over the lands (again representing the Cherokee as "roaming" and "wandering" over the lands and not as agriculturalists with established rights of property in the soil—a representation in direct contradiction with the known history and culture of the Cherokee as agriculturalists).

Marshall then turned to the Treaty of Hopewell, signed in 1785 with the Cherokee, to prove that the Cherokee acknowledged not only that they were "under the protection of the United States of America, and of no other power" but that they had benefited directly from said protections as evidenced by the subsequent treaties they signed with the United States.[37] (In other words, that the Cherokee kept signing treaties with the United States proved to Marshall that they not only benefited from said relations but were acknowledging the United States as the more powerful sovereign in the territory.) Consequently, Marshall purported, the Cherokee were not a sovereign equal in political status and rights to the United States, as might be suggested by the conventions of international law regarding the relationship between signatories. Rather, the Cherokee were a sovereign possessing partial or limited powers as dependent wards under the more supreme governing authority that it had recognized and benefited from in the United States.

Next Marshall addressed the matter of the Cherokee's relationship to Georgia as a state of the union. He argued that Georgia, as all states, recognized by their own statutes that it was the federal government that held exclusive rights and responsibilities to regulate relations with the Indian tribes "with which no state could interfere" by virtue of the U.S. Constitution's commerce clause. He concluded: "The Cherokee nation, then, is a distinct community, occupying its own territory, with boundaries accurately described, in which the laws of Georgia can have no force, and which the citizens of Georgia have no right to enter but with the assent of the Cherokees themselves, or in conformity with treaties and with the acts of Congress. The whole intercourse between the United States and this nation is, by our Constitution and laws, vested in the Government of the United States."[38]

The Court ruled that Georgia's 1830 act interfered with relations between the United States and the Cherokee, "the regulation of which, according to the settled principles of our Constitution, is committed exclusively to the Government of the Union." Marshall declared that Georgia's act was "in direct hostility with treaties, repeated in a succession of years, which mark out the boundary that separates the Cherokee country from Georgia; guaranty to them all the land within their boundary; solemnly pledge the faith of the United States to restrain their citizens from trespassing on it; and recognise the pre-existing power of the Nation to govern itself." Georgia's act was found to be "in equal hostility with the acts of Congress for regulating this intercourse and giving effect to the treaties." Marshall concluded that Georgia's laws were "unconstitutional and void" and granted Worcester a full pardon.[39]

Many have noted that U.S. president Andrew Jackson, who was instrumental in the passage of the Indian Removal Act of 1830, was so enraged by Marshall's opinion that he uttered something to the effect that Marshall had made his laws, let him enforce them. Jackson refused to send in the troops needed to defend Cherokee territory against Georgia's retaliatory encroachment and instead sent in commissioners to negotiate treaties for Cherokee removal to Indian Territory.[40]

Despite the superficial appearance of conflict in the Supreme Court's opinions in the Marshall trilogy, the decisions were in perfect keeping with the colonial objectives of the U.S. government at the time, a government that aimed to abrogate the means and abilities of Indian tribes to maintain their jurisdiction and territorial rights. The configuration of "Indian tribes" as being under the governing authority of the United States was neither adverse to nor undermining of the ultimate objective to dissolve Indian governments and dispossess Indians of their territories. And it certainly was not unique.

European nations likewise constructed themselves as sovereigns with abject rights to claim jurisdictional authority and territorial rights over indigenous peoples in their colonies throughout the Americas and the Pacific. The specific claims and exercises of their sovereign powers—militarily and otherwise—made almost incestuous use of each other's laws and policies to justify the dispossession, enslavement, and genocide of "their Indians." This is reflected in the opinions of Marshall's trilogy—which claimed that Indians had "passed under" U.S. plenary power, which in turn had a trust responsibility to govern the Indians as a matter of domestic policy—and in the ways that these rulings were taken up by England's Colonial Office to justify the usurpation of indigenous territorial rights in Canada, Australia, and New Zealand.[41]

Though informed by international debates, no previous legislative or court decision had defined the "doctrine of discovery" as such.[42] Marshall invoked it as though it were a well-founded legal principle of international law. It took on the force of precedence because Marshall invented a legal history that gave it that status. In this history, Marshall defined "aboriginal title," "domestic dependent nations," plenary power, and trust as inevitable evolutionary legal principles of a civilized state. The history constructed indigenous peoples under the civilized governing authority of the United States. In this tale, the United States, as all progressing nations, was charged with the demands of adhering to the principles of international law but also burdened with the responsibilities of civilizing/Christianizing Indians into those more civilized/Christian legal beliefs and practices.

The entire self-fulfilling narrative of legal, moral, and social superiority offered in such claims to doctrine as Marshall's discovery reinvented a sovereignty for indigenous peoples that was void of any of the associated rights to self-government, territorial integrity, and cultural autonomy that would have been affiliated with it in international law at the time.[43] In junction with the fact that the specific story Marshall told affirmed British and then U.S. title to the lands in North America on the basis of the legal precedence of discovery that it fictionalized, it is unsurprising that Marshall's trilogy was taken up by the Colonial Office in England to direct relations with indigenous peoples and its colonists in Canada and the Pacific. As in the United States, these relations were embedded with the ideologies of race, culture, and identity that legitimated the narratives.[44]

In response to the perceived problems with the colonial rebellion in the United States, and settler violence against indigenous peoples in Canada, Australia, New Zealand, and the Cape Colony, the Colonial Office established a firm "rule of law" framework for developing its guidelines for colonization.[45] Colonies were expected to adhere to the letter of the law, not to interpret the law according to their own want or personal interest.[46] However, geographical distance made it virtually impossible for the Colonial Office to oversee, let alone enforce, its guidelines. The result was an incredibly incongruous relationship between England, its colonies, and indigenous peoples.

The primary legal point of reference for the Colonial Office was the British Royal Proclamation of 1763. The Proclamation was issued by King George III after the cession of New France to England by the Treaty of Paris. Basically it determined English territorial boundaries and the terms for trade and governance within the Americas. In relationship to indigenous peoples, it asserted that the Crown possessed the sole right to acquire indigenous lands and prohibited the purchasing of lands by individuals from indigenous peoples. This directive necessitated that England enter into treaties with indigenous peoples in order to acquire title to desired areas before settlement.[47] Though not a law, the Proclamation was given the force of law by legislative action and court rulings in North America and the Pacific (including Marshall's trilogy).

Despite the Proclamation's directive, lands were occupied by English colonists without the required treaties in place. Violence against indigenous peoples occurred as individual colonies usurped lands from indigenous peoples and/or protected their interests to remain on lands they had illegally seized. The Aborigines in Australia, Maori in New Zealand, Beothuk in Newfoundland, and Tasmanians of Tasmania were some of the groups almost exterminated by colonists ignoring their own policy.[48]

In the 1830s and 1840s, Sir James Stephen was under-secretary of the Colonial Office (he had worked in the office as a legal advisor since the 1810s). Believing that the immediate genocide of Australian Aborigines had been "immoral," he turned to Marshall's opinion in *Johnson v. McIntosh* to help him write guidelines for William Hobson, the British consul in New Zealand, to treat with the Maori.[49]

> It [*Johnson v. McIntosh*] shows that the whole Territory over which those Tribes wandered was to be regarded as the property of the British Crown in right of discovery and conquest—and that the Indians were mere possessors of the soil on suffrance. Such is American Law. The British law in Canada is far more humane, for there the Crown purchases of the Indians before it grants to its own subjects. . . . Besides what is this to the case of New Zealand? The Dutch, not we, discovered it. Nearly a hundred years ago Captain Cook landed there, and claimed the Sovereignty for King George III. Nothing has ever been done to maintain and keep alive that claim. The most solemn Acts have been done in repudiation and disavowal of it. Besides the New Zealanders are not wandering Tribes, but bodies of men, till lately, very populous, who have a settled form of Government, and who have divided and appropriated the whole Territory amongst them. They are not huntsmen, but after their rude fashion, Agriculturalists.[50]

Stephen's invocation of *Johnson v. McIntosh* is based on Marshall's affirmation of the preeminence of English title within North America, as the first discoverers (agriculturalists), and of the Proclamation as the force of law in determining title. These affirmations were required by Marshall in order to make the claim that the passage of title from England to the United States had established U.S. entitlement to the lands and to jurisdiction over and within them. The rationale served English interests. Far more interesting than the predictably flippant remarks about "American Law" and the superiority of English civility over American barbarity in Stephen's directive is his treatment of the discovery doctrine as a well-established legal precept read back into the Proclamation and out of Marshall's opinion. This history provided Stephen with the legal framework that he needed in order to direct English colonists to treat with the natives as a distinction of English civilization. His directive concludes by ordering Hobson to treat with the Maori.[51] Hobson responded by initiating the negotiations that would result in the Treaty of Waitangi of 1840 (see Fiona Cram, "Backgrounding Maori Views on Genetic Engineering," this volume).[52]

Marshall's trilogy also influenced numerous Canadian court decisions. The discovery doctrine was taken as an extension of the principles set forth in the Proclamation, especially in regard to the notion that the Crown alone enjoyed the right to treat with and purchase lands from First Nation peoples.[53] As in the United States it was decided that title to lands that were unceded or unpurchased by treaty could still be found to have been "extinguished" if settlement within the area had progressed unfettered—a convenient displacement of the impact of overt military aggression and dispossession of indigenous peoples on the progress of said settlements. As in U.S. case history, this logic provided an efficient justification for Canadian nullification of "aboriginal title" by treaty, by purchase, or by the default of colonization.[54]

One of the other legacies of the Marshall trilogy was the configuration of indigenous peoples as welfare beneficiaries.[55] The notion that indigenous peoples are *weaker than*, *wards*, *dependent*, and *limited* in power in relation to their colonial states has perpetuated dominant ideologies of race, culture, and identity. Within these identificatory practices, "indigenous people" are marked as yet another ethnic group within the larger national melting pot, where the goal is to boil out cultural differences and the national jurisdictions and territorial boundaries of indigenous groups by boarding schools, farming programs, citizenship, and adoption.[56]

As I have argued elsewhere, the *making ethnic* or *ethnicization* of indigenous peoples has been a political strategy of the nation-state to erase the sovereign from the indigenous.[57] To the extent that the nation-state can maintain that indigenous peoples are nothing but welfare recipients under its trust, the very notion that indigenous peoples are members of sovereign political collectivities is made incomprehensible. This incomprehensibility works to collapse indigenous peoples into minority groups that make up the social rainbow of multicultural difference as a means of erasing their unique political status and rights under the precedence of international law.

The erasure of the sovereign is the racialization of the "Indian." These practices have had important consequences in shaping cultural perspectives about the relationship between indigenous identity and sovereignty, not only from the viewpoint of some dominant, privileged position but within indigenous communities as well.

On the one hand are all of the myriad social forces of oppression that have racialized (invented) an Indian identity that can be used to usurp indigenous sovereignty. These forces presuppose the legitimacy of an entire discourse of cultural authenticity, racial purity, and traditional integrity, which in turn legitimates assimilationist ideologies. In this discourse is the real Indian (the mythic full-blood traditionalist born and raised on the reservation in poverty and despair), romanticized as the last vestige of real Indian culture, and the fraud (the mythic mixed-blood urban Indian born and raised without any sense of Indian culture), demonized as the contaminant of all things Indian while serving as testimony to the successes of the colonial project. Nowhere in this discourse are real indigenous peoples permitted or heard to speak for themselves, and when they do, their self-definitions are incomprehensible.[58]

On the other hand are all of the ways that indigenous identity is foundational to the structure, exercise, and character of sovereignty. It is, in other words, impossible to separate Native Hawaiian identity from Native Hawaiian perspectives about and struggles for self-government; Chamorro identity from Chamorro struggles for jurisdictional integrity in Guam; Taíno identity from Taíno land rights; Makah identity from Makah whaling rights; Maori identity from Maori struggles for intellectual property rights. In the historical complexities and cultural richness and diversity of these and all indigenous communities is the truth of the heterogeneity of indigenous identity, not only in how indigenous peoples identify themselves and their cultures but in how their self-definitions inform the character of their unique political perspectives, agendas, and strategies for sovereignty.

Rearticulations

Following World War II *sovereignty* emerged as a particularly valued term within indigenous scholarship and social movements and through the media of cultural production. It was a term around which analyses of indigenous histories and cultures were organized and whereby indigenous activists articulated their agendas for social change. It was also a term through which indigenous artists represented their histories, cultures, and identities, often in opposition to the erasures of their sovereignty by dominant ideologies of race, culture, and nationalism coined in the discourses of eugenics and American patriotism.

This is not to say that the concept of sovereignty was new to indigenous peoples. Certainly by the early 1600s it was a familiar and often belligerent self-descriptive against relentless military invasions and the social forces of colonization. It was employed to claim nationhood status and so collective rights to territorial integrity and governance as well as to define a humanity that was denied by the discourses of missionization. For example, the adoption of the designation Five Civilized Tribes by the Cherokee, Muskogee (Creek), Choctaw, Chickasaw, and Seminole in relations with the United States was an interesting discursive maneuver in this regard.[59] So were the exchanges between the members of the Haudenosaunee Confederacy and early U.S. government leaders about democracy and personal freedom.[60] Paiute writer and activist Sara Hopkins Winnemucca wrote *Life among the Piutes* to make an intellectual intervention against assimilationist ideologies and toward affirming American Indian humanity, cultural vitality, and land rights.[61] These and other self-definitions by the status and rights of sovereignty disrupted the solidity of dominant representations of indigenous peoples as savage heathens.

One of the most important reasons why sovereignty took on renewed currency following World War II was the oppositional perspective it signified toward the racist ideologies of beneficiarism that settled national policies during the preceding assimilationist period. Sovereignty had come to represent a staunch political-juridical identity refuting the dominant notion that indigenous peoples were merely one among many "minority groups" under the administration of state social service and welfare programs. Instead, sovereignty defined indigenous peoples with concrete rights to self-government, territorial integrity, and cultural autonomy under international customary law.[62] By doing so, it served to link indigenous peoples across the territorial borders of nation-states, refuting their position under the domains of domestic policy and reclaiming their status under the conventions and relations of international law.

Again the strategy was learned from previous generations. Since the initiation of conquest, indigenous leaders had assumed the relevance of a legal discourse that was, conventionally speaking, "not their own" as a way of claiming a status, and its associated rights, against the ideologies and practices of colonialism.[63] Of course, translating indigenous epistemologies about law, governance, and culture through the discursive rubric of sovereignty was and is problematic.[64] Sovereignty as a discourse is unable to capture fully the indigenous meanings, perspectives, and identities about law, governance, and culture, and thus over time it impacts how those epistemologies and perspectives are represented and understood.

Despite the problems of translation, indigenous peoples learned that how they represented themselves in international affairs mattered in consequential ways to how they were related to and what rights they were perceived to be claiming.[65] Refuting minority status was a refutation of the assimilationist ideologies that constructed indigenous peoples as ethnic minorities under the governing authority of the nation-state and a claim of the attributes of sovereignty customarily associated with nations.[66]

These discursive strategies were key as the world community mobilized attention on the rights of minority groups after World War II and in the context of the formation of the United Nations.[67] Within the political forums and policy agreements of the UN, indigenous peoples insisted on being identified as *peoples* (political collectivities) and not as *people* (minorities). The stakes in being so identified originated with the UN Charter, which affiliated the rights of *peoples* to *self-determination*—a legal category that came to be defined by both group and individual rights not to be discriminated against on the basis of race, ethnicity, gender, sexual orientation, or physical or mental ability, and to determine one's own governments, laws, economies, identities, and cultures. By taking on the self-definition of peoples with group and individual rights to self-determination, indigenous leaders were claiming a difference from minorities and a status akin to the status of nations.[68] The UN community has not missed the political importance of such links, as has been true within the signatory process of the *Declaration on the Rights of Indigenous Peoples*.

Written by an international consortium of approximately one hundred indigenous leaders from around the world over a decade's time, the *Declaration* translates human rights principles for indigenous peoples into the specific rights of self-determination, including provision for aspects of tradition, custom, property, language, oral histories, philosophies, writing systems, educational systems, medicines, health practices, resources, lands, and self-definition. Though there are some troubles with the conceptualization of what these particular rights mean, and many feel that the definitions do not go far enough, what remains interesting is how those who participated in the process chose to represent the rights as *indivisible* and *interdependent* aspects of their identities as sovereigns.[69] Human rights for indigenous peoples, in other words, became translated to mean rights to a self-determination that was indelibly linked to sovereignty. So strong is this conceptualization that it is now virtually impossible to talk about what *sovereignty* means for indigenous peoples without invoking self-determination. As a consequence, sovereignty has been solidified within indigenous discourses as an inherent right that emanates from historically and politically resonant notions of cultural identity and community affiliation: "Sovereignty, in the final instance, can be said to consist more of a continued cultural integrity than of political powers and to the degree that a nation loses its sense of cultural identity, to that degree it suffers a loss of sovereignty."[70] "Sovereignty is inherent; it comes from within a people or culture."[71]

The link of sovereignty to peoples and cultures has been an important contribution to the precepts of human rights within international law by indigenous scholars and activists. The link has opened up debates about theories of humanity, notions of rights, and the authority of the nation-state to determine the legal substance of both. But it is also one of the most misunderstood and misrepresented aspects of how sovereignty matters. It is simultaneously and contradictorily true that many have mistaken an essentialist rhetoric for a politically strategic one, questioning what is perceived to be a gross reduction of everything from land rights to rug designs to sovereignty as a kind of raison d'être for all things indigenous.

The discursive proliferation of sovereignty must be understood in its historical context. The multiple social forces of globalization have reinvented colonial practices from the supposed confines of the nation as empire builder to the elusive networks of decentralized political economies and informatics.[72] These networks have perpetuated the kinds of exploitation of indigenous labor, products, resources, lands, and bodies conventionally ascribed to colonialism proper—that is, Colonialism with a capital C.[73] The almost aggressive self-definition of indigenous peoples by sovereignty is in large part a response to their continued experiences of exploitation and disempowerment under processes of globalization.[74] Fiercely claiming an identity as sovereign, and including multiple sociocultural issues under its rubric, has been a strategy of not merely deflecting globalization's reinvention of colonial processes but of reasserting a politically empowered self-identity within, besides, and against colonization.

It is also true that there is a troubling and troubled essentialism of sovereignty by indigenous scholars, community organizers, and cultural producers, evident in the moments when what it is or how it is important is taken-for-granted. Many find it troubling that indigenous histories and cultures are often framed through sovereignty without a consideration of the ways in which its ideological origins might predispose a distortion or negation of indigenous epistemologies of law and governance.[75] What this means for the actual decolonization of indigenous cultures is complicated by how those origins impinge upon real revitalization efforts or effective decolonization strategies. Others find the links between sovereignty and particular cultural practices, such as certain aspects of basket weaving or food preparation, to flatten out, distort, or even make light of the legal importance and political substance of sovereignty.

What is important to keep in mind when encountering these myriad discursive practices is that sovereignty is historically contingent. There is no fixed meaning for what *sovereignty* is—what it means by definition, what it implies in public debate, or how it has been conceptualized in international, national, or indigenous law. Sovereignty—and its related histories, perspectives, and identities—is embedded within the specific social relations in which it is invoked and given meaning. How and when it emerges and functions are determined by the "located" political agendas and cultural perspectives of those who rearticulate it into public debate or political document to do a specific work of opposition, invitation, or accommodation. It is no more possible to stabilize what *sovereignty* means and how it matters to those who invoke it than it is to forget the historical and cultural embeddedness of indigenous peoples' multiple and contradictory political perspectives and agendas for empowerment, decolonization, and social justice.[76]

The challenge, then, to understand how and for whom sovereignty matters is to understand the historical circumstances under which it is given meaning. There is nothing inherent about its significance. Therefore it can mean something different during its original uses in the politico-theological discourses of the Catholic church than it did during Marshall's delivery of the Supreme Court's decision in *Worcester v. Georgia*, differing again in its links to concepts of self-determination and human rights and in the contexts of Alaskan Native, Native Hawaiian, or Maori or Aborigine struggles.

Understanding the problems of translating indigenous concepts of law, governance, and culture through the discourses of sovereignty requires unpacking the social forces and historical conditions at each moment when it is invoked as well as the social relations in which it functions. How did those forces cohere? What social conditions were the social actors confronting? What kinds of identities did they have stakes in claiming and asserting? In relationship to what other identities?[77]

Concurrent with associating sovereignty with self-determination has been its linking to *self-government*.[78] In locating sovereignty within the idea of peoples who are collective political entities with inherent rights to decide their own laws and practice their own cultures, self-government has emerged as an attendant concept to signify rights to determine, practice, and transform multiple forms of social organization—in effect to decolonize social institutions from federal/state paternalism and to reformulate them along the lines of distinctive cultural perspectives. This is evident in everything from efforts to revitalize traditional forms of education and health care to reclamations of legal traditions and practices.

For instance a myriad of First Nation organizations in Canada—such as the Native Women's Association of Canada, Indian Women for Indian Rights, Assembly of First Nations, Native Council of Canada, Inuit Committee on National Issues, Inuit Tapirisat of Canada, Inuit Women's Association, and the Métis National Council—have almost unilaterally (though with important differences among them in political perspectives) made the assumption of band/reserve control over social programs and services like education, health care, child welfare, resource management, and economic development a key aspect of their movements to sovereignty by self-government. They have argued that not only should their unique cultural perspectives regarding education, health care, family, environmentalism, and communalism inform the structure and administration of these various types of social institutions but that sovereignty itself is a vacuous idea for indigenous peoples without providing for and guaranteeing their means and abilities to exercise it.[79]

Similarly, many indigenous peoples have revitalized their laws and legal practices in the contexts of their own juridical epistemologies and justice systems.[80] Several groups in Canada have returned to the model of the talking circle for deciding sentencing terms.[81] The Navajo have introduced the Peacemakers Court for mediation.[82] These efforts have been characterized by serious attention to inherited beliefs, stories, and ceremonies as well as a concern as to how best to entrench these cultural perspectives and practices within "tribal" law.[83]

One of the most powerful examples of these efforts is their implication for reforming nation-state policy, indicated by Australia's high court decision in *Mabo v. Queensland* in 1992. Eddie Koiki Mabo, Sam Passi, David Passi, Celuia Mapo Salee, and James Rice filed a legal claim of ownership to their "preconquest" lands on the island of Mer in the Torres Straight between Australia and Papua New Guinea. Their claim was based on their unique legal customs for naming (singing) territorial occupation, use, and responsibility. They argued that the said customs superseded English title, which had been illegally asserted without proper treaty or purchase in violation of the principles outlined in England's own Proclamation and wrongly justified on the basis of Marshall's discovery doctrine.[84]

In response to the claim, the high court of Australia required Queensland to determine the facts of the case. However, while the case was still pending, Parliament passed the Torres Strait Islands Coastal Act, which stated that "any rights that Torres Strait Islanders had to land after the claim of sovereignty in 1879 is hereby extinguished without compensation."[85] The challenge to the act was taken to Australia's high court in *Mabo v. Queensland*.[86]

In what would be an unprecedented ruling until Canada's Supreme Court decision in *Delgamuukw v. British Columbia* in 1997, Australia's high court found that indigenous customary law was a valid body of legal precedence for deciding aboriginal title. It held that title existed prior to Captain James Cook's maps of the area and the formal establishment of the neighboring English colony of New South Wales in 1788. The ruling overturned the discovery doctrine on which England had asserted title to indigenous territories in Australia. In recognizing that prior title in the lands existed with the Aborigines, the high court acknowledged that indigenous title still existed in any region where it had not been legally ceded.[87] Following the court's ruling, Parliament passed the Native Title Act in 1993, which provided indigenous peoples with the means to claim territorial rights to unalienated lands. These statutes have not only reversed the precedence for determining aboriginal title through discovery in Australia but have affirmed indigenous customary law as a credible source of precedence in matters of national jurisdiction.[88]

What all of these various political movements indicate is an attempt by indigenous peoples to be recognized as sovereigns and to be related to by their nation-states as forming legitimate governments with rights to direct their own domestic policies and foreign affairs, unmediated by the regional contours of state/provincial politics and corporate interests. Unevenly but steadily, the movements have impacted the direction of national law and policy, as nation-states have been held accountable to the increasing validation of indigenous epistemologies in matters of territorial rights and governance. Corollary terms like *nations within* and *government-to-government* have been deployed by indigenous peoples to position themselves as comprising fully self-determining political entities invested with the power to be related to as sovereigns in matters ranging from treaty to intellectual property rights.[89]

Indigenous opposition to being characterized as minorities by self-defining as peoples with the sovereignty of self-determination and self-government has met the challenge of conservative political interests that deploy the discourses of reverse racism to contest the terms of indigenous legal status, treaty and land rights, and economic self-sufficiency. The argument goes that indigenous peoples are only receiving these special funds and services on the basis of race and that such funds and services are therefore unconstitutionally discriminating against non-indigenous people.[90]

In the United States these discourses have been profoundly informed by anti–Affirmative Action movements that work to portray federal and state funding and services to indigenous peoples as nothing more than special benefits for a racial/minority group that perpetuates reverse discrimination. Therein anti-gaming, anti-recognition, and anti-sovereignty movements have coalesced by the reracialization of indigenous status and rights. Given their successes in challenging civil rights principles in university admissions and fellowship programs, and in recent Supreme Court decisions such as *Rice v. Cayetano* in 2000, many indigenous peoples in the United States and in U.S. territories such as Puerto Rico, Guam, and Samoa are justifiably concerned about the long-term implications of these efforts for treaty and land rights.[91]

These tensions likewise inform the now twenty-year revision process for the *Declaration on the Rights of Indigenous Peoples*, as member nations of the UN resist including the identification of indigenous groups as *peoples* because of the legal status that this would imply. At the UN meetings on race and human rights in South Africa in 2001, some nations conceded to the use of the term *peoples* as long as it was explicitly stripped of its legal connotations. As a result, indigenous peoples are identified as peoples in the *Declaration* but only as a matter of semantics.[92]

Reverberations

Despite the strategic deployments of sovereignty, many indigenous scholars have criticized its proliferation within indigenous discourses because of its etymological origins within European colonial law and Christian ideologies. In "International Law and Politics: Toward a Right to Self-Determination for Indigenous Peoples," Shawnee scholar Glenn T. Morris writes: "Indigenous peoples, as all colonized peoples, have come to realize the importance of semantics in their quest for self-determination."[93] As the ideological forces of colonialism bear down through the etymological origins, meanings, and histories of *sovereignty*, Morris questions "the usefulness of forcing indigenous reality into the forms [semantics] developed by Europeans."[94] Morris even anticipates an emergent field of inquiry within indigenous studies focusing on indigenous epistemologies of law and governance that move past the colonial legacies of concepts like sovereignty and nationhood.

A similar perspective is articulated by Mohawk scholar and activist Taiaiake Alfred in *Peace, Power, Righteousness: An Indigenous Manifesto* (1999) and "Sovereignty" (in this volume):

> But few people have questioned how a European term and idea—sovereignty is certainly not Sioux, Salish, or Iroquoian in origin—came to be so embedded and important to cultures that had their own systems of government since the time before the term *sovereignty* was invented in Europe. Fewer still have questioned the implications of adopting the European notion of power and governance and using it to structure the postcolonial systems that are being negotiated and implemented within indigenous communities today.[95]

For Morris, Alfred, and other indigenous theorists, sovereignty fails to interrogate the ideological bases on which it has emerged and functioned as a category. Accordingly, using it to theorize indigenous histories, governments, and epistemologies is not merely problematical but faulty because such configurations are perceived to distort rather than translate the representation and so understanding of indigenous epistemologies, laws, governments, and cultures. In order to decolonize indigenous peoples, they explain, a return to indigenous epistemologies and languages is required.

Paradoxically, Morris, Alfred, and others anticipate the need for a body of scholarship that has chosen to represent itself as "intellectual sovereignty."[96] What is common among these various writings is the explicit attempt by indigenous scholars to decolonize the theoretical and methodological perspectives used within analyses of indigenous histories, cultures, and identities from the legacies of intellectual colonialism. Fierce criticisms of the exploitative research practices of anthropology (ethnography) and history parallel attempts to revitalize and legitimize indigenous epistemologies as valid bodies of knowledge.[97]

What is interesting about the term "intellectual sovereignty" is its link to ongoing political and cultural movements working to rearticulate the rights of indigenous peoples to sovereignty by self-determination and self-government. While problematical for its occasional invocation of or reliance on racialized notions of cultural integrity and traditionalism, intellectual sovereignty has situated itself as a part of the various sociopolitical movements toward sovereignty, self-determination, and self-government and is understood by its authors to be an integral aspect of the configuration and import of their intellectual work.[98] Given ongoing social forces of intellectual exploitation and appropriation, it is understandable that indigenous scholars would want to mark their projects as oppositional by situating them as part of a sociopolitical movement for sovereignty.[99]

Conclusion

Sovereignty is historically contingent. What it has meant and what it currently means belong to the political subjects who have deployed and are deploying it to do the work of defining their relationships with one another, their political agendas, and their strategies for decolonization and social justice. Therefore to understand how it matters and for whom, sovereignty must be situated within the historical and cultural relationships in which it is articulated. The specific social conditions that produce its meanings must be considered. This is not to say that etymology is unimportant. Sovereignty carries the horrible stench of colonialism. It is incomplete, inaccurate, and troubled. But it has also been rearticulated to mean altogether different things by indigenous peoples. In its link to concepts of self-determination and self-government, it insists on the recognition of inherent rights to the respect for political affiliations that are historical and located and for the unique cultural identities that continue to find meaning in those histories and relations.

Notes

1. Vine Deloria, Jr., "Self-Determination and the Concept of Sovereignty," in *Economic Development in American Indian Reservations*, ed. Roxanne Dunbar Ortiz (Albuquerque: University of New Mexico Native American Studies, 1979), 22–28, see 22.

2. Kirke Kickingbird, Lynn Kickingbird, Charles J. Chibitty, Curtis Berkey, *Indian Sovereignty*, pamphlet (Washington DC: Institute for the Development of Indian Law, 1977), 64 pp., 1.

3. Deloria, "Self-Determination and the Concept of Sovereignty," 22.

4. S. James Anaya, *Indigenous Peoples in International Law* (New York: Oxford University Press, 1996), 13–19.

5. Anaya, *Indigenous Peoples in International Law*, 14–15.

6. Anaya, *Indigenous Peoples in International Law*, 13–19.

7. Kickingbird et al., *Indian Sovereignty*.

8. Glenn T. Morris, "International Law and Politics: Toward a Right to Self-Determination for Indigenous Peoples," in *The State of Native America: Genocide, Colonization, and Resistance*, ed. M. Annette Jaimes (Boston: South End Press, 1992), 55–86.

9. Anaya, *Indigenous Peoples in International Law*, 15.

10. Anaya, *Indigenous Peoples in International Law*, 15.

11. J. G. A. Pocock, "Waitangi as Mystery of the State: Consequences of the Ascription of Federative Capacity to the Maori," in *Political Theory and the Rights of Indigenous Peoples*, ed. Duncan Ivison, Paul Patton, and Will Sanders (Cambridge: Cambridge University Press, 2000), 25–35.

12. Robert F. Berkhofer, Jr., *The White Man's Indian: Images of the American Indian from Columbus to the Present* (New York: Vintage Books, 1979).

13. George E. Tinker, *Missionary Conquest: The Gospel and Native American Cultural Genocide* (Minneapolis: Fortress Press, 1993).

14. Ronald Niezen, *Spirit Wars: Native North American Religions in the Age of Nation Building* (Berkeley: University of California Press, 2000).

15. Christopher Vecsey, ed., *Handbook of American Indian Religious Freedom* (New York: Crossroad Publishing Company, 1993).

16. Paul Prucha, *American Indian Treaties: The History of a Political Anomaly* (Berkeley: University of California Press, 1994).

17. Sidney L. Harring, *White Man's Law: Native People in Nineteenth-Century Canadian Jurisprudence* (Toronto: Osgoode Society for Canadian Legal History, University of Toronto Press, 1998).

18. Tomás Almaguer, *Racial Fault Lines: The Historical Origins of White Supremacy in California* (Berkeley: University of California Press, 1994).

19. Vine Deloria, Jr., *Behind the Trail of Broken Treaties: An Indian Declaration of Independence* (Austin: University of Texas Press, 1974).

20. *Worcester v. Georgia* (1832).

21. Anaya, *Indigenous Peoples in International Law*, 16–19.

22. Harring, *White Man's Law*; Thomas Isaac, *Aboriginal Law: Cases, Materials, and Commentary*, 2nd ed., Aboriginal Issues Series (Saskatoon: Purich Press, 1999).

23. *Johnson v. McIntosh* (1823).

24. Pocock, "Waitangi as Mystery of the State," 27.

25. *Johnson v. McIntosh* (1823).

26. *Johnson v. McIntosh* (1823).

27. *Johnson v. McIntosh* (1823).

28. *Johnson v. McIntosh* (1823).

29. *Johnson v. McIntosh* (1823).

30. *Johnson v. McIntosh* (1823).

31. Marshall's "aboriginal title" was taken up by the colonies in Canada to justify land acquisition on the grounds that said title could be extinguished if the lands were not being used. See Antonio Mills, *Eagle Down Is Our Law: Witsuwit'en Law, Feasts, and Land Claims* (Vancouver: University of British Columbia Press, 1994). This argument was likewise used by the Indian Claims Commission in determining Western Shoshone extinguishment of title to Newe Segobia.

32. Quoted in Sharon O'Brien, *American Indian Tribal Governments* (Norman: University of Oklahoma Press, 1989), 57.

33. *Worcester v. Georgia* (1831).

34. *Worcester v. Georgia* (1831).

35. *Worcester v. Georgia* (1831).

36. Hopewell 1785; Holston 1791; Philadelphia 1794; Tellico 1798; Tellico 1804; Tellico 1805; Tellico 1805; Washington City 1805; Washington City 1816; Chickasaw Council House 1816; Cherokee Agency 1817; Washington City 1819 (*Worcester v. Georgia* 1831).

37. *Worcester v. Georgia* (1831).

38. *Worcester v. Georgia* (1831).

39. *Worcester v. Georgia* (1831).

40. Deloria, *Behind the Trail of Broken Treaties*, 8.

41. See Harring, *White Man's Law* and Mills, *Eagle Down Is Our Law*.

42. Some have suggested that the discovery doctrine was historically linked to the Spanish doctrine of "right of conquest." See, for example, O'Brien, *American Indian Tribal Governments*.

43. See Anaya, *Indigenous Peoples in International Law*, and Pocock, "Waitangi as Mystery of the State."

44. Brain W. Dippie, *The Vanishing American: White Attitudes and United States Indian Policy* (Middletown CT: Wesleyan University Press, 1982); Richard Drinnon, *Facing West: The Metaphysics of Indian Hating and Empire Building* (New York: New American Library, 1980); Robert A. Williams, Jr., *The American Indian in Western Legal Thought: The Discourses of Conquest* (New York: Oxford University Press, 1990).

45. Harring, *White Man's Law*, 19.

46. Harring, *White Man's Law*, 17.

47. Isaac, *Aboriginal Law*, 3.

48. Harring, *White Man's Law*, 19–20.

49. Harring, *White Man's Law*, 22.

50. Sir James Stephen, quoted in Harring, *White Man's Law*, 21–22.

51. Harring, *White Man's Law*, 22.

52. Harring, *White Man's Law*, 23.

53. Isaac, *Aboriginal Law*.

54. Mills, *Eagle Down Is Our Law*.

55. J. Kehaulani Kauanui, " 'For Get' Hawaiian Entitlement: Configurations of Land, 'Blood', and Americanization in the Hawaiian Homes Commission Act of 1920," *Social Text* 17, no. 2 (Summer 1999), 123–44, and "The Politics of Blood and Sovereignty in *Rice v. Cayetano*" *Political and Legal Anthropology Review* 25, no. 1 (2002), 110–28 (reprinted in this volume).

56. Andrew Armitage, *Comparing the Policy of Aboriginal Assimilation: Australia, Canada, and New Zealand* (Vancouver: University of British Columbia Press, 1995).

57. Joanne Barker, "Looking for Warrior Woman (Beyond Pocahontas)," in *This Bridge We Call Home: Radical Visions for Transformation*, ed. Gloria Anzaldúa and AnaLouise Keating (New York: Routledge, 2001), and "Indian(TM) U.S.A.," *Wicazo Sa Review: A Journal of Native American Studies* 18, no. 1 (Spring 2003).

58. Rayna Green, "The Pocahontas Perplex: The Image of Indian Women in American Culture," in *Unequal Sisters: A Multicultural Reader in U.S. Women's History*, ed. Ellen Carol DuBois and Vicki L. Ruiz (New York: Routledge, 1990), 15–21.

59. Angie Debo, *And Still the Waters Run: The Betrayal of the Five Civilized Tribes* (Princeton, NJ: Princeton University Press, 1940).

60. *Exiled in the Land of the Free: Democracy, Indian Nations, and the U.S. Constitution*, collectively edited by contributing authors (Santa Fe: Clear Light Publishers, 1992).

61. Sara Hopkins Winnemucca, *Life among the Piutes: Their Wrongs and Claims* (New York: Putnam, 1883).

62. Anaya, *Indigenous Peoples in International Law*, 13–19.

63. Morris, "International Law and Politics."

64. Taiaiake Alfred, *Peace, Power, Righteousness: An Indigenous Manifesto* (Toronto: Oxford University Press, 1999), and "Sovereignty," this volume.

65. Anaya, *Indigenous Peoples in International Law*.

66. Anaya, *Indigenous Peoples in International Law*; Franke Wilmer, *The Indigenous Voice in World*

Politics (Newbury Park: Sage Publications, 1993); Sharon Helen Venne, *Our Elders Understand Our Rights: Evolving International Law Regarding Indigenous Rights* (Penticton, British Columbia: Theytus Books, 1998). Joanne Barker, "The Human Genome Diversity Project: 'Peoples,' 'Populations,' and the Cultural Politics of Identification," *Routledge Journal of Cultural Studies*, forthcoming.

67. It would be challenging to try to figure out what the long-term implications of the normalization of the discourses of sovereignty for indigenous peoples have been for theorizing indigenous epistemologies and perspectives of law and governance, because it is tempting—almost irresistible from the context of dominant ideologies of race and culture—to mark the authentic from the inauthentic, the pure from the contaminated, the traditional from the colonial. The fact remains that after hundreds of years of cultural exchange between indigenous peoples and colonial states, sovereignty's currency within indigenous discourses has been long established, and not always or necessarily to detrimental or disastrous ends (Dan Taulapapa McMullin, "The Passive Resistance of Samoans to U.S. and Other Colonialisms," this volume; Donna Ngaronoa Gardiner, "Hands Off—Our Genes: A Case Study on the Theft of Whakapapa" [paper presented at Sovereignty 2000 conference, University of California, Santa Cruz, May 2000]).

Indigenous peoples have impacted sovereignty in important ways, changing what it means within international law and politics. For while ideologies of race and culture would like us to look at the exchanges between indigenous and colonial peoples from the authority of the colonial to erase the indigenous from historical significance, the fact is that indigenous peoples have made an important difference in what sovereignty means (Michael P. Perez, "Chamorro Resistance and Prospects for Sovereignty in Guam," this volume; Déborah Berman Santana, "Indigenous Identity and the Struggle for Independence in Puerto Rico," this volume). Understanding this requires the consideration of the heterogeneity of the "local," of the impact of locally specific cultural perspectives on what sovereignty is and how it matters.

68. Barker, "Human Genome Diversity Project."

69. Tony Simpson, *Indigenous Heritage and Self Determination: The Cultural and Intellectual Property Rights of Indigenous Peoples*, On Behalf of the Forest Peoples Programme, International Working Group for Indigenous Affairs Document no. 86 (Copenhagen: IWGIA, 1997), 138.

70. Deloria, "Self-Determination and the Concept of Sovereignty," 123.

71. Kickingbird et al., *Indian Sovereignty*, 1.

72. David Harvey, *The Condition of Postmodernity: An Inquiry into the Origins of Cultural Change* (Cambridge: Basil Blackwell, 1989).

73. Gardiner, "Hands Off—Our Genes."

74. Hence the reason why indigenous scholars have been resistant to theories of postcolonialism and why postcolonial theory does not often work in understanding indigenous histories, meanings, and identities (see Barker, "Human Genome Diversity Project").

75. Alfred, "Sovereignty."

76. Compare Lee Maracle, *I Am Woman: A Native Perspective on Sociology and Feminism* (New York: Press Gang Publishers, 1996); Patricia Monture-Angus, *Thunder in My Soul: A Mohawk Woman Speaks* (Nova Scotia: Fernwood Publishing, 1995); Haunani-Kay Trask, *From a Native Daughter: Colonialism and Sovereignty in Hawai'i* (Maine: Common Courage Press, 1993).

77. Lawrence Grossberg, "On Postmodernism and Articulation: An Interview with Stuart Hall," in *Stuart Hall: Critical Dialogues in Cultural Studies*, ed. David Morley and Kuan-Hsing Chen (New York: Routledge, 1996), 131–50.

78. Vine Deloria, Jr., and Clifford Lytle, *The Nations Within: The Past and Future of American Indian Sovereignty* (New York: Pantheon, 1984).

79. Harold Cardinal, *The Unjust Society: The Tragedy of Canada's Indians* (Edmonton: Hurtig Press, 1969); George Manuel, *The Fourth World* (New York: Free Press, 1974).

80. Bruce G. Miller, *The Problem of Justice: Tradition and Law in the Coast Salish World* (Lincoln: University of Nebraska Press, 2001).

81. Ross Gordon Green, *Justice in Aboriginal Communities: Sentencing Alternatives* (Saskatoon, Sasakatchewan: Purch Publishing, 1998).

82. Gloria Valencia-Weber and Christine Zuni, "Domestic Violence and Tribal Protection of Indigenous Women in the United States," *St. John's Law Review* (Winter–Spring 1995); Marianne O. Neilson and Robert A., Silverman, eds., *Native Americans, Crime, and Justice* (Boulder CO: Westview Press, 1996).

83. Alfred, *Peace, Power, Righteousness*, and "Sovereignty."

84. Mabo v Queensland No. 2 1992 (Cth), http://www.foundingdocs.gov.au (accessed January 5, 2002).

85. Torres Strait Islands Coastal Act (1982).

86. http://www.foundingdocs.gov.au.

87. http://www.foundingdocs.gov.au.

88. http://www.foundingdocs.gov.au.

89. Deloria and Lytle, *The Nations Within*; Curtis Cook and Juan D. Lindau, eds., *Aboriginal Rights and Self-Government: The Canadian and Mexican Experience in North American Perspective* (Montreal: McGill-Queen's University Press, 2000); Debra Harry, "The Human Genome Diversity Project," *Abya Yala News* 8, no. 4 (Fall–Winter 1993): 13–15, and "Biopiracy: The Theft of Human DNA from Indigenous Peoples" (paper, Sovereignty 2000: Locations of Contestation and Possibility, University of California, Santa Cruz, May 19, 2000).

90. For a list of some of the organizations, lobbyists, business people, and representatives making these arguments, see Adversity.Net's Web site for links and contact information at http://www.adversity.net. Adversity.Net is "a Civil Rights Organization for Color Blind Justice" that wants to "stop the divisive emphasis on race" in American law.

91. Kauanui, "The Politics of Blood and Sovereignty in Rice v. Cayetano."

92. See the Web site of the World Conference against Racism for information and documents on the debates at the conference, http://www.unhchr.ch/html/racism.

93. Morris, "International Law and Politics," 55–86.

94. Morris, "International Law and Politics," 27.

95. Alfred, *Peace, Power, Righteousness*, and "Sovereignty"; quoted text is from "Sovereignty," this volume.

96. Robert Allen Warrior, *Tribal Secrets: Recovering American Indian Intellectual Traditions* (Minneapolis: University of Minnesota Press, 1994); Elizabeth Cook-Lynn, "American Indian Intellectualism and the New Indian Story," *American Indian Quarterly* 20, no. 1 (Winter 1996): 57–76.

97. On exploitative practices see Linda Tuhiwai Smith, *Decolonizing Methodologies: Research and Indigenous Peoples* (New York: Zed Books/Dunedin, New Zealand: University of Otago Press, 1999). On revitalization see the following essays in the present volume: Guillermo Delgado-P. and John Brown Childs, "First Peoples/African American Connections"; Fiona Cram, "Backgrounding Maori Views on Genetic Engineering"; Kilipaka Kawaihonu Nahili Pae Ontai, "A Spiritual Defi-

nition of Sovereignty from a Kanaka Maoli Perspective"; Leonie Pihama, "Asserting Indigenous Theories of Change."

98. Louis Owens, *Mixedblood Messages: Literature, Film, Family, Place* (Norman: University of Oklahoma Press, 1998).

99. Laurie Anne Whitt, "Cultural Imperialism and the Marketing of Native America," *American Indian Culture and Research Journal* 19, no. 3 (1995): 1–31.

Taiaiake Alfred (Mohawk)

Sovereignty

Sovereignty. The word, so commonly used, refers to supreme political authority, independent and unlimited by any other power. Discussion of the term *sovereignty* in relation to indigenous peoples, however, must be framed differently, within an intellectual framework of internal colonization. Internal colonization is the historical process and political reality defined in the structures and techniques of government that consolidate the domination of indigenous peoples by a foreign yet sovereign settler state. While internal colonization describes the political reality of most indigenous peoples, one should also note that the discourse of state sovereignty is and has been contested in real and theoretical ways since its imposition. The inter/counterplay of state sovereignty doctrines—rooted in notions of dominion—with and against indigenous concepts of political relations—rooted in notions of freedom, respect, and autonomy—frames the discourse on indigenous "sovereignty" at its broadest level.

The practice of history cannot help but be implicated in colonization. Indeed most discussions of indigenous sovereignty are founded on a particular and instrumental reading of history that serves to undergird internal colonization. Fair and just instances of interaction between indigenous and non-indigenous peoples are legion; yet mythic narratives and legal understandings of state sovereignty in North America have consciously obscured justice in the service of the colonial project. From the earliest times, relations between indigenous peoples and European newcomers vacillated within the normal parameters that characterize any relation between autonomous political groups. Familiar relations—war, peace, cooperation, antagonism, and shifting dominance and subservience—are all to be found in our shared history. Yet the actual history of our plural existence has been erased by the narrow fictions of a single sovereignty. Controlling, universalizing and assimilating, these fictions have been imposed in the form of law on weakened but resistant and remembering peoples.

European sovereignties in North America first legitimated themselves through treaty relationships entered into by Europeans and indigenous nations. North American settler states (Canada and the United States, with their predecessor states Holland, Spain, France, and England) gained legitimacy as legal entities only by the expressed consent through treaty of the original occupiers and governors of North America. The founding documents of state sovereignty recognize this fact: all Dutch and French treaties with indigenous peoples, the Treaty of Utrecht, the Articles of Capitulation, and the Royal Proclamation (made in a context of military interdependency between the British and indigenous nations) all contain explicit reference to the independent nationhood of indigenous peoples. As the era of European exploration and discovery gave way to settlement, with its concomitant need for balanced peaceful relations with indigenous nations, the states' charter documents made clear reference to the separate political existence and territorial independence of indigenous peoples.

None of this historical diversity is reflected in the official history and doctrinal bases of settler state sovereignty today. Rather, Canada and the United States have written self-serving histories of discovery, conquest, and settlement that wipe out any reference to the original relations between indigenous peoples and Europeans. This *post facto* claim of European "sovereignty" is limited by two main caveats. The first is factual: the mere documentation of European assertions of hegemonic sovereignty does not necessarily indicate proof of its achievement. European control over actual territory was tenuous at best; and the political existence of European settler states was a *negotiated* reality until well into the nineteenth century (and not completely achieved, even in colonial mythology, until the end of the nineteenth century in the United States and to this day in Canada).

The second limitation is theoretical: the discourse of sovereignty upon which the current *post facto* justification rests is an exclusively European discourse. That is, European assertions in both a legal and political sense were made strictly vis-à-vis other European powers, and did not impinge upon or necessarily even affect in law or politics the rights and status of indigenous nations. It is only from our distant historical vantage point, and standing upon a counterfactual rock, that we are able to see European usurpations of indigenous sovereignty as justified.

If sovereignty has been neither legitimized nor justified, it has nevertheless limited the ways we are able to think, suggesting always a conceptual and definitional problem centered on the accommodation of indigenous peoples within a "legitimate" framework of settler state governance. When we step outside this discourse, we confront a different problematic, that of the state's "sovereignty" itself, and its actual meaning in contrast to the facts and the potential that exists for a nation-to-nation relationship.

Indigenous scholars have focused on this problematic to profound effect. Russel Barsh and James Henderson, for example, explored the process of intellectual obscurantism in close detail in *The Road: Indian Tribes and Political Liberty.*[1] Barsh and Henderson concentrated on the United States and the creation of a historical narrative that completely ignored basic principles of natural law and the philosophical underpinnings of American notions of liberty and equality. They trace the evolution of the doctrine of tribal sovereignty in U.S. law through judicial decisions and demonstrate the ways in which the process misrepresented the true potential of liberal principles—and even the United States Constitution—to accommodate notions of indigenous nationhood.

The Road is a landmark work. It embarked on a critique from within, arguing for recognition of indigenous peoples' rights *within* the historic and legal frame of state sovereignty. Ultimately, Barsh and Henderson subjected the rationale for indigenous or "tribal" liberty to criteria defined by the framers of the U.S. Constitution. The problem, they argued, was the subjection of principle to politics, and unprincipled decisions by the state judiciaries. Barsh and Henderson designed a "theory of the tribe in the American nation," and in doing so advanced the theoretical notion of a coexistence of indigenous and state sovereignty that was hamstrung as a conceptual tool by the weight of skewed legal precedent and the reality of the political context.[2] In this sense, *The Road* follows the trajectory—native sovereignty within and in relation to state sovereignty—first set forth in the 1830s in the Cherokee decisions, which suggested that tribes were "domestic dependent nations."

The entanglement of indigenous peoples within the institutional frame of the colonial state of course went beyond legal doctrines. The practice of sovereignty in the structures of government and the building of institutional relationships between indigenous governments and state agencies offered another forum for the subordination of principle. In two volumes, *American Indians, American Justice* and *The Nations Within*, Vine Deloria, Jr., and Clifford Lytle first outlined how the legal denial of indigenous rights in the courts was mirrored in governing structures that embedded the false notion of European superiority in indigenous community life.[3] The example of the usurpation of indigenous nationhood by the United States clarified how the state generally uses not only political and economic but also certain intellectual strategies to impose and maintain its dominance. Such linking of the intellectual and structural forms of colonialism have produced some of the deepest analyses of the issue.

In considering the question of the sovereignty of indigenous peoples within its territorial borders, the state takes various positions: the classic strategies include outright denial of indigenous rights; a theoretical acceptance of indigenous rights combined with an assertion that these have been extinguished historically; and legal doctrines that transform indigenous rights from their autonomous nature to contingent rights, existing only within the framework of colonial law. Scholars have documented fully the manifestation of these strategies in the various policies implemented by settler states in the modern era: domestication, termination, assimilation.

With the minor concession that in both Canada and the United States the federal government itself has maintained and defended its powers over indigenous peoples vis-à-vis states and provinces, the potential for recognition of indigenous nationhood has gone unrealized. There has been a total theoretical exclusion and extinguishing of indigenous nationhood, leading to what a recent United Nations Human Rights Commission study labeled the unjust "domestication" of indigenous nationhood.

Indigenous peoples nonetheless struggled to achieve a degree of freedom and power within the intellectual and political environment created out of the colonial domestication project and settler state sovereignty. For generations, indigenous peoples fought to preserve the integrity of their nations and the independent bases of their existence. They were successful in countering the colonial project to the extent that they survived (a monumental human achievement given the intensive efforts of two modern industrial states to eradicate them). Yet by the late 1980s, the increasing erosions of tribal governing powers in the United States and failed attempts to enshrine a recognition of indigenous nationhood in the Canadian constitution made it clear that the governments of Canada and the United States were incapable of liberalizing their relationships with "the nations within."

As they regained their capacity to govern themselves and began to reassert the earlier principles of the nation-to-nation relationship between indigenous peoples and states, indigenous people began to question seriously the viability of working within the system, of considering themselves "nations within." The questioning often came out of models—tribal and band councils dependent upon and administering federal funds, for example—that recognized indigenous sovereignty yet always subsumed it to that of the state. A new intellectual approach began to emerge in the critique of the fundamental pillars by which the United States and Canada claimed legal authority over indigenous peoples and lands. Reflecting critical trends in other academic disciplines, legal scholarship began the project of deconstructing the architecture of colonial domination. Perhaps the two most important strategies to reachieve a political plurality in the face of the dominance of state sovereignty have been woven together: on the one hand, the assertion of a prior and coexisting sovereignty, and, on the other, the assertion of a right of self-determination for indigenous peoples in international law.

The most thorough and illuminating of the critical legal studies of the indigenous-state relationship is Robert Williams's *The American Indian in Western Legal Thought.*[4] His description of how law—embodying all of the racist assumptions of medieval Europe—has served as the European colonizers' most effective instrument of genocide destroys the arguments of those who would defend the justice of the colonial state. Williams shows how the deep roots of European belief in their own cultural and racial superiority underlie all discussions of the interaction between whites and indigenous peoples on the issue of sovereignty. After Williams's critique, any history of the concept of sovereignty in North America must trace the manipulation of the concept as it evolved to justify the elimination of indigenous peoples. By examining the deep history of European thought on indigenous peoples—what he calls the "discourse of conquest"—Williams shows how the entire discussion of sovereignty in North America represents the calculated triumph of illogic and interest over truth and justice.

After the end of the imperial era and the foundation of the North American states, in no instance did principles of law preclude the perpetration of injustice against indigenous peoples. In Canada, the rights of indigenous peoples were completely denied in the creation of the legal framework for the relationship. And the United States Supreme Court's definition of tribal sovereignty—made by Chief Justice John Marshall in a series of nineteenth-century decisions centered on *Johnson v. McIntosh*—merely gave legal sanction to the unilateral abrogation of treaties by the United States and denial of the natural law rights of indigenous peoples. As Williams argues: "*Johnson*'s acceptance of the Doctrine of Discovery into United States law preserved the legacy of 1000 years of European racism and colonialism directed against non-Western peoples."[5] Recent assertions of prior and persistent indigenous power have come from two places: first, the intellectual and historical critiques of state legitimacy, and second, the revitalization of indigenous communities. Using "remnant recognitions" in colonial law, Indian critics have sought to deconstruct the skewed legal and institutional frame and to focus directly on the relationship between indigenous peoples and state sovereignty.

Core to this effort is the theoretical attention given to the entire notion of sovereignty as the guiding principle of government in states. What the Canadian philosopher James Tully calls the "empire of uniformity" is a fact-obliterating mythology of European conquest and normality.[6] Tully recognizes the ways in which injustice toward indigenous peoples is deeply rooted in the basic injustice of normalized power relations within the state itself. In his *Strange Multiplicity*, Tully considers the intellectual bases of dominance inherent in state structures, and he challenges us to reconceptualize the state and its relation with indigenous people in order to accommodate what he calls the three post-imperial values: consent, mutual recognition, and cultural continuity.

Taiaiake Alfred, in his *Peace, Power, Righteousness*, has engaged this challenge from within an indigenous intellectual framework.[7] Alfred's "manifesto" calls for a profound reorientation of indigenous politics and a recovery of indigenous political traditions in contemporary society. Attacking both the foundations of the state's claim to authority over indigenous peoples and the process of cooptation that has drawn indigenous leaders into a position of dependency on and cooperation with unjust state structures, Alfred's work reflects a basic sentiment within many indigenous communities: "sovereignty" is inappropriate as a political objective for indigenous peoples.

David Wilkins's *American Indian Sovereignty and the United States Supreme Court* amply illustrates the futility and frustration of adopting sovereignty as a political objective.[8] Wilkins traces the history of the development of a doctrine of Indian tribal sovereignty in the U.S. Supreme Court, demonstrating its inherent contradictions for Indian nationhood. From the central Marshall decisions in the mid-nineteenth century through contemporary jurisprudence, Wilkins reveals the fundamental weakness of a tribal sovereignty "protected" within the colonizer's legal system.

Wilkins's exhaustive and convincing work draws on postmodern and critical legal studies approaches to the law. Examining the negative findings of the Court, he deconstructs the façade of judicial objectivity, demonstrating that in defining sovereignty, the "justices of the Supreme Court, both individually and collectively have engaged in the manufacturing, redefining, and burying of 'principles,' 'doctrines,' and legal 'truths' to excuse and legitimize constitutional, treaty, and civil rights violations of tribal nations."[9] In the United States, the common law provides for recognition of the inherent sovereignty of indigenous peoples but simultaneously allows for its limitation by the U.S.

Congress. The logic of colonization is clearly evident in the creation of "domestic dependent nation" status, which supposedly accommodates the historical fact of coexisting sovereignties but does no more than slightly limit the hypocrisy. It accepts the premise of indigenous rights while at the same time legalizing their unjust limitation and potential extinguishment by the state.

Scholars and indigenous leaders, in confronting the ignorance of the original principles in politics today and in the processes that have been established to negotiate a movement away from the colonial past, have usually accepted the framework and goal of sovereignty as core to the indigenous political movement. New institutions are constructed in communities to assert indigenous rights within a "tribal sovereignty" framework. And many people have reconciled themselves to the belief that we are making steady progress toward the resolution of injustices stemming from colonization. It may take more energy, or more money than is currently being devoted to the process of decolonization, but the issue is always framed within existing structural and legal parameters.

But few people have questioned how a European term and idea—sovereignty is certainly not Sioux, Salish, or Iroquoian in origin—came to be so embedded and important to cultures that had their own systems of government since the time before the term *sovereignty* was invented in Europe. Fewer still have questioned the implications of adopting the European notion of power and governance and using it to structure the postcolonial systems that are being negotiated and implemented within indigenous communities today.

These are exactly the questions that have become central to current analyses of power within indigenous communities. Using the sovereignty paradigm, indigenous people have made significant legal and political gains toward reconstructing the autonomous aspects of their individual, collective, and social identities. The positive effect of the sovereignty movement in terms of mental, physical, and emotional health cannot be denied or understated. Yet this does not seem to be enough: the seriousness of the social ills that do continue suggests that an externally focused assertion of sovereign power vis-à-vis the state is neither complete nor in and of itself a solution. Indigenous leaders engaging themselves and their communities in arguments framed within a liberal paradigm have not been able to protect the integrity of their nations. "Aboriginal rights" and "tribal sovereignty" are in fact the benefits accrued by indigenous peoples who have agreed to abandon autonomy to enter the state's legal and political framework. Yet indigenous people have successfully engaged Western society in the first stages of a movement to restore their autonomous power and cultural integrity in the area of governance. The movement—referred to in terms of "aboriginal self-government," "indigenous self-determination," or "Native sovereignty"—is founded on an ideology of indigenous nationalism and a rejection of the models of government rooted in European cultural values. It is an uneven process of reinstituting systems that promote the goals and reinforce the values of indigenous cultures, against the constant effort of the Canadian and United States governments to maintain the systems of dominance imposed on indigenous communities during the last century. Many communities have almost disentangled themselves from paternalistic state controls in administering institutions within jurisdictions that are important to them. Many more are currently engaged in substantial negotiations over land and governance, matters hoped and believed to lead to significantly greater control over their own lives and futures.

The intellectuals' rejection of the cooptation of indigenous nationhood and the creation of assimilative definitions of sovereignty in Canada and the United States followed years of activism among indigenous peoples on the ground. That activism was the direct result of the retraditionalization of segments of the population within indigenous communities—rejection of the legitimacy of the state and recovery of the traditional bases of indigenous political society. In Canada the movement has taken the form of a struggle for revision of the constitutional status of indigenous nations, focused on forcing the state to break from its imperial position and recognize and accommodate the notion of an inherent authority in indigenous nations. In the United States, where a theoretical, redefined, and arbitrarily limited form of "sovereign" authority still resides with Indian tribes, the movement has focused on defending and expanding the political and economic implications of that theoretical right. In comparison, the struggles can be seen as philosophical vis-à-vis Canada and material vis-à-vis the United States.

There has been a much more substantive and challenging debate in Canada (linked to the struggles of indigenous peoples confronting the Commonwealth legal tradition in Australia and New Zealand) where actual political and legal stature is being contested, as opposed to the United States, where indigenous peoples tend to rely implicitly upon the existing legal framework. In Canada, more than any other country, indigenous peoples have sought to transcend the colonial myths and restore the original relationships. It is this effort to transcend the colonial mentality and move the society beyond the structures of dominance forming the contemporary political reality that will drive future activism and scholarship on the question of indigenous peoples' political rights and status in relation to states.

In spite of this progress—or perhaps because of it—people in many Native communities are beginning to look beyond the present, envisioning a postcolonial future negotiated at various levels. There are serious problems with that future in the minds of many people who remain committed to systems of government that complement and sustain indigenous cultures. The core problem for both activists and scholars revolves around the fact that the colonial system itself has become embedded within indigenous societies. Indigenous community life today may be seen as framed by two fundamentally opposed value systems, one forming the undercurrent of social and cultural relations, the other structuring politics. This disunity is the fundamental condition of the alienation and political fatigue that plagues indigenous communities. A perspective that does not see the ongoing crisis fueled by continuing efforts to keep indigenous people focused on a quest for power within a paradigm bounded by the vocabulary, logic, and institutions of sovereignty will be blind to the reality of a persistent intent to maintain the colonial oppression of indigenous nations. The next phase of scholarship and activism, then, will need to transcend the mentality that supports the colonization of indigenous nations, beginning with the rejection of the term and notion of indigenous "sovereignty."

A Post-Sovereign Future?

Most of the attention and energy thus far has been directed at the process of de-colonization—the mechanics of escaping from direct state control and the legal and political struggle to gain recognition of an indigenous governing authority. There has been a fundamental ignorance of the end values of the struggle. What will an indigenous government be like after self-government is achieved? Few people imagine that it will be an exact replica of the precolonial system that governed communities in the past. Most acknowledge that all indigenous structures will adapt to modern methods in terms of administrative technique and technology. There is a political universe of possibility when it comes to the embodiment of core values in the new systems.

The great hope is that the government systems being set up to replace colonial control in indigenous communities will embody the underlying cultural values of those communities. The great fear is that the postcolonial governments being designed today will be simple replicas of non-indigenous systems for smaller and racially defined constituencies; oppression becoming self-inflicted and more intense for its localization, thereby perpetuating the two value systems at the base of the problem.

One of the main obstacles to achieving peaceful coexistence is of course the uncritical acceptance of the classic notion of sovereignty as the framework for discussions of political relations between peoples. The discourse of sovereignty has effectively stilled any potential resolution of the issue that respects indigenous values and perspectives. Even "traditional" indigenous nationhood is commonly defined relationally, in contrast to the dominant formulation of the state: there is no absolute authority, no coercive enforcement of decisions, no hierarchy, and no separate ruling entity.

In his work on indigenous sovereignty in the United States, Vine Deloria, Jr., has pointed out the distinction between indigenous concepts of nationhood and those of state-based sovereignty. Deloria sees nationhood as distinct from "self-government" (or the "domestic dependent nation" status accorded indigenous peoples by the United States). The right of "self-determination," unbounded by state law, is a concept appropriate to nations. Delegated forms of authority, like "self-government" within the context of state sovereignty, are concepts appropriate to what we may call "minority peoples" or other ethnically defined groups within the polity as a whole. In response to the question of whether the development of "self-government" and other state-delegated forms of authority as institutions in indigenous communities was wrong, Deloria answers that it is not wrong but simply inadequate. Delegated forms do not address the spiritual basis of indigenous societies:

> Self-government is not an Indian idea. It originates in the minds of non-Indians who have reduced the traditional ways to dust, or believe they have, and now wish to give, as a gift, a limited measure of local control and responsibility. Self-government is an exceedingly useful concept for Indians to use when dealing with the larger government because it provides a context within which negotiations can take place. Since it will never supplant the intangible, spiritual, and emotional aspirations of American Indians, it cannot be regarded as the final solution to Indian problems.[10]

The challenge for indigenous peoples in building appropriate postcolonial governing systems is to disconnect the notion of sovereignty from its Western, legal roots and to transform it. It is all too often taken for granted that what indigenous peoples are seeking in recognition of their nationhood is at its core the same as that which countries like Canada and the United States possess now. In fact, most of the current generation of indigenous politicians see politics as a zero-sum contest for power in the same way that non-indigenous politicians do. Rather than a value rooted in a traditional indigenous philosophy, indigenous politicians regard the nationhood discourse as a lever to gain bargaining position. For the politician, there is a dichotomy between philosophical principle and politics. The assertion of a sovereign right for indigenous peoples is not really believed and becomes a transparent bargaining ploy and a lever for concessions within the established constitutional framework. Until sovereignty as a concept shifts from the dominant "state sovereignty" construct and comes to reflect more of the sense embodied in Western notions such as personal sovereignty or popular sovereignty, it will remain problematic if integrated within indigenous political struggles.

One of the major problems in the indigenous sovereignty movement is that its leaders must qualify and rationalize their goals by modifying the sovereignty concept. Sovereignty itself implies a set of values and objectives that put it in direct opposition to the values and objectives found in most traditional indigenous philosophies. Non-indigenous politicians recognize the inherent weakness of a position that asserts a sovereign right for peoples who do not have the cultural frame and institutional capacity to defend or sustain it. The problem for the indigenous sovereignty movement is that the initial act of asserting a sovereign right for indigenous peoples has structured the politics of decolonization since, and the state has used the theoretical inconsistencies in the position to its own advantage.

In this context, for example, the resolution of "land claims" (addressing the legal inconsistency of Crown or state title on indigenous lands) is generally seen as a mark of progress by progressive non-indigenous people. But it seems that without a fundamental questioning of the assumptions that underlie the state's approach to power, the bad assumptions of colonialism will continue to structure the relationship. Progress toward achieving justice from an indigenous perspective made within this frame will be marginal, and indeed it has become evident that it will be tolerated by the state only to the extent that it serves, or at least does not oppose, the interests of the state itself.

In Canada—to note a second example—recognition of the concept of "aboriginal rights" by the high court is seen by many to be such a landmark of progress. Yet those who think more deeply recognize the basic reality that even with a legal recognition of collective rights to certain subsistence activities within certain territories, indigenous people are still subject to the state's controlling mechanisms in the exercise of these inherent freedoms and powers. They must conform to state-derived criteria and represent ascribed or negotiated identities in order to access these legal rights. Not throwing indigenous people in jail for fishing is certainly a mark of progress, given Canada's shameful history. But to what extent does that state-regulated "right" to fish represent justice when you consider that indigenous people have been fishing on their rivers and seas since time began?

There are inherent constraints to the exercise of indigenous governmental authority built into the notion of indigenous sovereignty, and these constraints derive from the myth of conquest that is the foundation of mainstream perspectives on indigenous-white relations in North America. The maintenance of state dominance over indigenous peoples rests on the preservation of the myth of conquest and on the "noble but doomed" defeated nation status ascribed to indigenous peoples in the state sovereignty discourse. Framing indigenous people in the past allows the state to maintain its own legitimacy by disallowing the fact of indigenous peoples' nationhood to intrude upon its own mythology. It has become clear that indigenous people imperil themselves by accepting formulations of nationhood that prevent them from transcending the past. One of the fundamental injustices of the colonial state is that it relegates indigenous peoples' rights to the past and constrains the development of indigenous societies by allowing only that activity which supports its own necessary illusion—that indigenous peoples do not today present a serious challenge to the legitimacy of the state.

Indigenous leaders have begun acting on their responsibility to expose the imperial pretence that supports the doctrine of state sovereignty and white society's dominion over indigenous nations and their lands. State sovereignty can only exist in the fabrication of a truth that excludes the indigenous voice. It is in fact antihistoric to claim that the state's legitimacy is based on the rule of law. From the indigenous perspective, there was no conquest and there is no moral justification for state sovereignty, only the gradual triumph of germs and numbers. The bare truth is that Canada and the United States were "conquered" only because indigenous peoples were overwhelmed by imported European diseases and were unable to prevent the massive immigration of European, African, and Asian populations. Only recently, as indigenous people learned to manipulate state institutions and have gained support from others oppressed by the state, has the state been forced to incorporate any inconsistencies.

Recognizing the power of the indigenous challenge and unable to deny it a voice, the state's response has been to attempt to draw indigenous people closer. It has encouraged indigenous people to reframe and moderate their nationhood demands to accept the fait accompli of colonization, to help create a marginal solution that does not challenge the fundamental imperial premise. By allowing indigenous peoples a small measure of self-administration, and by forgoing a small portion of the moneys derived from the exploitation of indigenous nations' lands, the state has created an incentive for integration into its own sovereignty framework. Those indigenous communities that cooperate are the beneficiaries of a patronizing faux altruism. They are viewed sympathetically as the anachronistic remnants of nations, the descendants of once independent peoples who by a combination of tenacity and luck have managed to survive and must now be protected as minorities. By agreeing to live as artifacts, such coopted communities guarantee themselves a mythological role and thereby hope to secure a limited but perpetual set of rights.

Is there a Native philosophical alternative? And what might one achieve by standing against the further entrenchment of institutions modeled on the state? Many traditionalists hope to preserve a set of values that challenge the destructive, homogenizing force of Western liberalism and materialism: they wish to preserve a regime that honors the autonomy of individual conscience, noncoercive forms of authority, and a deep respect and interconnection between human beings and the other elements of creation. The contrast between indigenous conceptions and dominant Western constructions in this regard could not be more severe. In most traditional indigenous conceptions, nature and the natural order are the basic referents for thinking of power, justice, and social relations. Western conceptions, with their own particular philosophical distance from the natural world, have more often reflected different kinds of structures of coercion and social power.

Consider these different concepts of power as they affect one's perspective on the relationship between the people and the land, one of the basic elements of a political philosophy, be it indigenous nationhood or state sovereignty. Indigenous philosophies are premised on the belief that the human relationship to the earth is primarily one of partnership. The land was created by a power outside of human beings, and a just relationship to that power must respect the fact that human beings did not have a hand in making the earth, therefore they have no right to dispose of it as they see fit. Land is created by another power's order, therefore possession by humans is unnatural and unjust. The partnership principle, reflecting a spiritual connection with the land established by the Creator, gives human beings special responsibilities within the areas they occupy, linking them in a natural and sacred way to their territories.

The form of distributive or social justice promoted by the state through the current notion of economic development centers on the development of industry and enterprises to provide jobs for people and revenue for government institutions. Most often (and especially on indigenous lands) the industry and enterprises center on natural resource extraction. Trees, rocks, and fish become resources and commodities with a value calculated solely in monetary terms. Conventional economic development clearly lacks appreciation for the qualitative and spiritual connections that indigenous peoples have to what developers would call "resources."

Traditional frames of mind would seek a balanced perspective on using land in ways that respect the spiritual and cultural connections indigenous peoples have with their territories, combined with a commitment to managing the process respectfully and to ensuring a benefit for the natural and indigenous occupants of the land. The primary goals of an indigenous economy are the sustainability of the earth and ensuring the health and well-being of the people. Any deviation from that principle—whether in qualitative terms or with reference to the intensity of activity on the land—should be seen as upsetting the ideal of balance that is at the heart of so many indigenous societies.

Unlike the earth, social and political institutions were created by men and women. In many indigenous traditions, the fact that social and political institutions were designed and chartered by human beings means that people have the power and responsibility to change them. Where the human-earth relationship is structured by the larger forces in nature outside human prerogative for change, the human-institution relationship entails an active responsibility for human beings to use their own powers of creation to achieve balance and harmony. Governance structures and social institutions are designed to empower individuals and to reinforce tradition to maintain the balance found in nature.

Sovereignty, then, is a social creation. It is not an objective or natural phenomenon but the result of choices made by men and women, indicative of a mindset located in, rather than a natural force creative of, a social and political order. The reification of sovereignty in politics today is the result of a triumph of a particular set of ideas over others—no more natural to the world than any other man-made object.

Indigenous perspectives offer alternatives, beginning with the restoration of a regime of respect. This ideal contrasts with the statist solution, still rooted in a classical notion of sovereignty that mandates a distributive rearrangement but with a basic maintenance of the superior posture of the state. True indigenous formulations are nonintrusive and build frameworks of respectful coexistence by acknowledging the integrity and autonomy of the various constituent elements of the relationship. They go far beyond even the most liberal Western conceptions of justice in promoting the achievement of peace, because they explicitly allow for difference while mandating the construction of sound relationships among autonomously powered elements.

For people committed to transcending the imperialism of state sovereignty, the challenge is to de-think the concept of sovereignty and replace it with a notion of power that has at its root a more appropriate premise. And, as James Tully has pointed out, the imperial demand for conformity to a single language and way of knowing has, in any case, become obsolete and unachievable in the diverse (ethnic, linguistic, racial) social and political communities characteristic of modern states. Maintaining a political community on the premise of singularity is no more than intellectual imperialism. Justice demands a recognition (intellectual, legal, political) of the diversity of languages and knowledge that exists among people—indigenous peoples' ideas about relationships and power holding the same credence as those formerly constituting the singular reality of the state. Creating a legitimate postcolonial relationship involves abandoning notions of European cultural superiority and adopting a mutually respectful posture. It is no longer possible to maintain the legitimacy of the premise that there is only one right way to see and do things.

Indigenous voices have been consistent over centuries in demanding such recognition and respect. The speaker of the Rotinohshonni Grand Council, Deskaheh, for example, led a movement in the 1920s to have indigenous peoples respected by the members of the League of Nations. And more recently, indigenous leaders from around the world have had some success in undermining the intellectual supremacy of state sovereignty as the singular legitimate form of political organization.

Scholars of international law are now beginning to see the vast potential for peace represented in indigenous political philosophies. Attention focused on the principles of the Rotinohshonni *Kaienerekowa* (Great Law of Peace) in the international arena, for example, suggests the growing recognition of indigenous thought as a postcolonial alternative to the state sovereignty model. James Anaya, author of the most comprehensive and authoritative legal text on indigenous peoples in international law, writes: "The Great Law of Peace promotes unity among individuals, families, clans, and nations while upholding the integrity of diverse identities and spheres of autonomy. Similar ideals have been expressed by leaders of other indigenous groups in contemporary appeals to international bodies. Such conceptions outside the mold of classical Western liberalism would appear to provide a more appropriate foundation for understanding humanity." . . .[11]

But the state is not going to release its grip on power so easily. The traditional values of indigenous peoples constitute knowledge that directly threatens the monopoly on power currently enjoyed by the state. Struggle lies ahead. Yet there is real hope for moving beyond the intellectual violence of the state in a concept of legal pluralism emerging out of the critiques and reflected in the limited recognition afforded indigenous conceptions in recent legal argumentation. In a basic sense, these shifts reflect what many indigenous people have been saying all along: respect for others is a necessary precondition to peace and justice.

Indigenous conceptions, and the politics that flow from them, maintain in a real way the distinction between various political communities and contain an imperative of respect that precludes the need for homogenization. Most indigenous people respect others to the degree that they demonstrate respect. There is no need, as in the Western tradition, to create a political or legal hegemony to guarantee respect. There is no imperial, totalizing, or assimilative impulse. And that is the key difference: both philosophical systems can achieve peace; but for peace the European demands assimilation to a belief or a country, while the indigenous demands nothing except respect.

Within a nation, one might even rethink the need for formal boundaries and precedents that protect individuals from each other and from the group. A truly indigenous political system relies instead on the dominant intellectual motif of balance, with little or no tension in the relationship between the individual and the collective. Indigenous thought is often based on the notion that people, communities, and the other elements of creation coexist as equals—human beings as either individuals or collectives do not have a special priority in deciding the justice of a situation.

Consider the indigenous philosophical alternative to sovereignty in light of the effect sovereignty-based states, structures, and politics has had on North America since the coming of the Europeans. Within a few generations, Turtle Island has become a land devastated by environmental and social degradation. The land has been shamefully exploited, indigenous people have borne the worst of oppression in all its forms, and indigenous ideas have been denigrated. Recently however, indigenous peoples have come to realize that the main obstacle to recovery from this near total dispossession—the restoration of peace and harmony in their communities and the creation of just relationships between their peoples and the earth—is the dominance of European-derived ideas such as sovereignty. In the past two or three generations, there has been movement for the good in terms of rebuilding social cohesion, gaining economic self-sufficiency, and empowering structures of self-government within indigenous communities. There has also been a return to seek guidance in traditional teachings, and a revitalization of the traditions that sustained the great cultural achievement of respectful coexistence. People have begun to appreciate that wisdom, and much of the discourse on what constitutes justice and proper relationship within indigenous communities today revolves around the struggle to promote the recovery of these values. Yet there has been very little movement toward an understanding or even appreciation of the indigenous tradition among non-indigenous people.

It is in fact one of the strongest themes within indigenous American cultures that the sickness manifest in the modern colonial state can be transformed into a framework for coexistence by understanding and respecting the traditional teachings. There is great wisdom coded in the languages and cultures of all indigenous peoples—this is knowledge that can provide answers to compelling questions if respected and rescued from its status as cultural artifact. There is also a great potential for resolving many of our seemingly intractable problems by bringing traditional ideas and values back to life. Before their near destruction by Europeans, many indigenous societies achieved sovereignty-free regimes of conscience and justice that allowed for the harmonious coexistence of humans and nature for hundreds of generations. As our world emerges into a post-imperial age, the philosophical and governmental alternative to sovereignty and the central values contained within their traditional cultures are the North American Indian's contribution to the reconstruction of a just and harmonious world.

Notes

1. Russel Lawrence Barsh and James Y. Henderson, *The Road: Indian Tribes and Political Liberty* (Berkeley: University of California Press, 1980).

2. Barsh and Henderson, *The Road*, 205.

3. Vine Deloria, Jr., and Clifford M. Lytle, *American Indians, American Justice* (Austin: University of Texas Press, 1983), and *The Nations Within: The Past and Future of American Indian Sovereignty* (Austin: University of Texas Press, 1984).

4. Robert A. Williams, Jr., *The American Indian in Western Legal Thought: The Discourses of Conquest* (New York: Oxford University Press, 1990).

5. Williams, *American Indian in Western Legal Thought*, 317.

6. James Tully, *Strange Multiplicity: Constitutionalism in an Age of Diversity* (Cambridge: Cambridge University Press, 1995).

7. (Gerald) Taiaiake Alfred, *Peace, Power, Righteousness: an indigenous manifesto* (Toronto: Oxford University Press, 1999).

8. David E. Wilkins, *American Indian Sovereignty and the U.S. Supreme Court: The Masking of Justice* (Austin: University of Texas Press, 1997).

9. Wilkins, *American Indian Sovereignty*, 297.

10. Deloria and Lytle, *Nations Within*, 15.

11. S. James Anaya, *Indigenous Peoples in International Law* (New York: Oxford University Press, 1996), 79.

Suggested Readings

Alfred, Taiaiake (Gerald). *Heeding the Voices of Our Ancestors: Kahnawake Mohawk Politics and the Rise of Native Nationalism*. Toronto: Oxford University Press, 1995.

Asch, Michael, ed. *Aboriginal Treaty Rights in Canada: Essays on Law, Equality, and Respect for Difference.* Vancouver: University of British Columbia Press, 1997.

Bartelson, Jens. *A Genealogy of Sovereignty.* Cambridge: Cambridge University Press, 1995.

Biersteker, Thomas J., and Cynthia Weber, eds. *State Sovereignty as Social Construct.* Cambridge: Cambridge University Press, 1996.

Clark, Bruce A. *Native Liberty, Crown Sovereignty: The Existing Aboriginal Right of Self-Government in Canada.* Montreal: McGill-Queen's University Press, 1990.

Cornell, Stephen. *The Return of the Native: American Indian Political Resurgence.* New York: Oxford University Press, 1988.

Deloria, Vine, Jr. *We Talk, You Listen.* New York: Macmillan, 1970.

———. *Custer Died for Your Sins: An Indian Manifesto.* Norman: University of Oklahoma Press, 1988.

Fleras, Augie, and Jean Leonard Elliott, eds. *The "Nations Within": Aboriginal-State Relations in Canada, the United States, and New Zealand.* Toronto: Oxford University Press, 1992.

Foucault, Michel. *Power/Knowledge: Selected Interviews and Other Writings, 1972–1977*, ed. and trans. C. Gordon. New York: Pantheon Books, 1980.

———. *The Politics of Truth*, ed. S. Lotringer. New York: Semiotext(e), 1997.

Lyons, Oren, et al. *Exiled in the Land of the Free: Democracy, Indian Nations, and the U.S. Constitution.* Santa Fe: Clear Light Publishers, 1992.

Ivison, Duncan, Paul Patton, and Will Sanders, eds. *Political Theory and the Rights of Indigenous Peoples.* Cambridge: Cambridge University Press, 2000.

Rotman, Leonard Ian. *Parallel Paths: Fiduciary Doctrine and the Crown-Native Relationship in Canada.* Toronto: University of Toronto Press, 1996.

Royal Commission on Aboriginal Peoples (Canada). *Report.* 5 vols. Ottawa: Canada Communication Group, 1996.

Spinner-Halev, Jeff. *The Boundaries of Citizenship: Race, Ethnicity, and Nationality in the Liberal State.* Baltimore: Johns Hopkins University Press, 1994.

Wilkinson, Charles F. *American Indians, Time, and the Law: Indigenous Societies in a Modern Constitutional Democracy.* New Haven: Yale University Press, 1987.

Fiona Cram (Maori)

Backgrounding Maori Views on Genetic Engineering

The Maori version of *te Tiriti o Waitangi* (the Treaty of Waitangi), 1840, guaranteed the Maori chiefs the continuation of their *tino rangatiratanga* (sovereignty) over their lands. However, this promise was quickly set aside by a colonial government and we found ourselves marginalized within our own land. Colonization has robbed us of many things and continues to take on new faces and new forms of attack. One of the biggest threats we currently face is genetic engineering. Not only does genetic engineering undermine our role as *kaitiaki* (guardians) of this land; it threatens our very existence because of the nature of our belief systems. In this way, our rangatiratanga is undermined as others seek to control our destiny. Maori views on genetic engineering have been expressed in a number of forums. This chapter examines these views within the context of tino rangatiratanga and te Tiriti o Waitangi.

The Maori proverb "Kapo rere te kuri" (The dog snatches and runs away) sums up the situation.[1] Genetic engineering brings together a powerful mix of "science, cultural arrogance and political power" that strengthens the oppression and colonization of indigenous peoples.[2] Within the debate on genetic engineering our worldviews and our concerns are too often marginalized and our right to self-determination threatened. Such has been the case in this country even though our *tino rangatiratanga* (sovereignty) is guaranteed within *te Tiriti o Waitangi* (the Treaty of Waitangi), signed in 1840.

According to Donna Awatere, "Maori sovereignty is the Maori ability to determine our own destiny."[3] Yet there is resistance from our Treaty partner to acknowledging this guarantee. Their responsiveness to the Treaty is constructed within a discourse of Treaty 'principles' and the separateness of the three Treaty articles; both of which are poor proxies for the Treaty in its entirety. Within this chapter the right of Maori to rangatiratanga is addressed through an exploration of how genetic engineering is framed within a Maori worldview. First, the context for this is set by an examination of the Tiriti.

Te Tiriti o Waitangi

Te Tiriti o Waitangi is the founding document of Aotearoa–New Zealand. It was also an affirmation of the sovereign status of the Maori nation.[4]

The Treaty was first signed at Waitangi on 6 February 1840 by Maori chiefs and British officials. It paved the way for British settlement in Aotearoa–New Zealand while at the same time guaranteeing social and economics rights and privileges to Maori. The sharing of this land and its resources was acceptable to Maori. What was needed in order to facilitate this sharing was a constitutional code that would "articulate rights and responsibilities, regulate behaviors, and accommodate access rights of settlers without compromising the guardianship/ownership rights of Maori."[5] The Treaty was this code and the signing of it created this nation.

There were, however, two versions of the Treaty: an English version and a Maori language version. While not all chiefs signed the Treaty, those who signed did not all sign the same document. Whereas Maori sovereignty is ceded in the English version, its retention by the chiefs is guaranteed in the Maori version.[6] This sovereignty, or *tino rangatiratanga*, is defined by Claudia Orange as "the unqualified exercise of their chieftainship over their lands, villages, and all their treasures."[7]

The two versions therefore reflected the different intentions of the colonist and the Maori chiefs. Maori expected the Treaty to be honored and that we would remain physically and politically in control of our country and our destiny; that is, we would continue to have tino rangatiratanga. However the arrival of large numbers of settlers led to pressure for land, and their needs replaced the rights that were guaranteed to Maori in the Treaty. Taiaiake Alfred expresses this succinctly in his statement that the denial of sovereignty was based on "the gradual triumph of germs and numbers" rather than on any moral justification.[8]

In the years following the signing of the Treaty Maori were committed to maintaining tino rangatiratanga, whereas the newcomers were often perceived to be transgressing Maori sovereignty. Conflict was inevitable, and Maori reactions ranged from cooperation to passive resistance to antagonism and armed struggle in the 1860s. In 1877 the Treaty was declared a nullity by Judge Prendergast in the case of the *Bishop of Wellington v. Wi Parata*. Even so Maori have never stopped taking action aimed at ensuring that the Treaty is honored and that Maori tino rangatiratanga is recognized by our Treaty partner.

Aside from the Prendergast ruling in 1877 Moana Jackson, a prominent Maori lawyer and Treaty advocate, identifies two other key moves by the Crown to forestall the honoring of the Treaty. One is the passing of the Treaty of Waitangi Act in 1975 and the second is the reinvention of the Treaty as a series of principles. To this Papaarangi Reid adds the impact of treating the Treaty as a series of stand-alone articles.[9]

There is a guiding principle in English law, *contra proferentem*, that the interpretation of a treaty will favor the understanding that least disadvantages the accepting side (in this instance, the Maori language version). In the case of the Treaty of Waitangi this principle was effectively ignored for over 130 years and then effectively abolished. The issue of the two versions of the Treaty was addressed in 1975 with the passing of the Treaty of Waitangi Act and the establishment of the Waitangi Tribunal. The role of the Tribunal, when established, was to hear complaints about current breaches of the Treaty. The Treaty of Waitangi Act of 1975 did not specifically remove the contra proferentem rule; rather it required the Tribunal to give equal weight to both texts. The only remaining notion that the two texts might be weighted differently is when the Maori text is downplayed so as to balance our concerns against the concerns of all New Zealanders.[10]

In 1988 the Royal Commission on Social Policy described three principles that it saw as "crucial to an understanding of social policy and upon which the Treaty of Waitangi impacts," namely partnership, protection, and participation. These principles have become embedded in the Crown's Treaty discourse.[11] For example, rather than referring to the Treaty directly, legislation incorporated the "principles of the Treaty of Waitangi," as in section 4 of the Conservation Act of 1987: "The Act shall be so interpreted and administered as to give effect to the principles of the Treaty of Waitangi." The principles are problematic because they are not the Treaty. Instead they offer a poor interpretation that supports the breaching of Maori rights by the Crown. For example, the notion of "protection" is rooted in an assumption that indigenous peoples are childlike and require the protection of a superior authority. We would argue that the Crown has an obligation under the Treaty to allow us to protect our rights ourselves.[12]

Accompanying this promotion of principles was the dissection of the Treaty into its three component articles and the treatment of these articles as stand-alone entities. Thus Article 1 was seen to relate to good governance, Article 2 to tino rangatiratanga, and Article 3 to equality and equity between Maori and other New Zealanders. In addition, within the dominant, non-Maori, discourse Article 1 is read in its English version to support the argument that in signing the Treaty, Maori ceded sovereignty. However as Reid argues, the

Treaty is more than the sum of these parts, and tino rangatiratanga should not be confined to only one article.[13]

When each chief signed the Treaty in 1840 the British government's consul to New Zealand, Captain William Hobson, shook the chief's hand and said, "He iwi tahi tatou."[14] This translates as "We are one people," and we have endured a colonization process that has tried to make this so by making us all like our colonizers. However to this day we effectively remain two peoples with the impact of colonization evident in Maori poverty, ill health, and unemployment.[15] While some might say that now two peoples occupy the one land, I would argue that we continue to inhabit two very different lands. For Maori this land is Aotearoa; for the colonizer it is New Zealand.

The debate over genetic engineering has highlighted the lack of understanding the Crown has of our land and of us as *tangata whenua* (people of the land). This culminated in 2001 with the report of the Royal Commission on Genetic Modification, which offered yet another reinterpretation of the Treaty and of Maori rights within this country.[16] In the lead-up to this Royal Commission Maori views on genetic engineering were being expressed in many forums. It is to understandings and concerns that we now turn before examining Maori engagement with the debate over genetic engineering.

Maori and Genetic Engineering

Genetic engineering is different from traditional breeding for selected qualities in that genetic engineering involves a manipulation of the genetic makeup of an organism and often cross-species transfers of genetic material. Maori concerns about genetic engineering are based within our belief systems and culture. These concerns stem from our relationship with the land and the conservation of flora and fauna for future generations.[17]

The interconnectedness of life on this planet stems from all species being descended from Papatuanuku (Earth Mother) and Ranginui (Sky Father). Everything possesses a *mauri* (life force), including animals, fish, birds, land, forests, rivers, and seas.[18] Mauri is the source of the link between things. Cleve Barlow writes that "the flesh of a bird is different from the flesh of an animal, and that of a fish from that of a tree. The *mauri* makes it possible for a thing to exist within the bounds of its own creation."[19] Just as everything has a mauri, so everything has a *whakapapa* (genealogy). Whakapapa literally means the laying of one generation upon another, from the gods to the present generation and into the future.[20]

Maori inherited *Iratangata* or *Mauri-ora* (the life force of mortals) and are the repositories of Maori *whakapapa* (genealogies).[21] Of the species that exist humankind is the *teina* or youngest and therefore we do not have the right to dominate other species who are our *tuakana* or elders.[22] Our relationship with the land, the waters, and the animals and plants of Aotearoa is therefore one of respect and *kaitiakitanga* (guardianship). Genetic manipulation of the human genome places whakapapa at risk. Aroha Mead maintains that the "safety" of whakapapa is a fundamental concern for Maori and can only be guaranteed through guardianship rights.[23]

As *kaitiaki* (guardians), we have the responsibility to protect the mauri of species, including the mauri of genetic material. The Resource Management Act 1991 defines *kaitiakitanga* as the exercise of guardianship by the Maori of an area in accordance with *tikanga Maori* (custom), in relation to natural and physical resources, and includes the ethic of stewardship based on the nature of the resource itself. Maori have practiced kaitiakitanga for thousands of years and thereby protected and cared for our environment, our heritage. The purpose behind this practice is to ensure the protection of the mauri of all things inanimate or animate. Strict rules help prevent adverse effects on the people and the places.[24]

Calls for the recognition of the guardianship rights of indigenous peoples extend beyond our shores. For example, the 1993 Mataatua Declaration on Cultural and Intellectual Property Rights of Indigenous Peoples called upon state, national, and international agencies to recognize that indigenous flora and fauna are "inextricably bound to the territories of indigenous communities and any property right claims must recognise their traditional guardianship."[25] Similarly, in their *Principles and Guidelines for the Protection of the Heritage of Indigenous Peoples*, the Alaska Native Knowledge Network argues that "to be effective, the protection of indigenous peoples' heritage should be based broadly on the principle of self-determination."[26]

The mauri of a species is threatened by genetic engineering as genetic engineering interferes with the integrity of species.[27] In addition, because of the interrelatedness of our environment, "any mutilation, modification or unnatural desecration of any part affects the whole" by upsetting the balance of the mauri.[28] The integrity of this system is therefore essential to notions of sustainability and biodiversity.

At its very heart genetic engineering compromises tino rangatiratanga (sovereignty) as we are no longer able to exercise our kaitiakitanga (guardianship); we are no longer able to maintain our respectful relationship with our environment and ensure balance. "One of the loudest arguments against genetics and biotechnology is coming from our own *Kaumatua* [elders], who are saying very clearly that no one should corrupt or interfere with *whakapapa*. The sanctity and respect for whakapapa is to be maintained. Both *mauri* (life principle) and *wairua* (spirit) of living things are sacred. The responsibility falls on us to protect the legacy of our future generations and this includes the guardianship of *whakapapa*."[29]

A brief chronology of Maori engagement with genetic engineering discussions and debates is in order. This engagement has occurred over the past twelve to fifteen years and is sourced from within our traditional understandings as we have sought to come to grips with this new technology and the science discourse that often shelters it from critique.

An example of this science discourse appeared in the *New Zealand Herald* on 29 December 1999. In an article entitled "Sutton Keen to Cure 'Public Ignorance,' " the newly appointed minister of agriculture, Jim Sutton, is reported as saying that a lack of informed discussion on issues vital to New Zealand's agriculture-fueled economy hampered government decision making. The issue given as an example of this "lack of informed discussion" was the debate on genetically modified organisms. Of this particular issue Sutton is quoted as saying that the level of understanding is barely adequate to sustain a rational debate and that the promised commission of inquiry into genetic modification would raise public awareness and understanding and address this knowledge gap.

Perhaps one reason why Maori concerns are not often heard in the media is because Maori reactions can so easily be described as "nonrational." Many of our concerns are hardly mainstream "science." When Angeline Greensill became the first Maori to make a submission to the Environmental Risk Management Authority (ERMA) under the Hazardous Substance and New Organisms Act, she came up against this mainstream science as practiced by the Crown Agricultural Research Institute, AgResearch. Her submission was based on the clash between transgenic manipulation and her own worldview. Thus the scene was set for Maori views to enter more fully into the debate about the morality and ethics of genetic engineering. However this debate had begun some years earlier with a claim to the Waitangi Tribunal seeking redress for the Crown's denial of tino rangatiratanga with respect to cultural *taonga* (treasures), in particular native flora and fauna.

The Expression of Maori Views on Genetic Engineering

In 1991 the Wai 262 Indigenous Flora and Fauna Claim was lodged with the Waitangi Tribunal by Dell Wihongi (Te Rarawa), Haana Murray (Ngati Kuri),

John Hippolite (Ngati Koata), Tama Poata (Whanau a Rua, Ngati Porou), Katarina Rimene (Ngati Kahungunu), and Te Witi McMath (Ngati Wai). The Wai 262 claim relates to this country's biodiversity and seeks a reinstatement of Maori tino rangatiratanga "in respect of the knowledge of native plants and animals and cultural *taonga*."[30] This includes the right to make and to benefit from decisions about the application of technology, including genetic engineering, when it affects indigenous flora and fauna. The implications of this claim extend beyond flora and fauna to the guarantees contained in te Tiriti o Waitangi of our continued sovereignty over traditional Maori knowledge and ways of doing things more generally.[31] The Tribunal is still deliberating this claim.

In 1995 the Health Research Council held a Consensus Development Conference on human genetic information and subsequently published a conference report entitled *Whose Genes Are They Anyway?*[32] The conference drew a wide range of people and many Maori attended a preconference Maori *hui* (gathering). The key questions asked at the conference were: Who should have the right to know genetic information? What criteria should be used for genetic testing? What ethical and legal controls do we need?

The Maori caucus present at this conference reaffirmed the importance of whakapapa, genealogy, as the repository of our past, present, and future. They argued that any genetic research that includes Maori must be conducted from within a Maori worldview. Such research must also recognize that Maori retain ownership of any bodily material taken from us. Likewise a Maori definition of "quality of life" needs to be applied to any justification for genetic research and any application that purports to enhance quality of life.

There were substantive issues raised about whether scientific views of genetic information are relevant to Maori, who already map their being through whakapapa, which can never be alienated. This implies that no one except *whanau* (family), *hapu* (subtribe), and *iwi* (tribe) has the right to know genetic information unless with express permission, agreement, and management of access by Maori themselves.[33] The caucus concluded by acknowledging the potential of science to be yet another colonizer of Maori: "Whilst the spirit of science may be independent of commercial, political and religious interests, in reality it is often driven by those forces. Culturally unsafe scientific intrusion precludes acknowledgement of the Maori world view. This alienates Maori in yet another process of colonisation."

Following the conference the importance of consultation with Maori was emphasized in the Health Research Council's guidelines for researchers on Maori health research. A second Health Research Council conference was held in June 1998—the Foresight: Using Gene Technologies Conference. The report of this conference contains little evidence of Maori input.[34]

This country's first Talking Technology Conference was held in August 1996 and involved sixteen lay New Zealanders evaluating the use of gene technology in plants. Fourteen members of this panel were brought back together on 8 May 1999 and updated their opinions on plant technology.[35] Of the seven questions addressed by the panel, question 6 examined Maori values: How are the values of Maori going to be considered and integrated in the use of plant biotechnology in New Zealand?

The panel prefaced their response to this question by acknowledging that they were unable to provide a full answer about how Maori values could be taken into account in this debate. They were also explicit within their response that Maori values would be addressed through the Wai 262 claim and by consultation with iwi as part of the wider consultation that legislation related to genetically modified organisms requires. In addition, the addressing of Maori concerns was seen within the broader context of "underlying grievances related to Maori rights."

The panel did, however, support the distinctiveness of Maori cultural views within a predominantly Western European scientific discourse on plant biotechnology. In doing so they also reiterated the guarantees within the Treaty of Waitangi for the continuation of the "special relationship" Maori have with the lands, waters, air, flora, and fauna. Their conclusion was that Maori cultural and ethical concerns about genetic engineering therefore require "specific consideration by virtue of Maori status as tangata whenua [people of the land] and Treaty partners."

In 1996 the Crown passed the Hazardous Substances and New Organisms Act (HSNO Act) and a new organization, the Environmental Risk Management Authority (ERMA), was established to approve new organisms and hazardous substances. Sections 6(d) and 8 of the HSNO Act stipulate that the "relationship of Maori and their culture and traditions with their ancestral lands, water, sites, waahi tapu, valued flora and fauna, and other taonga shall be taken into account by all those working under the Act" and that "All persons exercising powers and functions under this Act shall take into account the principles of the Treaty of Waitangi (Te Tiriti o Waitangi)."[36] The provisions in the act for new organisms came into effect in 1998 and those related to hazardous substances came into effect in 2001.

Nga Kaihautu Tikanga Taiao (Nga Kaihautu), an advisory committee to the Environmental Risk Management Authority, was established under section 42 of the First Schedule to the HSNO Act. Nga Kaihautu provides direct advice to ERMA on Maori cultural and Treaty of Waitangi issues arising from applications to ERMA. The rationale behind the group's work is that genetic engineering is a relatively new technology for Maori, and that the impact of this technology on Maori should be widely debated (although it is noted that local hapu and iwi input to the consultation process must be also maintained).[37] Many of the issues raised by Maori making submissions to ERMA about local issues and by Maori during Nga Kaihautu consultations have been seen by Nga Kaihautu to be applicable to Maori in a wider context rather than as restricted to potential risks and impacts at a local level. These issues include:

- Cultural offense caused by the interspecies mixing of genes as this is an insult to the mauri inherent in whakapapa.
- Imbalances between physical and metaphysical states caused by the interspecies mixing of genes poses risks to Maori health.
- Health risks are also posed by the possibility of transgenic material entering the food chain and by the incineration of any human particulate.
- Negative impacts on Maori economic interests will arise if exports are disrupted by genetically modified organisms and/or food.

In addition, the ERMA Draft Summary Report on its national consultation notes that Maori opposition to genetic engineering is lessened when there is no impact on the mauri of the environment, the genetic material being engineered is not human, and there is the promise of positive health outcomes for current and future generations.[38] Similarly a June 1999 report to the Ministry of Health on Maori perspectives on genetically modified organisms and foods confirmed Maori concerns about whakapapa, the "need to protect taonga as guaranteed by the Treaty of Waitangi," and tino rangatiratanga.[39]

Many Maori have made submissions in response to applications to ERMA for field trials of genetically modified organisms (both plants and animals). However it appears that the burden of proof rests with Maori. In other words, it is not up to applicants to prove that no harm will be done; rather it is up to hapu and iwi to argue that there is a risk if the application is approved. As Jacqui Amohanga clearly outlines in her submission: "Our evidence clearly shows the high potential from a cultural/spiritual view point. However, we do not have the resourcing or the ability to assess Maori health effects given the time constraints. Surely this is the responsibility of either the applicant or the authority to ensure that all possible measures are undertaken to alleviate our concerns and particularly the concerns that many Tangata Whenua throughout Aotearoa would question."[40]

Even with the "newness" of genetic engineering many Maori recognize that the values governing the science of genetic engineering are not Maori values. For example, in response to the application to ERMA by Carter Holt Harvey Forests, Tikitu Tutua-Nathan states that "the [Tuwharetoa Maori Trust] Board does not consider that western scientific values should prevail over the kawa [rules] and tikanga of Ngati Tuwharetoa, and remains unconvinced that science will protect our taonga."[41]

In 1999 AgResearch applied to ERMA for permission to field test cattle that had been genetically modified to contain human genetic material. In response to this application Ngati Wairere, the tribal group within whose *rohe* (area) the field tests were to take place, requested that a moratorium be put in place until such time as protection mechanisms and a monitoring program were established with representative(s) of Ngati Wairere, and with results being submitted to Ngati Wairere.[42] Ngati Wairere's arguments were sourced from Maori cultural values, including whakapapa, tikanga (custom), and mauri. In her submission Jacqui Amohanga stated that "I am unaware of any instances where humans were permitted to mix species as this was traditionally within the domain of the Atua (gods). This application is a direct challenge on our tikanga and kawa and has been seen as culturally inappropriate by the people of Ngati Wairere."[43]

Nga Kaihautu were also clear in their advice to ERMA about the application: that the research proposed by the application is highly likely to cause cultural offense to Maori and that human gene experimentation should be declined until further public debate in general and more dialogue with Maori in particular has taken place.[44] Nga Kaihautu concluded: "It is clear . . . that the use of the human genome in inter-species experimentation is an issue for all Maori, and until this issue is debated widely, a comprehensive view on its impacts on Maori values will never be achieved. Consultation at a local level will not provide for this, and certainly not an adequate assessment of risk, benefits and costs for all Maori as guaranteed by the active protection principle of the Treaty of Waitangi (Section 8 of the HSNO Act)."[45] This argument, however, did not prevent this application from eventually being approved.

On 18 April 2000 the Labour Government announced a Royal Commission into genetic modification. This was seen by some as another avenue for Maori to express our views. However the Maori Council accused the government of ignoring Maori issues as the provisions of the Treaty of Waitangi had not been taken into account in the establishment of the Royal Commission.[46] The commission's warrant specified that it "consult and engage with Maori in a manner that specifically provides for their needs."[47]

The members of the commission were named as the Rt. Hon. Sir Thomas Eichelbaum (chair), the Rev. Richard Randerson (ethicist), Dr. Jean Feming (scientist), and Dr. Jacqueline Allan (Kai Mamoe ki Rakiura, Kai Tahu—Maori/Medical/Scientific/Technical). While the Royal Commission took place there was a voluntary moratorium on all applications for field testing and release of genetically modified organisms.

The commission received input from Maori through its public consultation and Maori-specific consultation. A number of Maori groups were also among those granted special person status and therefore made a more formal appearance before the commission. The commission reported in July 2001 and, while acknowledging Maori concerns, chapter 11 of the report on *Te Tiriti o Waitangi* once again moves past the Treaty to the establishment of Treaty principles, which the commission argues are relevant to the debate on genetic engineering. These principles are "active protection" of Maori interests by the Crown, and "cooperation" between Treaty partners, which the commission interprets as the requirement that the Crown consult with Maori. These principles bear little resemblance to the guarantee of tino rangatiratanga made in the Treaty.

Shortly after the Royal Commission began its deliberations Fiona Cram, Leonie Pihama, and Glennis Philip-Barbara completed a research project on Maori and genetic engineering.[48] During the course of this research Maori were asked for their thoughts on genetic engineering. Concerns about whakapapa dominated these conversations. The mixing of whakapapa through transgenic processes was viewed by many as unacceptable practice. The mixing of genetic material raised concerns in spiritual, cultural, and physical terms.

In addition, many aspects of tikanga Maori or custom were raised. One conclusion drawn was that there are clear indicators available to Maori within tikanga that may support decision-making processes and that provide guidelines for ethical frameworks for research generally and for genetic engineering research in particular. Te Tiriti o Waitangi was also viewed as the foundation for all processes regarding genetic engineering developments in Aotearoa.

Summary

Maori have views on genetic engineering, and these views have been expressed in many forums. The views are not new in the sense that we have always known of the importance of whakapapa and mauri. What is relatively new is the notion of genetic engineering and, in particular, the interspecies mixing of genes. However, discussion about genetic engineering and genetically modified organisms (GMOs) and food is accelerating within Aotearoa. Our role as kaitiaki of our environment and of our knowledge is a key factor within this discussion. And while an understanding of the science of genetics may also be desirable, it is important to recognize that the debate over genetic engineering is as much cultural, political, and economic as it is scientific.

Within this debate Maori knowledge should not be considered as an interesting aside to Western scientific knowledge. It must be acknowledged that Western scientific knowledge offers just one way of understanding the world and that this way is not the only way.[49] Moves are underway to incorporate Maori knowledge and values within the HSNO Act and other acts related to the regulation of genetic engineering.[50] It remains to be seen whether these changes will satisfy Maori calls for tino rangatiratanga.

The assertion by Maori of our tribal rights to full participation in the management of environmental resources reflects indigenous people's calls worldwide.[51] Situated directly from te Tiriti o Waitangi, tino rangatiratanga is about Maori having meaningful control over our own lives and cultural well-being and being able to exercise kaitiakitanga. As Ani Mikaere states, "The Treaty of Waitangi has never been the source of Maori authority in Aotearoa: all it did was confirm that authority and create a place for Pakeha to live, regulated by the Crown, but ultimately subject to *tino rangatiratanga*. There is nothing confusing about that."[52]

Acknowledgments

The author takes sole responsibility for this paper. However it would be improper to deny that her views have been informed and enriched by the talk and writings of many others, including Linda Smith, Papaarangi Reid, Moana Jackson, Aroha Mead, Leonie Pihama, and Bevan Tipene Matua, to name but a few.

Notes

1. "Just as a dog snatches food from its master's hand and runs away without obeying him, so is a person who listens to another but takes no notice of what is said." A. W. (Cliff) Reed, Aileen E. Brougham, and Timoti Karetu, *The Reed Book of Maori Proverbs* (Auckland: Reed, 1996), 69.

2. Linda Tuhiwai Smith, *Decolonizing Methodologies: Research and Indigenous Peoples* (New York: Zed Books/Dunedin, New Zealand: Otago University Press, 1999).

3. Donna Awatere, *Maori Sovereignty* (Auckland: Broadsheet Publications, 1984), 1.

4. Claudia Orange, *The Treaty of Waitangi* (Wellington: Allen and Unwin, 1987); Joanne Barker, "For Whom Sovereignty Matters," this volume.

5. Aroha Mead, "Speaking to Question 6: How Are the Values of Maori Going to Be Considered and Integrated in the Use of Plant Biotechnology in New Zealand?" in *Plant Biotechnology*, final

report and proceedings from Talking Technology Forums held 22–24 August and 8 May 1999 (Wellington: Talking Technology, 1999).

6. Jane Kelsey, "Te Tiriti o Waitangi and the Bill of Rights," in *Race, Gender, Class* (1986): 23–30.

7. Claudia Orange, *The Story of a Treaty* (Wellington: Bridget Williams Books, 1989), 30.

8. Taiaiake Alfred, "Sovereignty," this volume.

9. Tim McCreanor, "The Treaty of Waitangi—Responses and Responsibilities," in *Honouring the Treaty*, ed. Helen Yensen, Kevin Hague and Tim McCreanor (Auckland: Penguin, 1989); Moana Jackson, talk given at a health needs assessment hui, Kuratini Marae, Wellington, 2 March 2001 (author's notes); Papaarangi Reid, "Nga Mahi Whakahaehae a te Tangata Tiriti," in *Health and Society in Aotearoa New Zealand*, ed. Peter Davis and Kevin Dew (Auckland: Oxford University Press, 1999).

10. Jackson, talk at a health needs assessment hui.

11. Royal Commission on Social Policy, *The April Report. Vol. II* (Wellington: Government Print, 1988), 49.

12. Jackson, talk given at a health needs assessment hui.

13. Reid, "Nga Mahi Whakahaehae a te Tangata Tiriti."

14. Orange, *The Story of a Treaty*.

15. Te Puni Kokiri, *Progress Towards Closing Social and Economic Gaps between Maori and Non-Maori*, report to the Minister of Maori Affairs (Wellington: Ministry of Maori Development, 2000).

16. Royal Commission on Genetic Modification, *Report of the Royal Commission on Genetic Modification* (Wellington: Government Print, 2001, accessed 1 May 2003 at http://www.gmcommission.govt.nz).

17. Debra Harry, Stephanie Howard, and Brett Lee Shelton, *Indigenous People, Genes and Genetics: What Indigenous People Should Know about Biocolonialism. A Primer and Resource Guide* (Wadsworth NV: Indigenous Peoples Council on Biocolonialism, accessed 1 June 2003 at http://www.ipcb.org). See also Kilipaka Kawaihonu Nahili Pae Ontai, "A Spiritual Definition of Sovereignty from a Kanaka Maoli Perspective," this volume.

18. Cleve Barlow, *Tikanga Whakaaro: Key Concepts in Maori Culture* (Auckland: Oxford University Press, 1991).

19. Barlow, *Tikanga Whakaaro*, 83.

20. Barlow, *Tikanga Whakaaro*, 83.

21. Deborah Baird, Lloyd Geering, Kay Saville-Smith, Linda Thompson, and Tose Tuhipa, *Whose Genes Are They Anyway?* (Auckland: Health Research Council of New Zealand, 1995).

22. Angeline Greensill, *Statement of Evidence of Angeline Greensill in the Matter of Application for Approval to Field Test in Containment Any Genetically Modified Organism* (Wellington: Environmental Risk Management Authority, 1999).

23. Aroha Mead, "Human Genetic Research and Whakapapa," in *Mai i Rangiatea*, ed. Pania Te Whaiti, Marie McCarthy and Arohia Durie (Auckland: Auckland University Press, 1997).

24. Greensill, *Statement of Evidence*.

25. *Mataatua Declaration on Cultural and Intellectual Property Rights of Indigenous Peoples*, formulated at the First International Conference on the Cultural and Intellectual Property Rights of Indigenous Peoples, Whakatane, Aotearoa, 12–18 June 1993 (accessed 4 April 1999 at www.aotearoa.wellington.net.nz/imp/mata.htm).

26. Alaska Native Knowledge Network, *Principles and Guidelines for the Protection of the Heritage of Indigenous People*, elaborated by the Special Rapporteur, Mrs. Erica-Irene Daes, in conformity with

resolution 1993/44 and decision 1994/105 of the Sub-Commission on Prevention of Discrimination and Protection of Minorities of the Commission on Human Rights, Economic and Social Council, United Nations, E/CN.4/Sub.2/1995/26, GE. 95–12808 (E), 21 June 1995 (accessed 30 November 1999 at http://www.ankn.uaf.edu/protect.html).

27. Ministry for the Environment (1996) cited in Christine Simpson and Julie Browne, *A Brief Survey of Recent Consultations with Maori and of Published Maori Perspectives Relating to Genetically Modified Organisms and Genetically Modified Food* (Wellington: Ministry of Health, 1999).

28. Greensill, *Statement of Evidence.*

29. Cherryl Smith and Paul Reynolds, *Maori, Genes and Genetics: What Maori Should Know about the New Biotechnology* (available from the Whanganui Iwi Law Centre, telephone 06–345-9190, 2000).

30. Te Manutukutuku, "Wai 262 Hearings to Commence" and "Wai 262—Indigenous Flora and Fauna" (1997, accessed 31 May 1999 at http://www.knowledge-basket.co.nz/waitangi/welcome.html).

31. Smith and Reynolds, *Maori, Genes and Genetics.*

32. Baird et al., *Whose Genes Are They Anyway?*

33. Baird et al., *Whose Genes Are They Anyway?*

34. Health Research Council of New Zealand, *Gene Technologies Discussion Paper* (1996, accessed 1 June 2003 at http://www.hrc.govt.nz/biotech.html).

35. Talking Technology, *Plant Biotechnology*. Final report and proceedings from the Talking Technology Forums held 22–24 August 1996 and 8 May 1999 (Wellington: Talking Technology, 1999).

36. Ministry for the Environment, *Users' Guide to the Hazardous Substances and New Organisms Act 1996* (accessed 4 April 2000 at *http://www.mfe.govt.nz/about/laws/hsnouser.htm*).

37. Nga Kaihautu, *Tikanga Taiao Report: Application for Approval to Field Test in Containment Any Genetically Modified Organism* (Application Number: GMF98009 Genetically modified cattle [*Bos taurus*], July 1999).

38. Cited in Simpson and Browne, *A Brief Survey of Recent Consultations with Maori.*

39. Simpson and Browne, *A Brief Survey of Recent Consultations with Maori.*

40. Jacqui Amohanga, *Statement of Evidence of Jacqui Amohanga in the Matter of Application for Approval to Field Test in Containment Any Genetically Modified Organism* (Wellington: Environmental Risk Management Authority, 1999), section 2.4.15.

41 Tikitu Tutua-Nathan, *Statement of Evidence of Tikitu Tutua-Nathan, Project Manager, Environmental Services Division, Tuwharetoa Maori Trust Board, in the matter of Application for Approval to Field Test in Containment Any Genetically Modified Organism* (Wellington: Environmental Risk Management Authority, 1999).

42. Manuka Henry, *Statement of Evidence to* ERMA *in the Matter of the Application for Approval to Field Test in Containment Any Genetically Modified Organism* (AgResearch, 1999).

43. Amohanga, *Statement of Evidence.*

44. Nga Kaihautu, *Tikanga Taiao Report.*

45. Nga Kaihautu, *Tikanga Taiao Report*, section 3.5.

46. Maori Council, press release posted to the tino-rangatiratanga list-serve, 19 April 2000.

47. Maori Council, press release.

48. Fiona Cram, Leone Pihama, and Glennis Philip-Barbara, *Maori and Genetic Engineering* (Tamaki Makaurau [Auckland]: IRI Publications, 2000).

49. Leonie Pihama, "Asserting Indigenous Theories of Change," this volume.

50. Cabinet Paper 8, *Changes to More Appropriately Reflect the Treaty of Waitangi Relationship within the* HSNO *Act* (accessed 1 July 2003 at the Ministry for the Environment Web site, http://www.mfe.govt.nz/issues/organisms/legislation/).

51. Erica-Irene Daes, "Defending Indigenous People's Heritage" (keynote address, conference on Protecting Knowledge: Traditional Resource Rights in the New Millennium, hosted by the Union of British Columbia Indian Chiefs, Vancouver, Canada, February 2000); Dan Landeen and Allen Pinkham, *Salmon and His People: Fish and Fishing in Nez Perce Culture* (Lewiston ID: Confluence Press, 1999).

52. Ani Mikaere, "Challenging the Mission of Colonisation: A Maori View of the Treaty of Waitangi and the Constitution" (paper, conference on Liberty, Equality, Community: Constitutional Rights in Conflict, Auckland, 20–21 August 1999. Pakeha are non-Maori.

Guillermo Delgado-P. (Quechua) and
John Brown Childs (Massachuset/Brothertown-Oneida/Madagascan)

First Peoples/African American Connections

In the one hundred and eleven years since the creation of the Spokane Indian Reservation in 1881, not one person, Indian or otherwise had ever arrived here by accident. Walpinit, the only town on the reservation, did not exist on most maps, so the black stranger surprised the whole tribe when he appeared with nothing more than the suit he wore and the guitar slung over his back. . . . The entire reservation knew about the black man five minutes after he showed up at the crossroads. All the Spokanes thought up reasons to leave work or home so they could drive down to look the stranger over. . . . The black man waved at every Indian that drove by, but nobody had the courage to stop, until Thomas Builds-the-Fire pulled up in his old blue van.

"Ya-hey," Thomas called out.

"Hey," the black man said.

"Are you lost?"

"Been lost a while, I suppose."

"You know where you're at?"

"At the crossroads," the black man said . . .

African-American blues singer Robert Johnson comes to
Walpinit in Sherman Alexie's novel, *Reservation Blues*[1]

Thousands of volumes have been written about the historical and social relations existing between Europeans and the Native Peoples of the Americas and between Europeans and Africans, but relations between Native Americans and Africans have been sadly neglected. The entire Afro-Native American cultural exchange and contact experience is a fascinating and significant subject, but one largely obscured by a focus upon European activity and European colonial relations with "peripheral" subject peoples. Africans and Native Americans must now be studied together without their relations always having to be obscure by the separations established through the work of scholars focusing essentially upon some aspect of European expansion and colonialism.

Jack Forbes, *Africans and Native Americans: The Language
of Race and the Evolution of Red-Black Peoples*[2]

A Word on Co-Laboring

When members of the Native American Studies Research Cluster, sponsored by the Center for Cultural Studies at the University of California, Santa Cruz, invoked the need to carry out a serious of dialogues based on the notion of Indigeneity, we joyfully agreed to contribute to its success. The conference entitled Sovereignty 2000: Locations of Contestation and Possibility triggered our *transcommunal* thinking and we searched for the locations, for the place/spaces that would serve us as foundations to rebuild our memory.[3] We encountered them in the Red Clay/Blue Hills of Massachusetts and Alabama but also in the heart of the Andean mountains. We thought that both place/spaces spoke to the ideas of contestation and possibility. We even invented the term *place/space*, to implicate the relevance of space and place, which in indigenous thinking cannot be separated.[4]

In a way, we agreed to re/member (ourselves and our histories) following the notion that Indigenous narratives of histories have experienced—always—persistent dismemberment, dislocation, displacement and that even U.S. laws have been labeled with words like *removal* (e.g., Indian Removal Act of 1830) and *cleansing*. In South America, entire campaigns of colonial occupation were based on the terrible act of beheading. Names such as the Conquest of the Desert (in Argentina), the Campaign of the Extirpation of Idolatries (Peru), and the Pacification Campaigns of Rondón (Brazil) have become landmarks of official history. Violence is buried everywhere; history is buried too.

Events in 1992 commemorated five hundred years of European presence in the Americas, but they also reminded us about the demographic resilience Indigenous Peoples needed in that time. Time, after all, has placed peoples together against an inevitable history of coming together, something that colonizers did not foresee, as they pretended to impose their own invention of "racial purity." The reality is that peoples came and went, adding to the complexity of humanity already in place before the arrival of the Europeans. In this chapter, re/membering consists in looking at our ontological dwelling. We look at the power of place/spaces, and by offering such a glimpse, we find that it cannot be narrated without the spirit of languages, of place/spaces.

Hence, we divided the work in two main parts, the North American narrative (the Eagle) and the South American one (the Condor). Both re/member in terms of the past but also in terms of the present. In Aymara thought, we are told by Carlos Mamani Condori, the word for eye, *Nayra*, is also the prefix for the word meaning past: *Nayrapacha*.[5] By re/membering, naturally, we see our past before us, since the eye, Nayra, looks ahead but also looks back. This is an exercise inspired by Nayrapacha but also by Nayra and the Pacha (time and place/space). We, as authors, inscribe the past in the present; in a way we place the past ahead. We are looking for Punkapoag but also for *Punkupacha*, the word that contains the *door* to the roads of the *world*.

A Word about Sovereignty

We deliberately enhance the concept of sovereignty in the actual exercise of memory and language as means to illustrate decolonized Indigeneities. As such, we acknowledge a clear departure from modern and legal/structural definitions of sovereignty (which, by all means, frame concrete state-nation relations of modern theory). Our assumption is that Indigeneity continues to be constructed in this new century. In this context, sovereignty as a post-colonial concept illustrates the power to remember and to recall, in the same way that other Indigenous Peoples throughout the world have done. For us this remembering and recalling means bringing our Indigenous past along. This past, from the perspective of Indigeneity, has been sovereign—it has the power to endow us with the ability to question coloniality. Sovereignties are shaped by retrieval, by acknowledging the destructive forces of colonialisms, and by restoring the healing powers of pasts in the praxis of our own Indigenous languages and memories. The capacity to state and proclaim, with our own language and memory, from the bases of Indigeneity, can be seen as a sovereign act that reclaims a sense of self and affiliation. As colonialism has not been a synchronic movement, *sovereignty of thought* can be a concrete base to challenge it. This is what we intend to do here through bringing together two experiences of colonialism and Indigeneity.

Red Clay, Blue Hills: In Honor of My Ancestors

John Brown Childs

First, I must speak about my ancestors. It is from them that I have received the desire to contribute to the best of my ability, to what I hope is constructive cooperation among diverse peoples. I owe it to them to make these comments. What I have to say flows from two great currents, the African and the Native American, whose confluence runs through my family and infuses my spirit today.

The African-Malayo grandmother of my grandmother of my grandmother of my grandmother, known as "The Princess" to her captors, was born in Madagascar, an island peopled by populations from the Pacific and Africa.

In 1749, the Princess was a member of a Madagascan delegation on board a French ship bound for France, where she apparently was to go to convent school. Privateers captured their ship. All the Madagascans on board were captured and sold into slavery in the English colonies. My ancestress found herself in chains, being sold as property to a Thomas Burke, a leading colonial figure, to be given as a wedding present for his new wife at their ceremony in Norfolk, Virginia.[6]

The descendants of the Princess later established their families in the red clay country of Marion where they (as "property" of whites) had been transferred through the infamous network of the slave trade. Marion, in Perry County, Alabama, has for a long time been a dynamic wellspring of African-American life in that region. Marion is where my father's forebears, Stephen Childs and his family, created the Childs Bakery and Confectioners, Growers and Shippers store on Marion's main street after the Civil War. This store was an economic bulwark of the African-American community there. My father, born there in the heart of what had been the slaveholding region of the southern United States, was named after John Brown, the revolutionary fighter who gave his life in the battle against slavery. Marion is where one of my ancestors, James Childs, and nine other African Americans, newly liberated from slavery after the Civil War in 1865, established one of the first African-American–initiated schools in the South, the Lincoln Normal School.

The school's teachers were housed in a building that had been taken away from the white terrorist organization, the Ku Klux Klan, whose aim was to keep people of African descent in subordination and indignity. Lincoln Normal School went on to become an influential African-American educational institution. Through their creation of Lincoln Normal School, my Childs family relations, along with other African Americans in Marion, worked in the midst of Ku Klux Klan country to create a sustaining community institution that "would advance the black race" in the midst of a dangerous, often lethal environment of racial oppression. They sought to use their roots in the rural and small-town Deep South as a basis for construction of a bastion of justice and dignity.

I was born in 1942, in the Roxbury section of Boston, Massachusetts. My birthplace is only a few miles north of a state recreational park; there in the Blue Hills is a body of water still called by its Native American name Punkapoag, meaning "Place of Fresh Still Water." Punkapoag is where my mother's Native American ancestors originally lived. These relations of mine were members of the Algonkian confederacy known commonly by the name Massachuset—or to be more precise, Massachuseuck, which means "Place of the Big Hills." The Massachuset nation, like many Native American nations, was a noncentralized confederacy comprising several communities such as the Punkapoag, Nipmuck, Neponset, and Wesaguset.

European-introduced diseases such as smallpox heavily impacted the Massachuset along with many other Native Americans along the coast. The Massachuset population plummeted from an estimated thirty thousand to a few hundred by the mid 1650s. Surviving members of those nations that had been undermined as elders died, and land was taken from them, were forcibly concentrated into small villages called "praying towns," where they were supposed to adapt to and adopt Christianity. One of these towns was Punkapoag, originally the main home of the Massachuset but later turned into a mix of concentration camp and refugee center.

As a coherent cultural entity, the Punkapoag community of the Massachuset confederacy, with its members forced into exile and finding intermarriage with other peoples the only means of survival, ceased to exist as a social whole. Responding to decades of cultural erosion and assaults, a gathering of Christian Native peoples, including some of my ancestors, under the leadership of the Reverend Samson Occom—a Mohegan man, and a Presbyterian minister who had struggled against great odds to attain his "calling"—sought and were generously given land by the Oneida nation in what is now New York State. In 1774 at a ceremony in Johnson Hall along the Mohawk River, they were adopted as the "younger brothers and sisters of the Oneida." On that land they created a new community, Brothertown, or more precisely in their Algonkian language, *Eyamquittoowauconnuck*, "Place of Equal Peoples," which they hoped would allow them to (re)create a homeland free from subjugation.

My Native American ancestors, whose family name had become Burr, intermarried with the Oneida. Eventually, in the early 1800s they moved back closer to their ancestral homeland in the State of Massachusetts.[7] From these currents of Massachuset/Brothertown-Oneida and Africa came my mother Dorothy Pettyjohn, who was born in Amherst, Massachusetts. She became a teacher, who as a young woman went to "Cotton Valley" in Alabama of the 1930s to teach in a school for impoverished rural African-American children, not far from Marion and its Lincoln Normal School. It was there that she met and married my father. So the waves of oppression, crashing over many peoples driven from their land, forged them into complex syntheses of memory and belonging that link Africa and Native America for me.

In 1835, Alexis de Tocqueville's soon to be famous vast overview of the young United States, entitled *Democracy in America*, was published. Among his otherwise astute descriptions based on his travels in "America," de Tocqueville inaccurately pictures what he calls the "three races of the United States." These, he says, are "the white or European, the Negro, and the Indian," which he asserts are always distinctly separate populations. Concerning "the Negro" and "the Indian," he writes that these "two unhappy races have nothing in common, neither birth, nor features, nor language nor habits."[8]

If this assertion by de Tocqueville were accurate, then I could not exist, given the African and Native American currents that run together for more than two hundred years in my family histories. My family cannot be compartmentalized into the rigid sealed-off categories suggested by de Tocqueville. Nor can the depths of their courage be plumbed by his superficial description of the "unhappy races," a dismissal, no matter how terrible the tribulations as people flowed through so many valleys of oppression. Today I recognize that from Punkapoag in Massachusetts and Brothertown in New York State to Lincoln Normal School in Alabama, my relations were among those establishing roots in what they hoped would be sustaining communities that could buffer people against the forces of hatred, while offering solid ground for justice and dignity. I know that my connection to my ancestors is not only genealogical, as important as that is. My connection to them is also that of the spirit. I have for many years worked alongside those trying to create places of freedom from injustice. The springing hopes of my ancestors propel this work of mine.

I do not feel like one of those "crossing border hybrids" now so much discussed by scholars who examine postmodernity. Nor does the older Latin American term Zambo for "half black, half Indian" describe how I know myself. It is not in such a divided fashion that I recognize my existence. To the contrary, in the language of my Algonkian ancestors, I am a man who stands at *newichewannock*, the "place between two strong currents." Without these distinct streams there can be no such in-between-place to be named as such. But at the same time, this place is real and complete unto itself. In the same way I emerge a full man, not a simple bifurcated halfling, from the two strong currents of Africa and Native America. It is this newichewannock that marks the place of my spirit and that propels me today.

Compartmentalization of History and its Dangers

There are many well-known ways to obliterate histories. But the one I want to emphasize here involves a compartmentalized drawing of rigid boundaries among distinct histories that eliminates recognition of complexly fluid interminglings. As our opening quotation from Jack Forbes shows, such compartmentalization concerning Native Americans and African Americans results in ignoring the multiple and diverse crisscrossings of these two populations.

I suggest the importance of a crossroads or middle ground, the newichewannock between-strong-currents position, as yet another important angle on the rim of the circle of meaning, from which, along with perspectives from many other different starting points, we can reach a central location of shared understandings. As Guillermo Delgado-P. points out, the crossroads or *Tinkuqniypacha* has a special significance of strength and potential in the Andes. The Quechua term "*Tinku* (encounter/departure) is used to illustrate the coming together of pain and celebration. It also refers to the formation of space of dialogue and sharing, of struggle and conflict. Cyclically, Andean *ayllus* (communities) get together to move *inkamaykus* (milestones) that mark territorial boundaries. The purpose is to "read" nature's kinetics in order to proceed onward to a next stage of life. It implies readjusting territorial use, answering to the needs of seeds, planting, and irrigation. *Tinkuqniykuna* are simultaneous celebrations and commemorations of encounters and disencounters. They assume dialogues that, like seeds, will only later bear fruit.[9]

Similarly, for African-descent cultures in the Americas, the crossroads is also a place of great power and potential. From the vantage point of the crossroads, I can picture approaches that speak of the allied resistance of Africans and Seminoles against white, pro-slavery interests in the early 1800s and that also fundamentally address the way in which Native American removal and the massive stealing of Indigenous land is directly related to the rise of the slave economy on much of that illegally taken and (semi) vacated space. Those are diverse histories, but they are wrapped together forming a blood knot that is crucial to our understanding of the Americas. In this sense African-American, Native American, Latino/Latin American, and American studies projects in universities and colleges should consider including this tangled coming together of the ancestors of today's Indigenous Americans, Pacific Islanders, and African-Americans as we move into the twenty-first century.

There are too many crisscrossing paths from Mali to Oaxaca, from Angola to Choctaw and Cherokee lands in the United States, from Nigeria to the Arawak and Carib islands, and from Ghana to Peru to allow them to be lost under the pressure of imperial divide-and-rule mentality. Intellectually, we enrich our understandings of one another through such emphases on middle ground interactions of the African and Native American. Politically, we help to lay the groundwork for future hemispheric cooperation among Indigenous and African-American peoples. Such cooperation will become ever more necessary if we are to confront effectively the terrible onslaught of militarized globalizing economic forces that are sweeping all before them from body to soul, from air to water.

Curly Deer's Freedom

Seven men shot down by the authorities during a protest demonstration. This was the death count for a group described as "patriots" who were killed in a brawl with the British Army in Boston, Massachusetts, in the year 1770, the so-called Boston Massacre. This moment in U.S. history is often seen as a preliminary step toward the "Revolution for Independence." Among those killed was a young seaman named Crispus Attucks. I want to say a few words about Crispus Attucks. If he is mentioned as being distinctive at all (and such mention does not always occur), he is called a "a black man," being in part of African ancestry. However, Attucks was also apparently of Native American descent, coming from the same Massachuset background as do I. The name Attucks is a southern New England Algonkian word meaning deer. Crispus is apparently a Latinate derivation (it was common enough for slave owners to name their slaves after Romans), although in this case it is an adjective suggesting curly or "kinky" hair. His grave at Old South Church in Boston is not far from the Blue Hills Punkapoag homeland of many Massachuset people. He died too soon in the U.S. war for independence to have to grapple with what Carlos Fuentes, speaking of all the national independence wars in the Americas, observes: "These blacks . . . were the defeated troops of another revolt, "the insurrection of the other species" which soon recognized the reality of the wars of Independence; everyone wanted freedom for themselves, but no one wanted equality for the blacks."[10]

So Curly Deer (as we shall call him in translation), in his entwined Massachuset/African self, lay there on the cobblestoned, gunpowdered, bloodied streets of Boston, a martyr for freedom, dying alongside his white compatriots. His fate personified the contradiction of dying for freedom in a land that had enslaved his African ancestors and driven his Indigenous ancestors from their land (upon which Boston sits). Attucks personifies the connection among African Americans and Native Americans as well as their complex shared and difficult pathways in the midst of European domination.

African-American–Native American Connections

The massive abduction of millions of African people from their land and their enforced labor on plantations throughout the Americas were directly dependent on the European removal of Indigenous peoples from the land. The factory-like slave labor colonies of North America, the Caribbean, and South America were only possible because Indigenous people had either been killed or had been forced off those lands. It is not surprising therefore that in the United States, the place names of localities associated with racism, slavery, segregation, and black resistance are often also Indigenous place names that echo the original, pre–slave trade inhabitants.

As a former activist in the 1960s Civil Rights Movement in the United States, I still feel the haunted salience of names such as Natchez, Biloxi, Alabama, Mississippi, Mobile, and Tuscaloosa, to mention but a few places where legalized bloody racial subjugation was so deeply embedded. All of these are Native American place names. These same names are now burned into the memories of African Americans after centuries of slavery, segregation, lynching, and resistance in those very same sites. This coincidence of the significance of place names in the southeastern United States for both Native Americans and African Americans speaks, in the loudness of its often historically muted silence, to the crossing of the paths of these two peoples. The hemisphere-wide profit-driven European addiction for enslaved people to labor on conquered land, with its attendant corrosive consequences for both Indigenous peoples and African peoples, historically impacts both populations, albeit in different ways, while also bringing many of them into contact with one another in wide areas of the Western Hemisphere.

However, other complex parallels overlie this core fact. Even as Africa loomed as the land from which slave labor could be extracted, the European nightmare attempted not only to take Indigenous land but to use those driven from the land as slaves. Consider the following very partial listing.

1492 Columbus initiates the commercial enslavement of Native Americans, shipping them to the slave markets of Cadiz and Seville. In 1503 Queen Isabella of Spain grants permission to "capture" Native Americans for the slave markets of Europe, "paying us the share that belongs to us and to sell them and utilize their services."[11]

1501 Gaspar Corte Real (acting under Portuguese rule) kidnaps fifty-seven Beothuk Native Americans from the Labrador and Newfoundland coasts to be sold as slaves.[12]

1512 The Spanish Law of Burgos grants rights and legal doctrines to Spanish land grantees allowing and formalizing enslavement of Indigenous peoples under the encomienda system.[13]

1600s New England colonial governments sell Native Americans into slavery in the West Indies, in the aftermath of the crushing of Indigenous resistance, most notably in King Philip's Wars.[14]

1700s Some Portuguese slave plantations have more than a thousand Native Americans held on them in slavery in Brazil, with one Jesuit account asserting that some three million Indigenous people are held in slavery in the Rio Negro region alone.[15]

1784 After the crushing of the rebellion of the Inca leader Tupaq Amaru in Peru, some Inca nobility are sent into slavery in the Spanish-controlled Sahara. Thus, as Jack Forbes points out, "some (Native) Americans reached still another part of Africa.[16]

1600s–1880s Native Americans in what is now the southwestern region of the United States are consistently sold into slavery or semi-slavery, with some being shipped to the Caribbean and others such as the Yaqui being sold into the Yucatán.[17]

It is clear from the "importation" of millions of Africans that the Europeans could not and did not rely only on such Native American sources of forced labor. Yet the persistence of enslavement (formal or de facto) of Indigenous peoples in the Americas is another important dimension that must be considered. We must recognize the brutal enslavement impacting Indigenous peoples in the Americas that was a cousin to the totalitarian slave system imposed on African-descent peoples.

Of course in the spectrum of the human condition there have been those Native Americans who, as the Cherokee community leader and writer Wilma Mankiller illustrates, succumbed to the European system, adapting the international business of slavery as their own.[18] In effect they joined with some African kings on the opposite side of the Atlantic who similarly had no compunction about providing the ports, facilities, and captured people for transport to the Americas. There have been African Americans who, with various promises of freedom dangled in front of them, have fought Native Americans. There have also been blacks who betrayed their own people's resistance, as was the case in the defeat of the 1831 Nat Turner Rebellion in the State of Virginia. And there have been Native Americans who likewise undermined Indigenous efforts at resistance to the European advance.

But despite treachery and opportunism within their own communities and conflict across communal lines, there have also been important African–Native American alliances. Indeed, the nightmare of slavery and genocide has its own nightmare—the dream of freedom—among the oppressed. As long as Native Americans and African Americans were in proximity they constituted a dreaded threat of anticolonial alliance, imagined or real, actual or potential. It is not surprising that we find many laws in North America forbidding relations among these two populations from New England to the southern colonies. As "the Seminole Wars" from approximately 1816 to 1858 showed, slave owners had good reason to worry. From the late 1700s through the early 1800s, enslaved African resistors flocked to the safe haven of Florida, using the power politics of rivalry between the Spanish and the English-Americans, and the receptivity of the Seminole people to escaped slaves as allies. From leaders such as "Negro Abraham" to "John Horse" (or Golpher John), African-descent people in Florida played important roles in decades of resistance to white slave expansion from the north. As one shocked U.S. general exclaimed concerning the importance of the African-American allies of the Seminoles, "This is a Negro not an Indian War!"[19]

The African–Seminole alliance itself overlaps with a hemispheric stretch of "Maroon" communities from Florida to Jamaica, to Mexico, Guyana, Surinam, and Brazil, in which escaped Africans formed their own enclaves of independence. For example, the Garífuna of Central America from Honduras to Guatemala are of African and Native American (Carib) descent and speak the Garífuna language of the Carib linguistic family. As the Mayan writer Demetrio Cojti Cuxil points out, the Garífuna constitute one of the four major "peoples of distinct origins" in Guatemala.[20] In their African–Native American intertwinings they are yet another important example of the significance of in-between-place/*newichewannock* locations, peoples, communities, memories, and moments.

From some such enclaves and diasporic positions, African peoples could join with Native Americans in fighting subjugation by the Europeans. In the colonial Spanish Peruvian region, the great rebellion of the Indigenous leader Juan Santos Atahualpa in the early 1720s was "quickly joined" by enslaved Africans who had initially been brought in by the government to "control" the Indigenous peoples. When offered the choice of resistance or slavery, these Africans became strong allies of the rebels.[21] African-descent people in what is now Bolivia joined with Indigenous forces in anticolonial resistance in 1780–82.

In what is now the U.S. state of New Mexico the Pueblo Revolt of 1680, which drove the Spanish out for several decades, included among its leaders one Domingo Naranjo, whose "father was a black man, an ex-slave who had been included in the household of a soldier. His mother was a Tlascaltec

Indian."[22] Another account describes the meetings of the rebellion's leader Popé, at Taos pueblo with "a mysterious figure said to be the spokesman of the Pueblo war god. The Indians described him as a black giant with fiery yellow eyes; he seems actually to have been a mulatto from Mexico, one Diego de Santiago, who had come to New Mexico as a servant to the Spaniards. . . . Apparently he had married a woman of Taos and had taken up Indian ways. . . . The black giant appears to have been a guiding figure of the revolt, counseling Popé on the best way of defeating the Spaniards."[23]

These and countless other similar stories are part of a richly complex and significant panorama of diverse relations of many African communities with Indigenous cultures. Some such relations are cooperative, some competitive, and some antagonistic; some are about family, but all speak to intimate contacts boiling up from the cauldron of oppression. From North to South America interflowing destinies pull together significant portions of the African diaspora and Native American dimensions in a wide variety of crisscrossing currents.[24]

The Ophic Word—The Snake Word

Guillermo Delgado-P.

Aruskipasipxañanakasakipunirakispawa is a word that belongs to an ancient though still lively language in the South American Andes. If you listen to this word carefully, thirty-six letters are spelled out in one sequential staggered lingual utterance; it constitutes one rhythmical vocalizing. The term—announcing an unavoidable fact—voices the most important human need, that of communication. This breathtaking lexeme is key if not fundamental to this *agglutiNative* language known as Aymara. Aymara is a cousin to Quechua as the two simultaneously shared Kauki and Jaq'aru as parental languages. Linguists suggest that the Aymara-Quechua split occurred two thousand years ago in the Andes. These languages are technically unwritten—that is, if we refer to the Western conception of inscription. An *alterNative* story to this writing issue can be offered when the Aymara infuse meanings into puzzling icons carved on stolid monoliths that inhabit the plateau. When we are confronted by such codes it is as if we have been left with homework to do, messages to decipher.

Without mistake one could state that Spanish, the Iberian language, has had a hard time trying to unseat the persevering Quechuaymara languages. Upset they are, because linguistic cohabitation flexibly produced Quechuañol and Aymarañol. When written down—using the Spanish language phonetic system, the ophic word aruskipasipxañanakasakipunirakispawa is surprisingly entangled. Just listening to its cadence, and looking at it—written down—is defeating due to an assumed unintelligibility. Yet the meaning is there, echoing at you.

In the recently introduced language of Iberian conquerors of the area five centuries ago, aruskipasipxañanakasakipunirakispawa needs to be expressed using a few more words—with the Latin American flavor of the day—"estamos obligados a comunicarnos." To my knowledge only Mexicans have succeeded at expressing this idea with their "tenemos que platicar." And yet both phrases require three words showing the possibility to express the sense of aruskipasipxañanakasakipunirakispawa. In English, with appealing therapeutic nuances, it would be "let's get together for a chat," or "let's take a walk and talk." In Portuguese the sense of the Aymara word could be translated as "a gente precisa falar, vamos a batir um papo," celebrating in this expression the wont of extending time to relax, share, and befriend others. Note that in English, this ability to lengthen time shrinks, perhaps because of loyalty to the aphorism "time is gold."

Aruskipasipxañanakasakipunirakispawa springs in the aura of other linguistic systems decked with jewels, bearing its ophidian secrecy, since it is a complex word that slithers numinous energy. Yet despite such certitude, it continues to be loyal to its phylum, for it cannot fade in its endeavor to encourage dialogue against adverse circumstances, and it carries forth its *k'acha parlaq* (enunciated gracefulness) and *yachaq* (wisdom) to the end: aruskipasipxañanakasakipunirakispawa.

Amidst regular *jaqï* folks—that is, "real Aymara"—aruskipasipxajañanakasakipunirakispawa might sound like some esoteric message (*willaq*) impossible to capture by the conventions of writing and resembling instead entangled knots (*khipuqkuna*). Yet, aruskiwapasipxañanakasakipunirakispawa is inhabited by the prodigal daimon (*ajayuq*), thrown over to the space of archaic music (*ñawpa taquiq*) that endows or accompanies the human act of communication. True, it could be recorded among the ciphered languages as a case of language mountain building (*runasimi*), yet everyday enunciation by Andean people (*runakuna*) strips the word of intricacies and makes of it a plain communicative exercise: aruskipasipxañanakasakipunirakispawa—"let's take a walk and talk."

While this large word does not possess the ill-fated reputation of more cryptic or troublesome terms, it bears the *Illapa* (radiance), the effulgent and seductive peculiarity of things Aymara that endure over time and space. The ophic word materializes its tropological sense, "tropology being the study of tropes—and especially of the spiritual meanings concealed behind the literal meanings of religious scriptures."

Numerous *Runa* (human beings) who have communed with the world or universe (*Pacha*) have summed up their knowledge (*Yachaq*) of the Pacha and—transmitting it through purified forms—exercise their poetic powers inhabiting the word aruskipasipxañanakasakipunirakispawa.

To a restive reader the word might look like an *Amaru* (serpent), as it begins and ends with the letter *a*, containing ten of them from one end to the other. Wholly articulated, this term is built upon three essential vowels present in the language: *a*, *i*, and *u*. To my surprise, however, referring to this ophidian lexeme, my friend Juan de Dios Yapita, an Aymara linguist amidst very few, reminded me about his decision to add two more phonemes "to stress emphasis," telling me that now the word should be written as follows: aruskipasasapxajañanakasakipunirakispawa. "Stress" here means full attention, thinking, reflection, positioning, reasoning, and restituting the often displaced heartfelt emotions in the process of communication.

Making references to the Amaru, the serpent, other observers have noticed that healers recommend feeding the chthonic god— that is, the stone deity that lies in the Andean mountain chain. Its mouth and fangs are represented by a cave with quartz stalactites, and twice a year, in February and August, red roosters are sacrificed by Andean *Jaqïkuna* (real humans) at this precise place: *Amaruq Siminta*, Mouth of the Serpent. This is a sacred shrine inhabited by telluric deities. After all, without a mouth no words would materialize. Perhaps the Quechuaymara are not far wrong in providing special offerings at the Mouth of the Serpent. This might be because this Jaqï language is full of occlusives, affricates, fricatives, nasals, glides, glottals, gutturals, aspirations, laterals, metaterms all—available only to linguists.

Amaru, observes Jesús Urzagasti, a Chaco Boreal writer who was touched by the overwhelming attraction of Andean telluric forces, is the only animal attached to the earth (Pacha). In his book *En el País del Silencio* he writes: "Its whole body rests upon the ground, the *jallp'a*. But this metaphor, with all its suggestibility, doesn't exhaust the complex connotation of the snake's presence among human beings *Runa*; and instead of solving a riddle *imataqchá*, it simply brews a new one." For example, that the "cosmic serpent is narcissistic," and that "communication" is a sacred human zeal.[25]

The Andean Quechua and Aymara or for that matter our neighbors to the East, the Indigenous Peoples of the Amazon Basin, far from losing our way on a never-ending *Pampa* or in the immensity of the Amazon *Sachapacha*, erected vast dominions imitating the kinetic energy of words. That is, the knowledgeable Yachachïq of these Early States observed the flow of linguistic cadences and agglutinations and decided to apply them to configure the expansive periods of empire building. The early urban center was seen as the main root, the navel (*Qusqu*), and the suffixes became parts (*suyus*) of a larger entity. Not only that; languages themselves, throughout the Andes, flow in striated veins rather than nuclei. For "we are forced to communicate"—aruskipasipxañanakasakipunirakispawa is not an onomatopoeic locution or ephemeral decorum but a healer's square cloth that, bundled on his or her back, accommodates possessions of the most illustrious imagination, including shadows (*llant"uq*), hidden words that brew messages. After all, "the main purpose of language is to communicate," states David Crystal.[26]

The serpent word comes back to inspire other questions, as in the one posed by Jeremy Narby: "Why do life-creating, knowledge-imparting snakes appear in the visions, myths, and dreams of human beings around the world?"[27] And I would say: because there exists the human need to communicate with one another and because dreams are summed up in the ophic word aruskipasasapxajañanakasakipunirakispawa.

As we enter a new period marked by the millennium (*Pachakuti*), recent social movements of Jaqïkuna in the Andes have gained visible political recognition. As a matter of fact, whole Indigenous Peoples, First Nations, Originary Peoples, Natives, are carrying on a notable process of re/memberment. Tensions arise groggily from obscure corners of centuries of miscommunication. However, against that fragile background of history coming back to bite us, the ancient philosophy implied in the term *aruskipasasapxajañanakasakipunirakispawa* could now be loyal to its most profound meaning, "we must communicate with one another."

As Ways of Conclusion

In his classic *Custer Died for Your Sins: An Indian Manifesto*, Vine Deloria, Jr., usefully notes the importance of common issues for "Indians, blacks, and Mexicans."[28] He urges that both commonalities and differences should be carefully studied while also emphasizing that these populations are distinctive "social isolates" vis-à-vis one another.[29] We basically concur with the emphasis on comparison. But we must add that it is not only such a comparative intellectual project that is needed. Problematically, comparative studies can often retreat into compartmentalized parade-like formations in which groups are more or less juxtaposed, while interactive dimensions of their histories and present realities are obscured through a hermetically sealed set of analytic compartments.

We certainly need to recognize the significance of boundaries that communities use to delineate themselves. Such boundaries can be clear-cut and significant, contrary to the postmodern Geertzean emphasis on "blurring" of genres or borders while at the same time allowing for and facilitating interaction. The various allied African–Native American actions described are examples of people coming together either as groups or as individuals from distinct places who use their *own* rooted locations (i.e., exercising sovereignty as the basis for their interactions).

Consequently, we must comprehend the way in which the fabric of the Americas enfolds the warp and woof of Indigenous and African interactions that confront the complex multiple bloody consequences of the European invasion. So rather than a Western Hemisphere consisting of what Deloria calls "social isolates," we suggest drawing from interactive concepts and concepts of interaction, one of which is the Andean Indigenous concept of aruskipaskipxañanakasasakipunirakispawa, "the human need to communicate." It offers an aid to "dialogue against adverse circumstances."[30] For us, a key feature of this Andean approach to the world is, as noted elsewhere, "the multiple yet linked requirements that 'we communicate with each other / face to face / our feet rooted in the earth / with which we also must communicate / if we are to live.'"[31]

The great value of aruskipasipxañanakasakipunirakispawa is that it emphasizes the value of diverse points of origin while simultaneously focusing on the requirement of interaction among those places. This significant and supple concept could be a key building block in an activist and engaged scholarly strategy that emphasizes not just comparison but also communication. Such a communicative approach would reward and require an incorporation of dialogue about and within the African–Native American nexus. Elsewhere we term such dialogue transcommunal because it recognizes distinct positions (histories, locations, memories, cultures, and sacred sites) while also seeking out ways in which each may contribute to the larger picture.[32]

Transcommunal communication avoids the postmodern gnashing of teeth over blurring and "unending multiplicity" that seems to have no form, precisely because such transcommunality depends on distinct rooted cultural settings as the bases from which interaction occurs. By so doing we also avoid the contrary dilemma of assuming that distinct position implies no relationship among multiple perspectives. We can draw on Indigenous philosophy from the Andes to the Blue Hills as an aid to the construction of concrete interactions and related scholarly studies that draw from and enhance the African-American/Native American nexus throughout the Americas. By the same token, the shared crossroads meanings of *newichewannock*, and *Tinkuqniy-pacha*, along with the supple autonomy-oriented form of many Native American polities, offer intellectual guidelines for a communicative approach to the African American/Native American connection and to humanity in general.

Enhanced collaboration from North to South America, from the African American to the Native American to the Pacific Islands, will be an important social and cultural step we already are noticing. Today we still find many of our communities locked into settings of inequality and subordination. Co-operation that draws from distinctive cultural foundations is vital if we are to redress this harsh reality effectively. Moreover, in a world where the fabric of global understanding is undermined and shredded by hostilities and lack of mutual respect among peoples, such cooperation can play a vital role in helping humankind to survive and prosper.

Naturally, key elements in this process of re/membering involve our own ability not so much to speak unilaterally as to listen, to reach out, recognizing the value and capacity of every child, woman, man, elder. All contribute to the never-ending process of remembering. The co-laborating in the writing of this contribution demonstrates that self-reflexivity as well as a profound look at the linguistic meaning of Native languages, often undermined by persistent notions of neocolonialism, can trigger clear processes of decolonizing old, restraining orthodox modern discipline-bound thinking. This idea, of course, has been inspired in the process of rethinking unidirectional episteme, as shared with us by Maori thinker Linda Tuhiwai Smith in *Decolonizing Methodologies*.[33] We are convinced that rather than being an obstacle to intellectual growth, collaborating is methodologically and theoretically enriching.

Notes

1. Robert Johnson was the composer of the classic blues song "Crossroads Blues." Sherman Alexie, *Reservation Blues* (New York: Warner Books, 1995), 3–4.

2. Jack Forbes, *Africans and Native Americans: The Language of Race and the Evolution of Red Black Peoples* (Urbana: University of Illinois Press, 1993), 1. See also James F. Brooks, ed., *Confounding the Color Line: The Indian-Black Experience in North America* (Lincoln: University of Nebraska Press, 2002).

3. See the development and discussion of the concept of "transcommunality" in John Brown Childs, *Transcommunality: From the Politics of Conversion to the Ethics of Respect* (Philadelphia: Temple University Press, 2003).

4. For important discussions of places and spaces see Roxann Prazniak and Arif Dirlik, eds., *Places and Politics in an Age of Globalization* (New York: Rowman and Littlefield, 2001).

5. Carlos Mamani-Condori, "History and Prehistory in Bolivia: What about the Indians?" in *Conflict in the Archaeology of Living Traditions*, ed. Robert Layton (London: Unwin Hyman, 1989), 46–59.

6. Horace Mann Bond, *Black American Scholars: A Study of Their Origins* (Detroit, Michigan: Balamp Publishers, 1972), 22. Earlier versions of "Red Clay, Blue Hills" have appeared in John Brown Childs, *Transcommunality: From the Politics of Conversion to the Ethics of Respect* (Philadelphia: Temple University Press, 2003) and in Maurianne Adams et al., eds., *Readings for Diversity and Social Justice* (New York: Routledge, 2000).

7. Thomas L. Doughton, "Unseen Neighbors: Native Americans of Central Massachusetts, A People Who Had 'Vanished,' " in *After King Philip's War: Presence and Persistence in Indian New England*, ed. Colin G. Calloway (Hanover NH: University Presses of New England, 1998).

8. Alexis de Tocqueville, *Democracy in America* (New York: Vintage, 1954), 343.

9. Guillermo Delgado-P., "Tinkuqniypacha: Indigeneity in the Context of Transnational Dialogues" (keynote address, conference on Indigenous Mobilizations in the Americas: Forging Hemispheric Ties, Seattle: University of Washington, 2001), 1. See also Guillermo Delgado-P., "The Makings of a Transnational Movement" (NACLA/Report on the Americas. Vol XXXV (6), May/June, (2002), 36–39) and "El globalismo y los pueblos indios: De la etnicidad a la agresión benevolente de la biomedicina," in *Procesos Culturales de Fin de Milenio*, ed. José Manuel Valenzuela (Mexico: Centro Cultural Tijuana/Conaculta, 1998).

10. Carlos Fuentes, *The Campaign*, trans. Alfred MacAdam (New York: Farrar, Straus and Giroux, 1990), 173–74.

11. Alvin M. Joseph, Jr., *500 Nations* (New York: Alfred A. Knopf, 1994), 123.

12. Judith Nies, *Native American History* (New York: Ballantine, 1996), 75.

13. Carl Waldman, *Atlas of the North American Indian* (New York: Facts on File, 1985), 213.

14. Waldman, *Atlas*, 79–81.

15. Forbes, *Africans and Native Americans*, 58.

16. Forbes, *Africans and Native Americans*, 59.

17. Forbes, *Africans and Native Americans*, 58–59.

18. Wilma Mankiller and Michael Wallis, *Mankiller: A Chief and Her People* (New York: St. Martin's Press, 1993), 27.

19. Kenneth Littlefield, *Africans and Seminoles, from Removal to Emancipation* (Westport CT: Greenwood Press, 1979).

20. Demetrio Cojti Cuxil, "The Politics of Maya Revindication," in *Maya Cultural Activism in Guatemala*, ed. Edward F. Fisher and R. McKenna Brown (Austin: University of Texas Press, 1996), 27.

21. Fernando Santos-Granero and Frederica Barclay, *Selva Central: History, Economy, and Land Use in the Peruvian Amazonia*, trans. Elisabeth King (Washington: Smithsonian Institution Press, 1998), 30.

22. Joe S.Sando, *Pueblo Nations: Eight Centuries of Pueblo Indian History* (Santa Fe: Clear Light Publishers, 1992), 68. There is some scholarly debate as to whether Domingo Naranjo was indeed of African descent as the Jesuit chronicles indicated he was.

23. Robert Silverberg, *The Pueblo Revolt* (Lincoln: University of Nebraska Press, 1970), 99.

24. Earlier versions of portions of this preceding section appear in J. B. Childs, "Crossroads: Toward a Transcommunal Black History Month," in *Annales du Monde Anglophone: Écritures de l'Histoire Africaine Amèricaine*, ed. Hélène Le Dantec-Lowry and Arlette Frund (Paris: Institut du Monde Anglophone de la Sorbonne Nouvelle and Éditions L'Harmattan, 2003).

25. Jesús Urzagasti, *En el País del Silencio* (La Paz, Bolivia: HISBOL, 1987), 129; Jeremy Narby, *The Cosmic Serpent: DNA and the Origin of Knowledge* (New York: Penguin Putnam, 1998), 116.

26. David Crystal, *Linguistics* (Middlesex: Penguin Books, 1974), 239.

27. Narby, *Cosmic Serpent*, 114.

28. Vine Deloria, Jr., *Custer Died for Your Sins: An Indian Manifesto* (Norman OK: University of Oklahoma Press, 1969).

29. Deloria, *Custer Died for Your Sins*, 193.

30. Guillermo Delgado-P., "Ley ley del ayllu: La otra justicia," *Pulso* (June–July 2001), 4, 2.

31. Childs, *Transcommunality*, 77.

32. Childs, *Transcommunality*, 77.

33. Linda Tuhiwai Smith, *Decolonizing Methodologies: Research and Indigenous Peoples* (London: Zed Books/Dunedin, New Zealand: University of Otago Press, 1999).

J. Kēhaulani Kauanui (Native Hawaiian)

The Politics of Hawaiian Blood and Sovereignty in *Rice v. Cayetano*

In 1996 a white man named Harold F. Rice attempted to vote in the Hawai`i statewide elections for Office of Hawaiian Affairs (OHA) trustees and was turned away. Since the OHA's inception in 1978, trustee elections have been limited to residents of Hawai`i who, by blood quanta classifications, are "native Hawaiian" (those with 50 percent or more Hawaiian blood quantum) or "Hawaiian" (those with any amount less than 50 percent Hawaiian blood quantum).[1] Although Rice is a fourth generation Hawai`i state resident, he is neither native Hawaiian nor Hawaiian by their state constitutional or statutory definitions—where the terms signify race, not simply place of birth. As a result of being denied in the elections, Rice sued the state under the Fourteenth and Fifteenth Amendments. He lost in both the Federal District Court based in Honolulu, Hawai`i, and the United States Court of Appeals for the Ninth Circuit in San Francisco, California. However, in 1999, the Supreme Court agreed to hear the case.

On February 23, 2000, in *Rice v. Cayetano* (98–818) (146 F.3d 1075, reversed), the U.S. Supreme Court ruled that in denying Rice the vote in the Office of Hawaiian Affairs trustee elections, the state of Hawai`i violated the Fifteenth Amendment's guarantee that the citizens' right to vote shall not be denied or abridged on account of race, color, or previous condition of servitude by enacting race-based voting qualifications. Importantly, the court did not rule on the Fourteenth Amendment. On narrow grounds and in a split decision, the Supreme Court reversed the Ninth Circuit ruling that upheld Hawaiian-only voting for the Office of Hawaiian Affairs trustees.[2] This case is not easily recognized as having anything to do with blood quantum issues per se; on the surface, it looks like a simple case about the right to the franchise—a case between Hawaiians (of all amounts of indigenous ancestry) and non-Hawaiian residents of Hawai`i. But as I shall demonstrate, the two definitions of Hawaiianness (native Hawaiian and Hawaiian)—dictated by blood quantum classifications—played a key role in the court's decision.

The recurring use of blood logics with their implicit reference to race served to undermine Hawaiian entitlements in the *Rice v. Cayetano* decision. Blood quanta classifications have consistently been used to enact, substantiate, and then disguise the further appropriation of native lands while they obscured and erased a discourse of specifically Hawaiian sovereignty and identity as a relation of genealogy to place.[3] The definition of Hawaiian identity on the basis of blood logics was an American conception, a colonial policy developed through experience with American Indians. This policy presupposed long-term patterns of assimilation.[4] Moreover, these blood logics work to displace a discourse and recognition of Hawaiian sovereignty altogether.

This chapter examines the layering of legal-political discourses of blood, discourses that culminated in the intersections of voices in the Supreme Court case. I attempt to delineate the doubly contradictory place of Hawaiians. This place is contradictory because it relies on racialized identity imposed through a blood quantum criterion, yet when these mechanics are applied in the interest of Hawaiian body-politics, they are alleged to be racially discriminatory. I first offer a background on the history of U.S. colonialism in Hawai`i and then outline the trust issues surrounding Hawaiian land claims. I next briefly review the problematic terms of the passage of the Hawaiian Homes Commission Act (HHCA) of 1920—a formative piece of allotment legislation that informs the workings of the OHA—in relation to its blood racialization of Hawaiians and to the effacement of sovereign entitlements. I then turn to the issues of blood quantum raised in *Rice v. Cayetano* as they resonate with the development of the HHCA. In closing, I explore the predicaments involved in the current political terrain of indigenous status, predicaments that were heightened by the recent court case.

The Hawaiian Homes Commission Act first defined Hawaiians by blood quantum. Specifically, it defined "native Hawaiian" people as "descendants with at least one-half blood quantum of individuals inhabiting the Hawaiian islands prior to 1778," a classification that originated in the effacement of native assertions of sovereignty and aboriginal title.[5] As a land allotment act, the HHCA was originally billed as a native rehabilitation scheme.[6] But justification for the passage of the Act was tied in problematic ways to welfare notions constructing Hawaiians as a beneficiary class and, as such, racialized through blood criteria.[7] The operative logic in the debates prior to the passage of the HHCA differs little from that undergirding the recent Supreme Court decision, as these debates entail common problematic assumptions as to who should count as Hawaiian and what counting as Hawaiian means (and signifies). Both examples presumed two key interlocking notions: (1) the relationship between blood and competency and (2) the imperialist demands of assimilation regarding indigenous people under U.S. jurisdiction. Because the enfranchisement of Hawaiians entailed the domestication of a previously recognized sovereign entity, the project of erasing the Hawaiian people through discourses of deracination became essential.

Background

On November 28, 1993—in a joint Senate resolution known as Public Law 103–150—the U.S. government apologized to the Hawaiian people for its role in the illegal and armed overthrow of Queen Lili'uokalani and the Kingdom of Hawai`i in 1893. In 1893, the U.S. minister of foreign affairs, John L. Stevens, had organized a coup d'état with the support of a dozen white settlers, most of whom were American. Prior to that point, the kingdom had had ongoing diplomatic relations with the United States. These relations included five treaties and conventions to govern commerce and navigation in 1826, 1842, 1849, 1875, and 1887. Early U.S. influence in Hawai`i coincided with American missionary presence; in 1820 the American Foreign Board of Foreign Missionaries set out to Christianize the Hawaiian Islands, while in that same year John C. Jones was appointed to oversee American commercial interests. Even though the 1842 Tyler Doctrine asserted that Hawai`i was under the sphere of U.S. influence, it would be several more decades before the United States would assert formal colonial control in the islands.

Those who orchestrated the 1893 overthrow eventually formed the Provisional Government—established as the Republic of Hawai`i on July 4, 1894—with Sanford Ballard Dole as president.[8] In addition to asserting jurisdiction over the entire island archipelago, this group seized roughly 1.8 million acres of Hawaiian Kingdom government and Crown lands. In an attempt to remove any doubt that the republic was not rightly "heir and successor of the Hawaiian Crown," the new constitution declared the lands to be "free and clear from any trust of or concerning the same, and from all claim of any nature whatsoever."[9] This de facto government ceded these lands to the United States when it illegally annexed Hawai`i by joint resolution—also known as the Newlands Resolution—in 1898 despite massive Hawaiian opposition.[10] The Republic of Hawai`i ceded sovereignty of the islands to the United States under the terms of the joint resolution of annexation. Although the resolution provided for the cession of absolute title to the public lands (formerly the Hawaiian Kingdom and Crown lands), it also specified that the existing laws of the United States relative to public lands would not apply in Hawai`i. Moreover, the resolution provided that all revenue derived from the lands would be assigned for local government use and "shall be used solely for the benefit of the inhabitants of the Hawaiian Islands for educational and other public purposes."[11] Through a 1900 Organic Act, Hawai`i was incorporated as a territory and specific laws to administer the public lands were created.[12] These laws again affirmed that these lands were part of a special trust under the federal government's oversight.

Like many other colonial territories, in 1946 Hawai`i was inscribed onto the United Nations List of Non-Self-Governing Territories. As such, Hawai`i was eligible for decolonization under international law. However, the United States—in clear violation of UN policies and international law of the time and existing through the present—predetermined statehood as the status for Hawai`i. The 1959 ballot in which the people of Hawai`i voted to become a state of the union included only two options: incorporation and remaining a U.S. colonial territory.[13] By UN criteria the ballot also should have included independence as a choice. In addition—among those who were allowed to take part in the vote that eventually marked Hawai`i's supposed transition from colonial status—Hawaiians were outnumbered by settlers as well as military personnel.

The Hawai`i Admission Act for statehood transferred the "public lands" (former Crown and government lands) from federal to state control.[14] In doing so, it recognized the special status of these lands and reflected the earlier intent to return these lands to the new state.[15] Quite different from the legal treatment of land in other states, the federal government relinquished title to the new state for most of the ceded lands held at the time of statehood, with certain lands remaining the property of the United States with provisions allowing for their return to the state any time they are declared unnecessary to federal needs. Thus we find one of the crucial differences between Hawaiians and other indigenous people, to which we will return when we turn back to *Rice*.

The Hawai`i State Constitution provides that lands ceded to the State of Hawai`i by the federal government at the time of admission to the United States shall be "held by the State as a public trust for native Hawaiians and the general public" (article 7, section 4). Section 5(f) of the Hawai`i State Admissions Act details five purposes for the income and proceeds derived from the leases of these lands. These purposes include support of public education, the development of farm and home ownership, public improvements, provision of lands for public use, and "the betterment of the conditions of native Hawaiians."[16] Hawaiians are included in the act because the 1920 HHCA was carried through statehood in 1959 when the Territory of Hawai`i acknowledged the trust obligation toward "native Hawaiians" as a condition of admission to the union. In doing so, the state also accepted the definition of "native Hawaiian" as per the 50 percent blood rule that was codified in the 1920 Act. While statehood has determined the trust for "native Hawaiians," the courts have not delineated the public trust concept. As Mari Matsuda has found, the "special designation of native Hawaiians as beneficiaries plausibly indicates that Hawaiians are entitled to benefits as Hawaiians over and above any benefit as state citizens, but court decisions have made it difficult for Hawaiians to pursue trust benefits."[17]

In the late 1960s, just one decade after statehood, the contemporary Hawaiian movement was at its nascent stage. Increasingly through the 1970s, Hawaiians island-wide protested their own social conditions as well as the displacement of other (mostly Asian) locals as a result of overnight development when multinationalization and foreign investments led to a steady boom in tourism. Developers evicted, dispossessed, and displaced many Hawaiians and other locals from lands to make way for the building of subdivisions, hotel complexes, and golf courses. Haunani-Kay Trask notes that in the early seventies, communities resisting this kind of development identified their struggles in terms of the claims of "local" people, which included both Hawaiian and non-Hawaiian long-time residents of Hawai`i. "The residency rights of local people were thus framed in opposition to the development rights of property owners like the state, corporations, and private estates."[18] But as the decade proceeded Hawaiians increasingly asserted their rights as indigenous and historically unique from other "locals."[19]

Due in part to the requests of Hawaiian activists during the 1970s, the state held a constitutional convention in 1978. At this convention the vast majority of voters agreed to the creation of an Office of Hawaiian Affairs to look out for Hawaiian interests. The OHA is organized as a state agency to be governed by a nine-member elected board of trustees and holds title to all real or personal property set aside or conveyed to it as a trust for "native Hawaiians" (defined by the 50 percent blood rule). The OHA was also established to hold in trust the income and proceeds derived from a pro rata portion of the trust established for lands that were earlier granted to the state.[20] Further, the OHA is restricted to using its public lands trust funds for the benefit of its beneficiaries who meet the 50 percent rule, while the Hawai`i state constitution does not establish a source of funding for "Hawaiians" who do not meet the 50 percent definition. But because the State Admission Act did not determine a formula for allocation of public land trust income among the five specified purposes, the 1978 constitutional amendment that created the OHA did not define the pro rata share.[21] In 1980 in response to the new constitutional prerequisite, the Hawai`i state legislature set the share at 20 percent. This is no doubt because "the betterment of the conditions of native Hawaiians" was only one of the five trust purposes detailed in the Admission Act. The one-fifth of the revenue from these lands is to be transferred to the OHA for the benefit of Hawaiians who meet the 50 percent rule. However, due to state neglect and conflicts about the trust relationship, the state has not transferred these revenues as stipulated.

By the 1990s after decades of protest and a rapidly growing Hawaiian sovereignty movement, even federal representatives responded to the call for the United States to recognize the near century-long (neo)colonial legacy that began with the 1893 overthrow. Specifically, Hawai`i state senator Daniel Akaka—with support from the entire Hawai`i congressional delegation—pushed for the passage of the 1993 Apology. Besides delineating a detailed account of U.S. encroachment and betrayal, the resolution maintains that "the indigenous Hawaiian people never directly relinquished their claims to their inherent sovereignty as a people or over their national lands to the United States, either through their monarchy or through a plebiscite or referendum." Importantly, the Apology defined "native Hawaiian" as "any individual who is a descendent of the aboriginal people who, prior to 1778, occupied and exercised sovereignty in the area that now constitutes the State of Hawaii." No reference to blood quantum was made. Hence this recognition was extended to *all Hawaiians* in a way that accounts for lineal descendancy. Certainly the Apology can be understood as an emergent federal discourse on the eve of the Rice case. But it was also the culmination of Hawaiian demands that the United States acknowledge the crimes of 1893. The Apology, the potential of which remains unfulfilled, not only served as a finding of fact; a legal and educational tool, it has also been a focal point of mobilization. The passage of the law empowered the island's sovereignty movement, and Hawaiians increased their initiatives for self-determination.

There is currently a whole range of Hawaiian sovereignty projects. These projects span a wide variety of models for self-governance, from proposals for an independent nation-state (including interest in restoring a kingdom) to various proposals for working within U.S. state and federal policy. The answer to any question of "inclusion" related to Hawaiian sovereignty is thoroughly dependent on two factors: the land base targeted for reclamation and the attendant form of self-governance advocated in relation to this land base. On the one hand, the sovereignty groups with the most moderate political model—such as the nation-within-a-nation model compatible with U.S. federal policy for Native Americans—do not include citizenship entitlements for non-Hawaiians. The goal in that framework is to gain some of Hawai`i—that is, control of specific Native trust lands—for Hawaiians. On the other hand, groups striving for independent Hawaiian nationhood aim to reclaim all of Hawai`i for all of its residents.

The ongoing practice of blood quantum identification has had some effect on contemporary Hawaiian sovereignty politics. As the right to self-definition is a crucial part of self-determination, the issues of identity and identification are clearly part of the larger struggle for indigenous autonomy. Hawaiian groups aiming for self-governance within a limited land base especially emphasize the connection between ancestral descent and land claims.

The Hawaiian Homes Commission Act of 1920

The HHCA set aside approximately 200,000 acres of land for residential, pastoral, and agricultural purposes, with ninety-nine-year lease provisions at one dollar per year. In the act as already noted, eligibility was restricted to "native Hawaiians" defined as "descendants with at least one-half blood quantum of individuals inhabiting the Hawaiian Islands prior to 1778." Although the act allotted lands to Hawaiians for leasing, the origins of this blood racialization of Hawaiians are rooted in a broader context of dispossession; the legal construction of the rule was determined within the context of U.S. colonial land appropriation from 1898 to 1920. The goal of rehabilitating Hawaiians—a goal that provided the impetus for the HHCA—was imagined and argued for, in relation to questions of racial-political status, entitlement, and American citizenship. In earlier work, I trace the HHCA debates that took place in Washington DC during the three different hearings before the Committee on Territories in February 1920, December 1920, and June 1921.[22] There I trace the shift from the originally inclusive definition of "Hawaiian" to the more exclusive rule that resulted from the effacement of indigenous land title. Through the debates, discursive constructions of Hawaiianness deflected recognition away from Native entitlement and refocused on white property interests.

Debates over the HHCA put a spotlight on the 1898 annexation and whether the federal government had a trust obligation to the Hawaiian people. Contention over the nature of *which lands* counted as "public" and whether they might rightly be Hawaiians' collective entitlement was central. Hawaiian advocates saw the leasing of these particular lands as connected to the goals of native rehabilitation. Advocates also justified leasing as a form of reparations for the overthrow of the kingdom and even earlier forms of dispossession.[23] Hawaiian entitlement to these lands rested upon a dual claim: first, that Hawaiian commoners were unfairly provided for in the kingdom's land division and, second, that they were further dispossessed after the overthrow and subsequently in the illegal U.S. annexation of Hawai`i. Representatives suggested that the HHCA could provide an opportunity for the U.S. government to place itself above the actions of the monarchy.[24]

The first territorial bill leading to the HHCA included no designated blood quantum. This bill was specifically written for the rehabilitation of Hawaiians "in whole or in part."[25] Early on, Hawaiian advocates for the bill argued against any sort of racial differentiation based on blood logics because the claim to the lands for rehabilitating Hawaiians was based on their assertion of collective Hawaiian entitlement. Still the second draft presented to Congress specified a Hawaiian blood criterion of one thirty-second. Through the various articulations of Native rehabilitation, these critical issues of political status and land title fell by the wayside, as did any discussion that called U.S. claims into question. Politicians who opposed parts of the bill seized on the ill-defined concept of rehabilitation while sidestepping or directly opposing the issue of Hawaiian legal claims to the land.[26]

Because there was no consensus on what would constitute rehabilitation and upon what basis that rehabilitation was in order, the idea of putting needy Hawaiians back on the land was justified as charity and a form of protection. Here the focus shifted to discussions of how best to "preserve" the Hawaiian people. These representatives even went so far as to propose that the definition be restricted to "full-blood." This restriction allowed for an easy move away from the issues of trust obligation and land title claims. Once the issue of legal entitlement was sidestepped, limiting the number of Hawaiian beneficiaries was key.[27] Hence it is not surprising that the issue then foregrounded was *who was in need* of rehabilitation. Those involved in determining the future land laws grappled with defining who would count as Hawaiian through different evocations of the "full-blooded Hawaiian" and the "part-Hawaiian."

The shifting proposals for defining Hawaiian were debated ardently until the very end of the hearings.[28] Along the way sharp distinctions between "full-blooded" and "part" Hawaiians emerged. These different constructions were tied to notions of assimilation and degrees of competency as they related to qualities attributed to American citizenship-subjectivity. In the debates, mixed-race Hawaiians were said to be, for the most part, "indistinguishable from a white person" and "for all intents and purposes white." However, such estimations ignored indigenous modes of reckoning identity and belonging. Using a Hawaiian genealogical framework, a wide range of mixed Hawaiians could still be distinguishable as Hawaiians. However, in the colonial "common sense" about race that operated at the time (and arguably still exists today), out-marriage was assumed to be an index of assimilation away from Hawaiianness. But Hawaiian society had long been incorporative.[29]

During the debates, in the equations casting "part-Hawaiians" (a term from the debates) as "practically white," the subject was always presumed (in unmarked ways) to have only white along with Hawaiian ancestry. For example, in those debates, a person of Hawaiian, white, and Chinese ancestry was not figured as "practically white" but was considered "alien." Moreover, Hawaiians of mixed Chinese ancestry were figured as a substantial threat to white property rights. It was therefore important to find rhetoric of identity whereby to exclude them. "Part-Hawaiians" who did not meet the 50 percent blood quantum rule were considered fully competent in their American citizenship and, as such, able to secure private property (and hence not in need of land leasing).

By the time the act was adopted, the criterion of Hawaiian ancestry had changed to one-half blood quantum. This dramatically revised legal definition decreased the potential number of applicants for leasing the Hawaiian Home Lands allotted in the act. The compromise of defining Hawaiians by the one-half blood criterion seems largely a last ditch effort to pass the bill. Indeed, after it failed passage by the U.S. Senate in 1920, it was taken back to the territorial legislature in Hawai`i, where it was radically transformed by various amendments that reflected the prominence of sugar and ranching interests. Hawaiian complicity, on the part of the congressional delegate Jonah Kuhio along with Hawaiian members of the territorial legislature, in negotiating those plantation interests was at odds with rehabilitative homesteading.[30] Still, the plantation interests were primarily behind the 50 percent model. The colonial form of land expropriation won out in the final version of the bill that created the HHCA.[31] Though the act was said to rehabilitate natives, it merely reinstitutionalized the forces acknowledged to be displacing Hawaiians in the first place. By facilitating sugar and ranching advancement, the act had an adverse impact on small farmers at large. The act was signed into law on July 9, 1921. The rehabilitation section was relegated to an explicitly minor role in this omnibus bill that finally secured congressional approval to restructure Hawaii's land laws. At the time of its passage, the act did not even have a statement of purpose.[32]

The Case

On behalf of the Respondent, Hawai`i's governor Benjamin Cayetano, the state argued that the OHA's limitation on the right to vote was based not on race but on the unique status of Hawaiian people in light of the state's trust obligations. Hence the limitation on the right to vote for the OHA trustees was based on a legal classification determined by those who constitute the beneficiaries of the trust managed by that office. Importantly, the state also submitted that this classification met rational basis review under *Morton v. Mancari* 417 U.S. 535 (1974), the U.S. Supreme Court case that upheld American Indian preferences as constitutional. *Morton v. Mancari* established a precedent that the Fourteenth Amendment's equal protection guarantees are not infringed by legislation that benefits American Indians due to their political relationship to the United States.

In *Rice v. Cayetano* Hawaiians were in a fraught position, as they had no direct voice in the case that was central to Hawaiian concerns.[33] Governor Cayetano, notorious for his anti-Hawaiian veto power, was held accountable for the voting practices of the OHA because it is a state agency. Moreover, the claim of Hawaiians' position being analogous to that of American Indians meant articulating a position that compromised *already recognized* Hawaiian historical claims that exceeded the U.S. federal framework under U.S. policy on Native American self-determination. The state had to argue that analogy, but the comparison was problematic in that, by definition, it entailed affirming congressional plenary power over Hawaiians. As a result, Hawaiians fell through the cracks in legal precedent by not being seen as having a sufficient claim to a genealogy linked to Indian case law and being held to the equal protection clause of the U.S. constitution.[34] Because the U.S. federal government and the Supreme Court do not recognize Hawaiians collectively as a sovereign entity, the state was compelled to articulate a likeness to American Indians by citing a long history of legislation (dating back to 1903) for "Native Americans" that includes "Native Hawaiians." Specifically, Congress has enacted numerous special provisions of law for the benefit of Native Hawaiians in the areas of health, education, labor, and housing. Along with American Indians and Alaskan Natives, Native Hawaiians have been included in over 160 federal acts for Native Americans. To some degree, the U.S. Congress recognized the special relationship that exists between the United States and the Native Hawaiian people when it extended to Native Hawaiians the same rights and privileges accorded to American Indian, Alaska Native, Inuit, and Aleut communities. Relevant legislation includes the Native American Programs Act of 1974 (42 USC 2991 et seq.), the American Indian Religious Freedom Act (42 USC 1996), the National Museum of the American Indian Act (20 USC 80q et seq.), the Native American Graves Protection and Repatriation Act (25 USC 3001 et seq.), the National Historic Preservation Act (16 USC 470 et seq.), and the Native American Languages Act (25 USC 2901 et seq.). Also, under Title VIII of the 1975 Native American Programs Act, American Indians, Alaska Natives (Inuits and Aleutians), Native Hawaiians, Samoans, and other native Pacific Islanders are defined as Native Americans.[35] There are also several Hawaiian-specific federal acts comparable to those providing for American Indians and Alaskan Natives, such as the Native Hawaiian Health Care Act and the Native Hawaiian Education Act. It is important to note that in all of these acts, Hawaiians are defined by the most inclusive definition: "any individual who is a descendent of the aboriginal people who, prior to 1778, occupied and exercised sovereignty in the area that now constitutes the State of Hawaii."

The state maintained that the voting classification was *rationally* tied to its fulfillment in upholding a congressional requirement because the United States has a "special relationship" with—and obligation—to "native Hawaiians." Moreover, it argued that this connection is analogous to the federal government's relationship with American Indian tribes.[36] Thus the defense in the Rice case rested upon the claim that Congress has the power to enter into special trust relationships with indigenous peoples, a power that is not confined to tribal Indians, and that the state "stood in for" the United States as concerns land claims and related claims.[37] This analogy seemed most threatening to the Court.

However, these state obligations to Hawai`i's indigenous people—and the claim that this case is analogous to that of the U.S. federal–American Indian relationship—did not convince the Supreme Court of the unique political situation of Hawaiians that may have justified the exclusive OHA election process. Also, the majority ruling in the case refused to decide whether Hawaiians were analogous to Indian tribes for the purposes of constitutional analysis. Even so, the majority justices distinguished *Morton v. Mancari* as being restricted to the Bureau of Indian Affairs (and not extended to the OHA).

Favoring Rice, the majority Supreme Court opinion based its ruling on three major findings. First, the OHA was understood only as an arm of the state and not as a mechanism to perform the trust commitments delegated to the state by the federal government. Hence because the state, rather than a separate quasi-sovereign (such as a federally recognized tribal government) administers the OHA trustee elections, they are elections to which the Fifteenth Amendment applies. Second, the court found that the limited voting franchise failed to comply with the Fifteenth Amendment. Third, it was not clear to the court that the voting classification was symmetric with the beneficiaries of the programs that OHA administers, because while the bulk of funds appear to be designated for "native Hawaiians" (as per the 50 percent rule, originating in the HHCA), both "native Hawaiians" and "Hawaiians" who reside in the state are allowed to vote in the OHA elections. The majority of the court identified what it saw as an asymmetrical relationship between the Hawaiian-specific voting process and the beneficiaries of the trust.[38] This identification seems curious given that the OHA is restricted to using its public lands trust funds for the benefit of beneficiaries who meet the 50 percent rule. Still, these two definitions of beneficiaries were implicated in the court's decision.

Blood Logics

In defining who should count as Hawaiian, the operative logic in the 1920 HHCA debates differs little from that in the recent Supreme Court case of *Rice*. But in neither instance was there any basic common understanding of actual blood quantum modes of classification and their genealogies. Instead, the HHCA debates and *Rice* relied on the logics of dilution to undermine inclusive conceptualizations of Nativeness. As mentioned earlier, because the enfranchisement of indigenous peoples in the United States entailed the domestication of previously recognized sovereign entities, the project of erasing their distinctiveness through discourses of deracination was essential to and remains a key feature of contemporary neocolonial entrenchment.

It is also important to note that in both the 1920 debates and the Court's decision in *Rice*, those who opposed inclusive definitions of Hawaiian, such as one thirty-second, compared them to grandfather clauses during Reconstruction.[39] What is the significance of citing the grandfather clause within these different discussions of an inclusive policy for Hawaiians? First, these citations suggest a radical misreading of the one thirty-second definition for Hawaiians by equating this definition with rules used during Reconstruction to disenfranchise people of African descent further from full citizenship. Inclusive definitions of "Hawaiian" are not comparable to the exemptions that undergirded grandfather clauses such as the poll taxes and literacy tests imposed on descendants of those who were previously ineligible to vote due to enslavement and servitude. And still, in a contradictory move, the final argument regarding the blood quantum in the HHCA was offered by Harry Irwin—attorney general of Hawai`i at the time—who stated that the one thirty-second definition was changed in order to do away with territorial opposition to the bill and was successfully dismantled when it had been said that a person of one thirty-second Hawaiian ancestry was "to all intents and purposes a white person."[40]

Similarly in the *Rice* case, Justice Scalia also focused on low blood quantum but in more absurd terms. This focus arose in the Court when it was brought to his attention that there are already legal definitions of Hawaiian that are most inclusive. That is to say, they are not defined by the 50 percent rule, where "native Hawaiian" is defined inclusively for anyone of Hawaiian ancestry. Judge Scalia found such inclusive definitions of Hawaiian most troubling. With regard to all inclusive definitions based on ancestral descent, he impatiently stated, "And you are defining Native Hawaiian now to mean any Hawaiian. . . . So 148 [sic] will do it . . . . [even] if you have 195th Hawaiian blood."[41] Scalia's hypothetical figures were invoked as a rhetorical device for pushing the arbitrary point, or the point that one's ancestry is arbitrary.

This point also became evident when Justice Breyer attempted to clarify that a more inclusive definition of Hawaiian (other than that based on 50 percent blood quantum) was covered in one way or another by two separate trusts under the OHA. He declared: "That I think is the problem. It seems to me . . . that everyone who has one Hawaiian ancestor at least gets to vote, and more than half of those people are not Native Hawaiians. They just have a distant ancestor."[42] Here the subtext of the discussion and summation seems concerned with phenotype and racial recognizability. Even after lawyers in the case pointed out to him that U.S. Code allows for tribal membership defined in terms of lineal descendancy, Justice Breyer repeatedly evoked the figure of the "remote" aboriginal ancestor, seemingly to dismiss native identification based on such inclusive regard for ancestry. For example, he asked: "How do we extend that to people 10 generations later, who had 10 generations ago one Indian ancestor? I mean, that might apply to everybody in the room. We have no idea. . . . You just have one ancestor 10 generations ago."[43] Breyer's assumption is that such matters of ancestry are both arbitrary and irrelevant. Also he refused to take account of the fact that one cannot have an ancestor from ten generations without also having that same line be just one generation removed.

In his concurrence with the majority opinion on the case, Breyer specifically targeted Hawaiian ways of accounting for indigenous ancestry as meaningless. He declared: "There must . . . be . . . some limit on what is reasonable, at the least when a State (which is not itself a tribe) creates the definition. And to define that membership in terms of 1 possible ancestor out of 500, thereby creating a vast and unknowable body of potential members—leaving some combination of luck and interest to determine which potential members become actual voters—goes well beyond any reasonable limit." Breyer's limit seems most *unreasonable*; ignoring cultural specific differences regarding kinship, he presumes that genealogy is the arbitrary modality of identity when it would seem that blood quantum is not only arbitrary; it is abstract and restrictive. Moreover, where blood quantum is always about the individual body, genealogy enlarges the collective social body.

The mixed-race status of Hawaiians is both a desired outcome of assimilation and also a condition that disqualifies them from land rights and other benefits. It is in the majority opinion in the case that we see how the issues of descendancy, in relation to Hawaiian entitlements (or even, as one could argue, inheritance rights), provoked the deployment of race as a stand-in category for lineage. The court's majority opinion declared:

> The state maintains that this is not a racial category at all but instead a classification limited to those whose ancestors were in Hawaii at a particular time, regardless of their race. . . . Furthermore, the State argues, the restriction in its operation excludes a person whose traceable ancestors were exclusively Polynesian if none of those ancestors resided in Hawaii in 1778; and, on the other hand, the vote would be granted to a person who could trace, say one sixty-fourth of his or her ancestry to a Hawaiian inhabitant on the pivotal date . . . these factors, it is said, mean the restriction is not a racial classification. We reject this line of argument. . . . Ancestry can be a proxy for race. It is that proxy here.[44]

Here the court clearly privileged duration and residency over genealogy and sovereign status. Indeed, indigeneity was billed as a farce.

This case marks the impossibility of using the discourses of "race" and the apparatus of liberal discourses of discrimination and equality to account for pressing issues of constituencies, inheritance, and native title. It is not that the state is using ancestry as a proxy for race; it is that blood quantum inherently mobilizes racial categories as a proxy for ancestry. For many Hawaiians, what this case highlights is the necessity for insistently articulating discourses of genealogy with their attendant notions of responsibility to place and to descendants, as a basis of Hawaiian discourse of sovereignty.

Taking the Apology Seriously

In his dissenting opinion in *Rice v. Cayetano*, Justice Stevens points to one of the more salient predicaments for Hawaiians today: "It is a painful irony indeed to conclude that native Hawaiians are not entitled to special benefits designed to restore a measure of native self-governance because they currently lack any vestigial native government—a possibility of which history and the actions of this [U.S.] nation have deprived them."[45]

This is not ironic; it is neocolonial. Therein lies the challenge: to protect lands and entitlements in the face of further diminishment under conditions where Hawaiians are inconsistently recognized as indigenous peoples with sovereignty claims. On the one hand, Hawaiians are caught between extensive inclusions in congressional legislation for Native Americans. And on the other, Hawaiians are subject to the equal protection clause under the Constitution, unlike American Indians. Hawaiians maintain historical sovereignty claims and yet persist without sovereign recognition. Although the relationship is typically not recognized as such, the United States retains a colonial relationship with the Hawaiian people—not despite the fact that Hawai`i is a state but perhaps because of it. It is precisely this misrecognition of the colonial correlation that perpetuates that same relationship.

In March 2000, in the wake of the ruling in *Rice*, Hawai`i's congressional delegation formed a Task Force on Native Hawaiian issues, chaired by Senator Daniel Akaka. As its immediate goal, the Task Force aimed to clarify the relationship between Hawaiians and the United States through the U.S. Congress. Soon Akaka introduced federal legislation during the 106th Congress. This bill proposed to recognize that Hawaiians are an indigenous people and have a "special relationship" with the United States and hence a right to self-determination under federal law. The passage of the bill would lay the foundation for a nation-within-nation model of self-governance like that of over five hundred federally recognized tribal nations. However, Akaka's bill did not pass at that time and has since been reintroduced to Congress, where it has survived committee hearings and still awaits final vote in both the House and the Senate.[46] Whatever the outcome, it is but part of a larger struggle and not a simple issue, as the diversity of Hawaiian responses to the legislation shows.[47]

For some Hawaiians, a proposal such as Akaka's is seen as a crucial opportunity. But many sovereignty groups have persistently and consistently rejected the application of U.S. federal Indian law that would recognize a Hawaiian domestic dependent nation—as ward to guardian—under the plenary power of Congress. In other words, the proposed legislation to recognize Hawaiians as "Native Americans" with "a political trust relationship to the U.S. similar to that of American Indians and Alaska Natives" is a violation of Hawaiians' inherent sovereignty and self-determination as recognized by the U.S. Apology. Taking that apology seriously, one must conclude that if Hawaiian sovereignty and self-determination are inherent, then they need not be legislated by the

United States. Still, federal recognition raises a key question: how to protect Hawaiian lands while international claims are pursued? Legal suits were soon filed to dismantle all federal and state-supported Hawaiian programs, including the Office of Hawaiian Affairs.

As soon as March 2002, U.S. District Judge Susan Oki Mollway denied a temporary restraining order requested by a group of Hawai`i residents who tried to stop programs offered by the Office of Hawaiian Affairs and the Hawaiian Homes Commission.[48] The sixteen plaintiffs—Earl F. Arakaki, Evelyn C. Arakaki, Edward U. Bugarin, Sandra P. Burgess, Patricia Carroll, Robert M. Chapman, Brian L. Clarke, Michael Y. Garcia, Roger Grantham, Toby M. Kravet, James I. Kuroiwa, Jr., Fran Nichols, Donna M. Scaff, Jack H. Scaff, Allen Teshima, and Thurston Twigg-Smith—are currently challenging the constitutionality of both agencies because of allegations that their "race-based programs" discriminate against non-Hawaiians. Still, although the judge denied their immediate request, the plaintiffs had standing to go forward with their lawsuit because, as taxpayers, they can challenge the use of state money to fund programs by OHA and the state Department of Hawaiian Home Lands. Indeed in March 2003 the case was filed in federal court on their behalf.

It would seem that while pressing international claims, Hawaiians might have a better chance at de facto self-determination by remaining under the current state situation and by resisting federal recognition that would foreclose legitimate claims to independence. But this too is questionable, because it was the willful neglect of the state to uphold the trust agreement that was the very impetus for the movement to restore Hawaiian sovereignty and the full exercise of self-determination.[49] Moreover, as a state agency the OHA still struggles to enforce the trust obligations in order to receive all of the revenues meant for allocation from the so-called ceded lands. Similarly, the Department of Hawaiian Home Lands has also been exposed for its failure to implement the leasing programs set aside for Hawaiians through the HHCA. Fewer than five thousand "native Hawaiians" are currently leaseholders, covering only a small area of these lands, mostly marginal in the first place. In any case, the controversy over land administration is only one aspect of Hawaiian self-determination. Nonetheless, the challenge seems to be how Hawaiians can continue to pressure the state government to meet its trust responsibilities while also negotiating a position to determine what modalities of self-governance would enhance the indigenous position without extinguishing aboriginal title to Hawaiian lands. However, this neocolonial predicament has been intensified by the ruling in *Rice*, which some fear has laid the essential groundwork for further assaults on Hawaiian lands and people.

It should not go unmentioned that Rice himself was financed by the Campaign for Color-Blind America and Robert Bork; Americans against Discrimination and Preferences; the United States Justice Foundation; the Center for Equal Opportunity; New York Civil Rights Coalition (Carl Cohen and Abigail Thernstrom); and the Pacific Legal Foundation—all of which submitted legal briefs on his behalf. Each of these institutional think-tanks has been central in the nationwide attack on affirmative action and other civil rights gains. Moreover, Theodore Olsen—well known for his legal representation of George W. Bush in *Bush v. Gore* and later the U.S. solicitor general—was also legal counsel for Rice. Finally, the ruling in *Rice* has provoked concern regarding the continued political assaults on American Indians' classification as distinct sovereign peoples and further raises various questions about the constitutional rights of those residing in the U.S. insular territories.[50] Clearly the Rice case has implications beyond the Hawaiian situation.

One thing is certain: because the right of self-definition is an integral part of indigenous sovereignty and self-determination, Hawaiians will continue to contest blood quantum identification and to assert culturally integral models of reckoning belonging, such as those found in persistent genealogical practices. Just as the frameworks currently available for the exercise of Hawaiian self-determination do not do justice to the specific sovereignty claims outlined, blood quantum classification cannot account for the relatedness of genealogical practice and forms of identification that serve to connect people to one another, to place, and to the land. These connections are grounded in sovereignty, self-determination, and citizenship—not racialized beneficiary status.

Acknowledgments

This article, in a slightly different form, was previously published in the *Political and Legal Anthropology Review* 25, no. 1 (2002), 110–28, and is reprinted here with permission of the American Anthropological Association, which holds copyright. It is based on a conference paper entitled, "Racialized Genealogies: Blood Quanta Politics in *Rice v. Cayetano*," prepared for the Sovereignty 2000: Locations of Contestation and Possibility conference held at the University of California at Santa Cruz in May 2000. Thanks to Joanne Barker for her encouragement. The work here was also supported by the following scholars and institutions who invited me to present my research on this topic and to whom I offer *mahalo*: Elena Creef and the Hawai`i Club, the Office of Equal Opportunity and the History, Political Science, and Peace and Justice Studies departments at Wellesley College; Jocelyn Linnekin and the Anthropology

Department at the University of Connecticut; Ellen Shimakawa and the McNair fellows at Chaminade University; Wendy Ho and the Asian Pacific Cultural Studies Research Cluster at the University of California, Davis; Leti Volpp and the Latino Critical Theory Conference Committee of 2000; Judith Raiskin and the University of Oregon, Eugene; Marilyn Halter of Boston University, who organized the conference on the Limits of American Citizenship: Local Culture, Hawaiian Identity and Mainland Influences in Hawai`i; and Henry Abelove, director of the Center of Humanities at Wesleyan University, for his mentorship, and colleagues at the center during our time as fellows there in the fall semester of 2001. *Aloha* to Anne Keala Kelly for her enthusiasm for my scholarship and for her political passion, which continues to inspire me; and Marvette Perez and Noenoe Silva, with whom I heard the *Rice v. Cayetano* case presented before the U.S. Supreme Court, for their care and solidarity. Thanks also go to the three anonymous reviewers, who offered invaluable critical comments on the draft of this article and to the guest editors—Susan Gooding and Eve Darian Smith. The research conducted for this work was supported by a National Science Foundation Minority Predoctoral Fellowship. The findings and mistakes herein are my own and do not reflect the National Science Foundation or any of the people whom I have acknowledged.

Notes

1. The state residency restriction itself is profoundly problematic for off-island Hawaiians who assert their own claims in relation to the trust. See J. Kehaulani Kauanui, "Off-Island Hawaiians 'Making' Ourselves at 'Home': A [Gendered] Contradiction in Terms?" *Women's Studies International Forum* 21, no. 6 (1998): 681–93, for an exploration of Hawaiian diaspora in relation to the Hawaiian sovereignty movement.

2. J. Breyer and J. Souter concurred with the majority, with Breyer offering their concurrence. The two took their concurrence one step further than the court's opinion in that they denied the analogy between the Native Hawaiian relationship to the U.S. federal government and that of American Indians. Furthermore, they argued that there is no trust for Native Hawaiians and that the OHA's electorate, defined by statute, did not sufficiently resemble an "Indian tribe." J. Stevens and J. Ginsberg each offered a dissent.

3. Hawaiians recite, evoke, declare, chant, practice through naming, and deploy genealogical invocation at specific moments appropriate to their own positioning. The word for genealogy in modern Hawaiian is *mo'oku'auhau*. One of the many meanings of *mo'o* is a succession or series, while *ku'auhau* is defined as genealogy, pedigree, lineage, old traditions, genealogies, historian, and to recite genealogy. See Mary Kawena Pukui, *Hawaiian Dictionary* (Honolulu: University of Hawaii Press, 1986), 254. It is interesting to note that the word *'auhau* is used to mean an assessment, tribute, levy, or tax. I do not provide these definitions in hopes of finally translating *mo'oku'auhau* into English but rather to suggest that the word Hawaiians use for genealogy does not inherently carry the racial, genetic, or blooded meanings that genealogy does. Hawaiian

genealogical practices are also bi-lineal and allow for reckoning through female and/or male lines of descent. Questions about one's genealogy may sometimes be coupled with questions about one's fraction of "blood." But Hawaiians are more likely to go by genealogy over and above blood degree in order to decide who counts as Hawaiian.

4. Thomas Biolsi, "The Birth of the Reservation: Making the Modern Individual among the Lakota," *American Ethnologist* 22, no. 1 (1995): 28–53. Strong similarities operate between the approaches to American Indian and Hawaiian racialization: issues of colonization, land allotment, blood quanta determinations, and assimilation policies as both legal and ideological precedents. See Avtar Brah, *Cartographies of Desire: Contesting Identities* (London: Routledge, 1996), 187, for her concept of "differential racialization." There she describes this concept as a key component of her framework, enabling a rejection of binary racial formulations by exploring "how different racialised groups are positioned differently *vis-à-vis* one another" (15). Her concept of differential racialization opens space for comparative examinations of "Native" for Hawaiians and American Indians where whiteness is figured as a solvent of native blood. Occupying a racially mixed subjectivity has not only been afforded to Natives—both American Indian and Hawaiian—it has tended to be prescriptive. Mixed-race family histories have been routinely evoked to disqualify Natives who don't "measure up" for entitlements and benefits.

5. This marks the year that Captain Cook landed in Hawai`i.

6. Davianna Pomaika`i McGregor, "Aina Ho'opulapula: Hawaiian Homesteading," *Hawaiian Journal of History* 4 (1990): 1–38; Alan Murakami, "The Hawaiian Homes Commission Act," in *Native Hawaiian Rights Handbook*, ed. Melody MacKenzie (Honolulu: Native Hawaiian Legal Corporation and the Office of Hawaiian Affairs, 1991), 43–76; Marylynn Vause, "The Hawaiian Homes Commission Act, 1920: History and Analysis" (Ph.D. diss., University of Hawaii, 1962).

7. J. Kehaulani Kauanui, " 'For Get' Hawaiian Entitlement: Configurations of Land, 'Blood,' and Americanization in the Hawaiian Homes Commission Act of 1920," *Social Text* 59 (1999): 123–44, and "Rehabilitating the Native: Hawaiian Blood Quantum and the Politics of Race, Citizenship, and Entitlement" (Ph.D. diss., University of California, 2000).

8. Ulla Hasager and Jonathan Friedman, *Hawai`i Return to Nationhood* (Copenhagen: International Working Group for Indigenous Affairs, 1994), Document no.75; Noel J. Kent, *Hawaii: Islands Under the Influence*, 2nd ed. (Honolulu: University of Hawaii Press, 1982).

9. Thomas Marshall Spaulding, *The Crown Lands of Hawaii* (Honolulu: University of Hawaii, 1923), 16.

10. Noenoe K. Silva, "Kanaka Maoli Resistance to Annexation," *'Oiwi: A Native Hawaiian Journal*, December 1998.

11. *Native Hawaiian Rights Handbook*, ed. Melody Kapilialoha MacKenzie (Honolulu: Native Hawaiian Legal Corporation and the Office of Hawaiian Affairs, 1991), 15.

12. Congressional Record, United States Congress, *The Act of Congress Organizing Hawaii into a Territory, An Act to Provide a Government for the Territory of Hawaii*, April 30, 1900.

13. Mililani Trask, "The Politics of Oppression," in *Hawai`i Return to Nationhood*, ed. Ulla Hasager and Jonathan Friedman (Copenhagen, IWGIA, 1994) Document 75, 68–87.

14. MacKenzie, *Native Hawaiian Rights Handbook*, 26.

15. MacKenzie, *Native Hawaiian Rights Handbook*, 18.

16. Congressional Record, United States Congress, *State Admissions Act of March 18, 1959, 73 Stat. 4*. United States House of Representatives.

17. Mari Matsuda, "Native Custom and Official Law in Hawaii," *Law and Anthropology* 3 (1988): 139.

18. Haunani-Kay Trask, *From a Native Daughter: Colonialism and Sovereignty in Hawai`i* (Monroe ME: Common Courage Press, 1993), 89–90.

19. Trask, *From a Native Daughter*, 91.

20. MacKenzie, *Native Hawaiian Rights Handbook*, 33.

21. MacKenzie, *Native Hawaiian Rights Handbook*, 33.

22. Kauanui, " 'For Get' Hawaiian Entitlement," and "Rehabilitating the Native."

23. To argue their case, they pointed to the 1848 privatization of collective land holdings under Kamehameha III (commonly known as the Mahele), a disaster for Hawaiian commoners, who received only 28,000 acres of land in the division. Kamehameha III, along with the chiefs and land stewards, secured 1,619,000 acres, 984,000 of which were held for the crown, thus providing a source of income and support for the kingdom. See Congressional Record, U.S. House of Representatives, 1920, *Proposed Amendments to the Organic Act of the Territory of Hawaii*, Hearings before the Commission on the Territories, 66th Congress, Second Session, February 3, 4, 5, 7, 10, 1920.

24. Congressional Record, U.S. House of Representatives, 1920, *Proposed Amendments to the Organic Act of the Territory of Hawaii*, Hearings before the Commission on the Territories, 66th Congress, Second Session, February 3, 4, 5, 7, 10, 1920.

25. Territory of Hawaii, *Journal of the House of Representatives*, Tenth Legislature of the Territory of Hawaii, Regular Session, Commenced on Wednesday, the Nineteenth Day of February, and Ended on Wednesday, the Thirteenth Day of April, 1919.

26. A. G. M. Robertson, *The Hawaiian Rehabilitation Bill: An Argument Against the Bill* (Honolulu: H.R. Union Calendar No. 269, 66th Congress, Second Session, 1920).

27. Congressional Record, United States House of Representatives, May 21, 1920; *Proposed Amendments to the Organic Act of the Territory of Hawaii*, Hearings before the Commission on the Territories, 67th Congress, First Session, on H.R. 7257, June 9, 10, 1921.

28. Congressional Record, United States Senate, *Hawaiian Homes Commission Act, 1920, Hearings Before the Committee on the Territories*, 66th Congress, Third Session, on H.R. 13500, December, 1920.

29. Clarence E. Glick, "Interracial Marriage and Admixture in Hawaii," *Social Biology* 15, no. 4 (1970): 278–91; A. Marques, "The Population of Hawaii: Is the Hawaiian a Doomed Race? Present and Future Prospects," *Journal of the Polynesian Society* 2 (1894): 253–70.

30. Territory of Hawaii, *Senate Journal*, Tenth Legislature of the Territory of Hawaii, Regular Session, Opening Day—Wed., February 19, 1919, Closing Day—Wed., April 30, 1919, and *Senate Journal*, Eleventh Legislature of the Territory of Hawaii, Regular Session (Honolulu: New Freedom Press, 1921).

31. Congressional Record, United States Congress, *Proposed Amendments to the Organic Act of the Territory of Hawaii*, Hearings before the Commission on the Territories, 67th Congress, First Session, on H.R. 7257, June 9, 10, 1921.

32. McGregor, "Aina Ho`opulapula"; Murakami, "Hawaiian Homes Commission Act"; Congressional Record, *Hawaiian Homes Commission Act of July 9, 1921, c42, 42 Stat 108.*

33. Some Hawaiian groups, including those pressing for federal recognition of a native governing entity, submitted *amicus* briefs on behalf of the Respondent. The State Council of Hawaiian Homestead Associations, Hui Kako`o 'Aina Ho`opulapula, Kalama`ula Homestead Association, and the Hawaiian Homes Commission collectively submitted a brief. Another was collectively

submitted by the Office of Hawaiian Affairs, Ka Lahui, the Association of Hawaiian Civic Clubs, Council of Hawaiian Organizations, Native Hawaiian Convention, Native Hawaiian Bar Association, Native Hawaiian Legal Corporation, Native Hawaiian Advisory Council, Ha Hawai`i, Hui Kalai'aina, Alu Like Inc., and Papa Ola Lokahi. The Kamehameha Schools Bishop Estate Trust also offered amici curiae, as did the Hawai`i Congressional Delegation and the National Congress of American Indians. Moreover, the solicitor general of that time—Seth Waxman—wrote a brief representing the Department of Justice in support of Cayetano. The state governments of Alabama, California, Nevada, New Mexico, Oklahoma, Oregon, Washington, the Territory of Guam, and the Commonwealth of the Northern Mariana Islands did as well. It should not go unmentioned that among the briefs of amici curiae for the petitioner, one was submitted from a Hawaiian group called Hou Hawaiians and a man named Maui Loa—who identified themselves as "Native Hawaiian beneficiaries." They backed Rice and claimed that the OHA—by allowing Hawaiians who do not meet the 50 percent blood quantum rule to vote—violated the trust for those Hawaiians who do.

34. Besides a focus on the applicability of Indian case law for Hawaiians, this situation also begs the question of what precedence, if any, insular case law holds; that is, how past rulings on the insular territories implicate Hawaiians.

35. However, it is important also to point out that data for Native Hawaiians, Samoans, and other Pacific Islanders are all too often aggregated with data for Asian Americans under the rubric "Asian and Pacific Islanders." This practice obscures both the differences between the Asian and the native Pacific Islander subpopulations and the similarities in outcomes for native Pacific Islanders and American Indians/Alaska Natives. One hopes the new "Hawaiian and other Pacific Islander" classification option in the 2000 census, outside the "Asian" category, will inspire the OMB to direct agencies collect their data accordingly.

36. The court determined that it would review the legislation in question with a rational basis analysis rather than subject the case to strict scrutiny dictating all other cases understood as race-based. In *Adarand Constructors, Inc. v. Pena* (515 U.S. 200, 1995), the Supreme Court ruled that "a group classification such as one based on race is ordinarily subjected to detailed judicial scrutiny to ensure that the personal right to equal protection of laws has not been infringed. Under this reasoning, even supposedly benign racial classifications must be subject to strict scrutiny."

37. The perversion here is that Hawaiians—as a people—cannot press land claims against the state because of their wardship status.

38. J. Breyer and J. Souter concurred with the majority but took their opinion one step further in that they denied the analogy between the Native Hawaiian relationship to the U.S. federal government and that of American Indians. Furthermore, they argued that there is no trust for Native Hawaiians and that the OHA's electorate, defined by statue, did not sufficiently resemble an "Indian tribe."

39. For example, under North Carolina voting laws, all men were required to pay poll taxes except those whose ancestors had been eligible to vote prior to 1 January 1867, and to pass a literacy test. That amendment would take effect on 1 July 1902, but white men (whose ancestors could have voted) would not have to take the literacy test until 1908. See Glenda Elizabeth Gilmore, *Gender and Jim Crow: Women and the Politics of White Supremacy in North Carolina 1896–1920* (Chapel Hill: University of North Carolina Press, 1996), 20, 120. It was this kind of exemption that was known as a "grandfather clause."

40. Congressional Record, United States Senate, *Hawaiian Homes Commission Act, 1920, Hearings*

Before the Committee on the Territories, 66th Congress, Third Session, on H.R. 13500, December, 1920. In the 1920 debates, Senator Chamberlain (of Oregon) compared the one thirty-second blood degree to a definition of "one thirty-third," as if this was possible in the mathematical schema of blood quantum (U.S. Senate 1920).

41. United States Supreme Court, Official Transcript Proceedings before the Supreme Court of the United States, *Harold F. Rice, Petitioner v. Benjamin J. Cayetano, Governor of Hawaii*, Case no. 98–818, Wednesday, October 6, 1999, 54.

42. *Rice v. Cayetano*, Official Transcript, 39.

43. *Rice v. Cayetano*, Official Transcript, 47–48.

44. *Rice v. Cayetano*, Opinion of the Court (2000), Justice Kennedy, 9.

45. *Rice v. Cayetano*, Dissenting Opinion (2000), Justice Stevens.

46. There have been several different versions of this legislation since the 106th Congress. The current proposal, S. 147, is still before the 109th Congress for a vote in the Senate. See http://www.stopakaka.org for a comprehensive delineation of the proposals and for a range of political responses to them.

47. Other useful web sites that represent a variety of Hawaiian positions on sovereignty include: *http://www.hawaii-nation.org*; http://www.kalahui.org; and http://www.HawaiianKingdom.org.

48. See Pat Omandam, "Judge Denies Bid to End Native Hawaiian Funding," *Honolulu Star Bulletin*, 13 March 2002, 1.

49. John F. Dulles II, *A Broken Trust: The Hawaiian Homelands Program: Seventy Years of Failure of the Federal and State Governments to Protect the Civil Rights of Native Hawaiians, Hawai`i Advisory Committee to the United States Commission on Civil Rights* (Los Angeles: United States Commission on Civil Rights, 1991); Susan Faludi, "Broken Promise: How Everyone Got Hawaiians' Homelands Except the Hawaiians," *Wall Street Journal*, 9 September 1991, 1); Federal-State Task Force on the Hawaiian Homes Commission Act, *Report to the United States Secretary of the Interior and the Governor of the State of Hawai`i* (Honolulu: United States Department of the Interior, August, 1983).

50. This is clear when one considers the so-called Native American Equal Rights Act introduced before the House, during the 106th Congress, which aimed to be the basis for repealing Indian preference laws (mistaken as "racial preferences") of the United States, citing the ruling in *Rice v. Cayetano* as an instrument. There are also questions as to what the constitutional rights of U.S. citizens who live in the U.S. territories include. What are the rights and privileges of the residents (indigenous and non-indigenous) of these islands under the U.S. Constitution and international law? Which provisions of the U.S. Constitution apply in these islands?

Dan Taulapapa McMullin (Samoan)

The Passive Resistance of Samoans to U.S. and Other Colonialisms

Preface

Tulouna le Manu'a, tulouna lau afioga Tuimanu'a 'o lo'o e afio i le Fale'ula, afio mai laia i ou epa ma lou faleto'a, alāla maia fa'atui, alāla mai 'oulua Vaimagalo, mamalu mai 'outou to'oto'o o le Fale'ula, mamalu mai 'oulua le Manu'a. Tulouna 'oe le motu tapua'i, tulouna le tapua'iga le motu a Salaia, tulouna Sua ma le Vaifanua, tulouna Fofō ma Itulagi. Tulouna 'oe Pule, tulouna a Tumua, tulouna āiga i le tai, tulouna alataua ma itu'au, tulouna va'a o Fonotī. 'Iā Samoa 'uma. With apologies for errors and omissions but with hope this essay will contribute to our discussion.[1]

Introduction

Currently there is no great grassroots movement toward independence for American Samoa or reunification with independent Samoa among the American Samoa people, although there is a strong nationalism that identifies as Samoan.[2] Western institutions, even nationhood, have not been the main definition of Samoan identity; it is in the *fa'asamoa* (Samoan language, culture, and way of life) and *fa'amatai* (Samoan chiefly system) that Samoans identify and live as a people. Therefore Samoan sovereignty as expressed by the American Samoa people is through the decentralized, diffuse small local family fa'amatai that also connects with Samoans in independent Samoa and worldwide. The danger for Samoans is that the U.S. centralization of authority always incorporates the fa'asamoa and by its nature and relationship attempts to dissolve the fa'amatai.[3] The communal land ownership system administered by the fa'amatai is not defined or protected by Western systems of law; but it is presumed to be.

The 2001 and 2002 attempts to remove the U.S. Territory of American Samoa from the United Nations List of Nations to be Decolonized were justified to

American Samoa based on the belief that "we are not a colony" because of the fa'asamoa and good U.S. relations.[4] Although the attempt was ostensibly and publicly pushed forward by Samoan leadership, its impetus came from the U.S. government and was not truly debated or voted in American Samoa. Were this de-decolonization to happen, like previous removals of Hawaii by the United States and Tahiti by France from the decolonization list, it would presage U.S. attempts at further colonization and eventual incorporation.

The Many Immovable Circles

"On Samoa the difficulty is not to know who is a chief but to know who is not."[5] Samoa practices decentralization of authority in the fa'amatai and indigenous family ownership of communal land even while under colonialism and globalization.[6] In Samoa although the *matai* (chiefs) determine the use of the land, communal land may not be alienated or sold from the family/village without the consensus of the entire family/village; individuals of the family do not own the land. "The *ali'i* [noble matai] is the guardian of the honors and dignity of the family or *e tausia le mamalu o le aiga*. He is the peacemaker and mediator in family friction and is to be the repository of wisdom or *tofa mamao*. The *tulafale* [orator matai] is the custodian and protector of family genealogies and history or *uputuu* . . . tulafale are the workers or *o e faaeleelea* consequently their larger numbers."[7]

Le Tagaloa writes: "Within a *nu'u* [village] five basic societal groups can be found to constitute the socio-metric wheel of the fa'amatai interacting in a social system performing economic, political and legal functions: the groups are the *tama'ita'i* or daughters of matai, *faletua ma tausi* or wives of matai, *'aumaga* or sons of matai, *tamaiti* or young children, and *sa'ofaiga* or matai council."[8] This is quite inclusive as the head of every family is a matai and as gender has become a nonissue in matai selection regarding women and *fa'afafine* (transgender individuals) who take a lead with their families.

Saleimoa Vaai writes: "A holder of a matai title may not confer on or assign the title held (*faaui le ula*) to any other person as the title is not property personal to the holder but is familial property which reverts back to the family on the death of the holder or may be revoked by the family for justifiable reasons under its constitutive authority."[9] The handing down of matai authority within a village and/or family is decided by consensus in the *fono* (village/family meeting), and even if the *mavaega* (parting words) of the previous matai favor one candidate, only in the fono is it finally decided. Succession is based on many factors, including ability, *tautua* (past service), and knowledge of tradition and leadership as well as genealogy. By taking on a matai title one assumes the privileges of *faaloalo* (respect) and the responsibility of *pule* (distribution). Colonization brought the intervention of Western-based court systems for cases of succession, in favor of candidates with Western-based education and wealth. The chief justice and associate justices of the American Samoa judiciary system's High Court are appointed by the U.S. secretary of the interior and not by the local government. The High Court, which at one time went to the extreme of settling American Samoa disputes of chiefly titles outside Samoa, in Hawaii, has shifted toward trying to settle disputes out of court and within the family from the urging of many families in American Samoa.

In 1901 the first great court case against the fa'amatai in American Samoa between the United States and a Samoan chief was called the Trial of the *Ipu* (meaning the '*ava* cup; 'ava or *kava* is the ceremonial and sacred drink of Polynesia). Given much press both sympathetic and racist in the United States, the case put on trial the ceremonial rights of the Tui Manu'a title itself, the oldest chiefly sovereign's title of Samoa and of Polynesia. The U.S. Navy, in taking control of Pago Pago Bay after the 1899 Treaty of Berlin, which divided the Samoa Islands, installed Australian E. W. Gurr as the local administrator. Giving himself many titles and offices, he monopolized the copra industry, suppressing Samoan merchants while secretly pocketing the profits, for which he was convicted years later.[10]

In conflict with the highest chief of American Samoa, the Tui Manu'a Elisala, over the missing tax revenues from the copra industry, Gurr sent—accompanied by a U.S. gunboat—the high chief of Pago Pago, who paid a visit to the Manu'a Islands and there demanded to be served by the 'ava name of the Tui Manu'a, which was against Samoan customary law. When Manu'a attempted to punish the local matai who served up the 'ava cup name of the Tui Manu'a, a trial was called by the United States, establishing U.S. law above Samoan law. The U.S. judge called the Pago Pago high chief "a Samoan chief of no less rank than Tui Manu'a."[11] This ignored the *fa'alupega* (title-kinship order) of Samoa.[12] The Navy commandant called the Tui Manu'a Elisala to his ship and reinforced the U.S. judge's decision.[13] These actions led to the Deed of Cession of Manu'a, which followed the Deed of Cession of Tutuila, both island groups forming the U.S. Territory of American Samoa.[14]

After World War II when the Department of the Interior moved in Washington to take over the territory of American (Eastern) Samoa from U.S. naval authority, it first attempted to make the territory a part of the United States through Organic Act 4500, at about the same time as New Zealand began to work with the United Nations toward independence for Western Samoa. High

Orator Chief Tuiasosopo Mariota and a group of other young matai in American Samoa sought to establish a legislature and declared that "the proposed Organic Act 4500 now in Washington and pending a hearing before Congress will not in the conviction of Samoa safeguard their land and customs."[15] To "rescue such happiness and [our] own way of life" they helped defeat the act in the U.S. Congress.[16] In promoting the Organic Act 4500 to Samoans the Department of Interior cited U.S. treaties with other nations, such as the Cherokee and Iroquois. As the United States did not honor its deeds and treaties with these nations, American Samoa cannot expect different treatment when the needs of the United States change.

Ultimately the removal of the Tui Manu'a title did not diminish the fa'amatai, nor did the creation of a legislature enhance it. " 'O nei faiga 'uma e i lalo o le pule'aga malosi e tasi. 'O lea pule'aga le fono a le nu'u po o le village council."[17] In other words, the village council rules in Samoa; although some Samoans, often emigrants, choose not to live under the fa'amatai because of issues of accountability. Before the introduction of money into Samoan society about 150 years ago the fa'amatai system of obligations was based on exchange of food and fine mats. And whereas previously pule distribution was in full public view on the *malae* (sacred village green), now pule has various levels of publicity, the fono retaining responsibility for making the process transparent and accountable to the people, whether for fine mats or land use.

The United States maintains to the UN that "the traditional communal system provides the basis for a strong Government whereby leaders are responsible not only for preserving the social order but also for the economic welfare of the extended family. The federal Government underwrites most of the cost of preserving this system."[18] However, since the fa'amatai is just as well preserved in independent Samoa as in American Samoa, it cannot be truly said that the fa'amatai system requires any outside support for its preservation. It is the will of the Samoan people that it continue.

The Changeable Center

It has been said of the Samoa archipelago that here, God is the village, and the culture of the people is the fa'asamoa: " 'A fa'a'upu e papālagi le Fa'asamoa o le culture lea a tagata e toto Sāmoa."[19] Some Samoans see Christian faith in opposition to fa'asamoa and try to discourage "the culture," although Samoan churches have been the shelter of fa'asamoa, especially for youth and especially in diaspora communities. In independent Samoa "all lands given for use of the churches should revert to the original title holders when they were no longer needed for church purposes," but not in American Samoa.[20] The Samoan village is intensely Christian yet may be said to be polytheistic in source and therefore structure. And the centralization of a U.S. colonial authority may be said to be monotheistic in source and structure.

Centralization of Polynesian nations grew out of need for representation in foreign affairs with Western nations. Nineteenth-century relationships between Polynesian nations and imperialist Western nations were strengthened by the centralization of authority. Paramount chiefs became monarchs. Families such as the Kamehameha in Hawaii, the Pomare in Tahiti, the Malietoa in Samoa, and the Cakobau in Fiji gained prominence, with the arrival of westerners sometimes causing the decline of many lesser chiefs. The Samoa Civil Wars of the late nineteenth century saw various high chiefs creating alliances with opposing Western powers, pitting the Germans, British, French, and Americans against one another.

In 1878 when the British declared Samoa subject to their jurisdiction, the government of chiefs in 'Upolu sent their secretary of state Le Mamea to Washington DC, where he signed a treaty with the United States for protection and for the use of Pago Pago harbor on behalf of Samoa.[21] However in 1882 when paramount chief Malietoa Laupepa in 'Upolu asked the U.S. Navy to establish his representative in Pago Pago in respect of the Le Mamea agreement, his request was declined.[22] Thereafter the United States supported High Chief Mauga of Pago Pago as the central chiefly authority in now eastern (American) Samoa—that is, until the Deeds of Cession of Tutuila and Manu'a were secured and the U.S. naval commandant took full authority.

According to the oral traditions of Western Polynesia, more than a thousand years ago the Tui Manu'a ruled over all the archipelagos of the southwest Pacific where Polynesians had settled, including Manu'a, Samoa, Tonga, Fiji, the Cook Islands, and more. Over the centuries and as peoples settled into their present nations, the rule of the Tui Manu'a diminished to just the Manu'a Islands of Samoa. About seven hundred years ago the chiefs of Tonga came to rule southwest Polynesia, including Samoa except Manu'a. Throughout this Tongan colonization the local fa'amatai system continued until the Tongans were driven out. Currently the Tui Manu'a title has not been held by anyone since the U.S. takeover, but the title still exists and is often addressed in Samoan speeches and songs. The paramount titles of independent Samoa if faced with reunification might have to acknowledge a Tui Manu'a, but this would not influence the fa'amatai system itself, which is decentralized, or the central state where authority has shifted.

When the U.S. Navy took over Manu'a, the Tui Manu'a Elisala, seeking funds to found a school in Manu'a, had written a letter to the U.S. president requesting the use of Manu'a's own copra tax funds for education in Manu'a.[23] Upon receipt of the letter, the U.S. Navy leveraged education funding against the signing of the Deed of Cession of Manu'a.[24] Frustrated by the withholding of copra tax funds, Tui Manu'a Elisala eventually agreed to the Deed of Cession signing, which took place in 1904. Thereafter the Tui Manu'a Elisala was addressed as district governor of Manu'a by the U.S. Navy.[25]

Thus was one of the most ancient continuous titles of Polynesia and perhaps the world quietly relegated to keeping desk at a salary less than that of the local *fitafita* (soldier). The loss to Samoa was not an insurmountable one, but history was neglected and replaced by three much-repeated myths about American Samoa. One involves the Tui Manu'a Elisala saying that after him there would be no other Tui Manu'a, which there is no tradition of anyone hearing him say.[26] Another myth is that the chiefs of Tutuila and Manu'a signed the deeds for gold watches, when their reasons were various and complex but mostly due to superior U.S. weaponry. And the third myth is that the United States does not really want to retain possession of American Samoa at all, since the U.S. reason for retaining the territory has little to do with Samoans and everything to do with the Pacific Ocean. The U.S. representative to the UN 2001 Decolonization Committee said "the United States could not agree with the implementation in the draft resolution that the mere presence of military activities and bases in the Non-Self-Governing Territories was harmful to the rights and interests of the people of those Territories."[27]

When first presented with the opportunity to elect the governor of American Samoa locally, "the voters went to the polls three times [in the 1970s] before they would approve the change and accept the responsibility of electing their own governor"—indicating then a lack of faith in Western institutions of local governance.[28] Today U.S. centralization of authority in American Samoa is localized in the power of the governor. "The Governor of American Samoa has item veto power and the liberal use of that power has been a source of frustration to the legislature. Governor Haydon once vetoed everything in an appropriation bill including explanatory statements. Governor Coleman followed suit by x-ing out an entire bill except totals."[29] Disputes are referred to the U.S. secretary of the interior, who has final decision. However, the legislature's complaint is: "First the Executive never calls or invites requests from individual members during the preparatory phase of the preliminary budget request. Second the governor waits . . . close to the Washington deadline before presenting. Third and biggest complaint by the Fono legislature over this issue is that the Governor frequently undid changes after the legislative review."[30]

The late governor Tauese at the United Nations Decolonization Committee said: "Independence is a noble ideal; however, the path of decolonization is littered with internal strife and human suffering. . . . The very thought of putting a timeframe to such a quest is most presumptuous and unrealistic . . . the people of American Samoa take exception to the term "colony." In their unique relationship with the United States of America, they view themselves as an integral part of the U.S. family of states and territories enjoying individual rights and freedoms under an evolutionary political process."[31] Here the term *evolutionary* suggests Department of Interior authority.

The comptroller general of the United States wrote in a report: "We believe the Department of the Interior has not provided effective oversight and technical assistance to help [the Government of American Samoa] achieve greater self-support. Interior's neglect to clarify the U.S. roles and responsibilities is a contributing factor to American Samoa not developing a greater self-help capability. Because Interior has the ultimate responsibility for the administration of [Government of American Samoa] we believe it should establish its role and responsibilities and how it will exercise them."[32] The Department of the Interior responded in the same report: "The people of American Samoa acting through their locally elected Legislature and Governor exercise nearly complete self-government. The Department of Interior does not administer the territory and the basic decision-making and formulation of policies and programs rest with the local government."[33]

The United States further subverts the fa'amatai by maintaining "American" standards across departments, not just through the Department of Interior. For instance, the U.S. Department of Agriculture imposed a ban in 2003 on meat imported into American Samoa from Samoa, disrupting the all-important gift exchange system.[34] "Taking into consideration our cultural and blood ties imposing such a ban would harm one of our cultural obligations when it comes to funerals and other Samoan obligations."[35] This continues a process that began when the U.S. Navy assumed control over Pago Pago and at that time suppressed the practices of *lagi* (funeral games), *malaga* (traveling parties), and *fai'aiga* (cohabitation), just as the missionaries since the 1830s had been banning traditions such as tattooing in Manu'a.

In the forming of the constitution of independent Samoa "there was the position where Samoans from American Samoa could take titles in Western Samoa [because of family ties] although the reverse was not allowed."[36] A recent governor of American Samoa received a matai title in Savai'i in independent Samoa, and at a public gathering there he was asked why it was becoming more difficult for Samoans from Samoa to enter American Samoa. His response was that it was not his decision but the decision of the lieutenant governor, echoing the U.S. Department of Interior's deferring of responsibility for American Samoa to a leadership funded by the U.S. Department of the Interior. In the 2001 UN Decolonization meeting, Congressman Faleomavaega, the representative for American Samoa in the U.S. Congress, said: "American Samoa enacts its own laws, including the power of taxation, and controls its own borders through local immigration statutes and an immigration department." Immigrants include Samoans from independent Samoa who are treated as aliens in American Samoa.

The Land and Samoan Sovereignty

"Customary land is not land belonging to individuals. Land is under the protective authority of the *Ali'i* and *Faipule* [noble chiefs and orator chiefs]. Subject to this is the *pule* [power of distribution] of the matai which authorizes the exploitation and usage of family land."[37]

In Samoan communities everywhere there is some sense of communal property. However only in the two Samoas is communal land protected by law, both Samoan and Western. Here even the downtown areas of Pago Pago and Apia are divided into communal villages run by the fa'amatai system.

"A village or *nu'u* to the Samoans is not just a geographical entity but has a prescriptive and descriptive identity which 'goes beyond the physical setting. As well nu'u encompasses all the cultural values and practices.' "[38] In Samoan diaspora communities in the United States, Aotearoa–New Zealand, Australia, Fiji, and the United Kingdom the fa'amatai system continues, sustained through the family, the church, and cross-border traffic of *malaga* (large group visitation) and gift exchange, as can be confirmed by anyone who has waited in airport check-in lines where Samoan families travel with caravans of large boxes, bales, and bags of fine mats, food, and clothes.

When the United States and the European powers met to divide Samoa among themselves, "the Treaty of Berlin also enacted henceforth . . . there should be a complete prohibition on all sales, mortgages and other dispositions of Samoan lands to the citizens or subjects of any foreign country."[39] But it was also "the beginning of the marginalization of indigenous authority and law, which were made subservient to Western law under the Treaty. It was for instance assumed in discussions on the settlement of land disputes and inserted in the Treaty that Samoa did not have a land tenure system and land claims by Europeans were accordingly determined largely by concepts of Western law."[40]

When the United States finally agreed with the Germans to the U.S. portion being eastern Samoa for Pago Pago harbor, the U.S. Regulation to Prohibit the Alienation of Native Lands in Tutuila and Manu'a was promulgated: "From and after the coming into force of this regulation the alienation of native lands within the limits of the jurisdiction of the United States Station Tutuila is prohibited.

"[U.S. Navy governor] Tilley's 'non-alienation' promulgation became the basis for all land protection legislation passed since and is one of the twin pillars of the territorialized political development, the other . . . is the protection of matai titles."[41] Thus the matai were assured of what mattered most to them under the terms of sovereignty.

In terms of sovereignty, *indigenous* and *native* are words rarely used in Samoa or American Samoa and are words sometimes considered racist by Samoans; indeed the terms are often based on race in the West, but in the fa'asamoa these terms are substituted by terms of genealogy and titles. Whether the United States will always honor our Polynesian custom and fa'asamoa, which support communal land and titles, or will attempt issues of conflict with its own laws and constitution as it does now with the Hawaiian Kanaka Maoli, will become apparent.

The philosopher Deleuze says regarding intellectual discourse on human rights that "these declarations are never made as a function of the people that are directly concerned . . . it's a question of territory, not one of the 'rights of man,' not a question of justice, but a question of jurisprudence."[42] Whether the laws of the United States and the United Nations can protect the territories of peoples and nations like eastern Samoa cannot be decided without the full and equal participation of indigenous people bringing to the discussion native or in this case Samoan law.

The Ocean and U.S. Hegemony

The history of Europe tells of many nations that rose to prominence within democratic institutions, becoming imperialist powers by increasing centralization of authority or becoming centralized by increasing imperial powers. The history of the United States in the Pacific has often been the history of U.S. presidents seeking greater domain against the will of the U.S. Congress.

Following the U.S. Civil War, a new U.S. imperialism in the Pacific found its planner in Alfred T. Mahan, who in 1870 founded the Naval War College.

Ironically, Mahan was a naval captain with distaste for the ocean. He wrote: "Sea Power was more than a strong navy. It was an economy that could produce goods for export. It was trade ships that could carry the goods. It was colonies that could supply raw materials and markets. And it was overseas naval bases that could defend U.S. interests far from home."[43] As was acted upon by Presidents McKinley and Roosevelt and the young Republicans of the late 1800s, Mahan wrote in 1890: "The affair of the Samoa Islands, trivial apparently, was nevertheless eminently suggestive of European ambitions. America then roused from sleep as to interests closely concerning her future. At this moment internal troubles are imminent in the Sandwich Islands [Hawai'i], where it should be our fixed determination to allow no foreign influence to equal our own."[44]

In the UN Decolonization Committee on December 10, 2001, "the representative of the United States said that his country was fully supportive when countries chose independence and was proud to work with them on an equal and sovereign basis." However "the United States could not support the draft resolution on the implementation of the Declaration on the Granting of independence to Colonial Countries and Peoples. The draft resolution unfairly applied a single and narrow standard for decolonization. Indeed for the United States the term 'non-self-governing' was of questionable applicability," and "the United States could not support language that would infringe on the sovereign right of the United States."[45]

While American Samoa works ostensibly within U.S. political boundaries, independent Samoa finds itself working within U.S. economic boundaries by way of international free trade agreements, which, while privatizing public corporations and improving access to international trade, are submitting independent Samoa to internal requirements that try to bring the fa'amatai and nu'u communal land system closer to Western systems. Samoa because of its independence has "modernized" in ways that American Samoa cannot. Both have their issues and problems; this essay addresses mainly American Samoa, part of an inter-island dialogue that continues in ways private and public. The two Samoas may well say to each other in the words of the Samoan proverb: "We will meet again through our children."

Afterword

U.S. hegemony in the territorialized Pacific Islands and Ocean helps maintain a class system in the United States that is moving away from equality toward a polarized American society based on wealth. The fa'amatai is an assemblage that also implicates processes of deterritorialization, movements of deterritorialization. Practices similar to fa'asamoa practice of communal ownership of lands and titles can become an acceptable alternative to Western individualism and capitalism outside Samoa, though the responsibilities of fa'asamoa are many.

In the colonialisms of the nineteenth and twentieth centuries the United States protected Samoa from encroachments by England, Germany, Japan, and other foreign nations like itself, if only for its own interests. At this time American Samoa may well ask: will U.S. protectionism in the twenty-first century improve our quality of life or diminish it? Will its patronage maintain our people and way of life or dissolve us in the American melting pot? Only through public dialogue will any decisions happen with a truly informed consensus of the Samoan people.

Notes

1. *O le a sosopo le manu vale i le fogatia.* I quote often from the works of Vaai, Le Tagaloa, Meti, Sunia, and Simanu, and ask their pardon for any miscontextualization.

2. There was a 1920s independence movement, the American Samoa mau, which was suppressed by the United States, its leader Samuel Sailele Ripley exiled from American Samoa. Interview with Samuel Sailele McMullin, Sr., September 2001.

3. The time span involved dates from the Wilkes Expedition of the 1830s, which marked eventual territorialization of American Samoa.

4. U.S. Congressman Faleomavaega and late Governor Tauese at the United Nations Caribbean Regional Seminar to Review the Political, Economic and Social Conditions in the Small Island Non-Self-Governing Territories, Havana, 23–25 May 2001.

5. George Turner, *A Hundred Years Ago and Long Before* (London: London Missionary Society, 1884).

6. In both Samoas over 90 percent of the people are Samoans and over 90 percent of the lands are communal or nationalized.

7. Saleimoa Vaai, *Samoa Faamatai and the Rule of Law* (Apia: National University of Samoa Le Papa-I-Galagala, 1999).

8. A. F. Le Tagaloa, "The Samoan Culture and Government," in *Culture and Democracy in the South Pacific* (Port Moresby: Institute of Pacific Studies, University of Papua New Guinea Press 1992).

9. Vaai, *Samoa Faamatai and the Rule of Law*, 49.

10. Articles in *Samoanische Zeitung* (Apia), 1901–4.

11. Edwin Gurr, "Decision in Trial of the Ipu," *Samoanische Zeitung*, 1901.

12. In the preface to this essay are state fa'alupega for Manu'a, Tutuila, and western Samoa, as quoted in Agustin Kramer, *The Samoa Islands*, vol. 1 (Honolulu: University of Hawaii Press, 1995).

13. Anonymous letter, "Correspondence," *Samoanische Zeitung*, 16 August 1901.

14. Letter from Commandant Sebree to Assistant Secretary of the Navy, June 30, 1902, National Archives–San Bruno.

15. Resolution No. 6 of the American Samoa Fono.

16. During the same time period Western Samoa was struggling toward independence from New Zealand and "annoyed with the attitude of the New Zealand government a meeting of all Samoa was convened in Lepea . . . on 13 November [1946] which overwhelmingly supported a request for an United States Protectorate. The Samoans however were persuaded by Tupua Tamasese and Malietoa Tanumafili II to remain with New Zealand and to adapt instead a petition to the United Nations seeking self-government for Western Samoa" (Vaai, *Samoa Faamatai and the Rule of Law*).

17. Aumua Mataitusi Simanu, *O Si Manu a Alii: A Text for the Advanced Study of Samoan Language and Culture* (Honolulu: Pasefika Press–University of Hawaii Press, 2002).

18. UN Working paper on American Samoa prepared by the Secretariat, United Nations General Assembly, A/AC.109/2002/12, May 14, 2002, Special Committee on the Situation with regard to the implementation of the Declaration on the Granting of Independence to the Colonial Countries and Peoples (accessed at *http://ods-dds-ny.un.org/doc/UNDOC/GEN/N02/381/74/PDF/N0238174.pdf?Open Element*).

19. Simanu, *O Si Manu a Alii*, 65.

20. Lauofo Meti, *Samoa: The Making of the Constitution* (Apia: Government of Samoa Press, 2002).

21. Treaty of the Tumua and Faipule and the U.S., January 17, 1878.

22. Letter from Captain Skerrett in response to letter from Mauga and other chiefs, January 15, 1882, National Archives–San Bruno.

23. Letter from Tui Manu'a Elisala to the U.S. President, October 26, 1903, National Archives–San Bruno. See also anonymous reprint of *San Francisco Chronicle*, August 1, 1903, itself a reprint of *Omaha Gazette* July 31 article, in *Samoanische Zeitung*, August 29, 1903; letter from (U.S. Navy governor) Tilley to the Assistant Secretary of the Navy, May 7, 1901, National Archives–San Bruno.

24. Letter from Commandant Underwood to Assistant Secretary of the Navy, July 18, 1904, National Archives–San Bruno.

25. Letter from Commandant Sebree to Secretary of the Navy, September 6, 1902, National Archives–San Bruno.

26. Interview with Fofō Sunia, January 2000.

27. UN Working paper on American Samoa, A/AC.109/2002/12.

28. Fofō Sunia, *The Story of the Legislature of American Samoa* (Pago Pago: Fono of American Samoa Press, 1998).

29. Sunia, *Story of the Legislature*, 236.

30. Sunia, *Story of the Legislature*, 244.

31. UN working paper on American Samoa, A/AC.109/2002/12/

32. *Report by the Comptroller General of the United States* CED-78–154, September 22, 1978.

33. *Report by the Comptroller General*, appendix 6, p. 76 (letter, July 7, 1978).

34. Another U.S. standard is imposed by the ban on importation of cheaper cigarettes to American Samoa from Samoa, which favors the importation of more expensive cigarettes from the U.S. because they have been determined to be "healthier."

35. Faleomavaega, Eni quote, *Samoa Observer*, May 26, 2003.

36. Meti, *Samoa: The Making of the Constitution*, 217.

37. Chief Justice Tiavaasue, "Record of Land and Titles Seminar Proceedings," as quoted and translated in Vaai, *Samoa Faamatai and the Rule of Law*, 49.

38. A. F. Le Tagaloa, "Samoa Village Society," *Courier* (Brussels), no. 99 (September–October 1986): 72; Vaai, *Samoa Faamatai and the Rule of Law*, 36.

39. Meti, *Samoa: The Making of the Constitution*, 216.

40. Vaai, *Samoa Faamatai and the Rule of Law*, 244.

41. Sunia, *Story of the Legislature*, 12.

42. *L'Abécédaire de Gilles Deleuze, avec Claire Parnet*, 1996 TV program directed by Pierre-André Boutang (accessed in 2003 at http://www.langlab.wayne.edu/CStivale/D-G/ABC1.html).

43. Alfred T. Mahan quoted, "The Making of a Nation #144," *Voice of America* (accessed in 2003 at http://www.voa.gov/special/nat-foreign-policy-late-1800s-060701.html).

44. Alfred T. Mahan, "The United States Looking Outward" (*Atlantic Monthly* 64 (1890): 816–24 (accessed at http://www.nv.cc.va.us/home/nvsageh/Hist122/Part2/Mahan.htm).

45. UN Working paper on American Samoa, A/AC.109/2002/12.

Robert J. Miller (Eastern Shawnee Tribe of Oklahoma)

Tribal Cultural Self-Determination and the Makah Whaling Culture

American Indian tribes and Alaskan and Hawaiian natives have long suffered under the cultural oppression of European and American societies. As a result many tribal traditions, cultures, and languages have disappeared from the North American continent and Hawaiian Islands. Today tribes and native individuals are still forced to fight to preserve and to exercise their remaining traditions and cultural practices.[1] These entities are fighting to overcome the influence of the dominant American society and to avoid being assimilated into the American "melting pot." This struggle will continue into the foreseeable future as these native societies, governments, and individuals try to maintain the diversity of their native cultures and set the agenda for their own cultures—in essence to exercise cultural self-determination and sovereignty for their groups.

This chapter defines cultural self-determination as "the right of a distinct and identifiable group of people or a separate political state to set the standards and mores of what constitutes its traditional culture and how it will honor and practice that culture."[2] Defined as such, cultural self-determination is intimately tied to tribal sovereignty and the rights of self-determination for American Indian and Alaska Native tribes. This is so because native groups will decide for themselves what cultural practices to preserve, and they will use their political power and sovereign status to fight for those rights.

The political, sovereign struggle to preserve a tribal culture and to practice it on its own terms is well exemplified by the recent Makah whale hunts. The tribe is a good example of a culture that preserved its important traditions, even during a long dormant period, and then revived its cultural, religious, and legal rights by resuming its traditional practice of whaling. The Makah relied on their sovereign powers and the tribal government to fight for this right, and the tribe also relied on its political relationship with the United

States. The Makah plan to continue to preserve this cultural and religious tradition into the future.

In May 1999, after years of legal, cultural, and religious preparations, members of the Makah Tribe put to sea in a traditional cedar canoe and killed a California gray whale. This was the first whale hunt for the tribe in over seventy years. The uproar of media coverage, the outrage of some animal rights groups, and the outpouring of support for the Makah were intense. The tribe also hunted gray whales, albeit unsuccessfully, in the spring of 2000. Decisions by the Ninth Circuit federal court of appeals in June 2000 and December 2002 have temporarily prevented the tribe from further whaling and have raised some question as to whether the tribe will ever be allowed to whale again. The federal government, however, has taken and appears to be ready to take further steps that will ensure continuation of Makah whaling in the future.

The Makah situation demonstrates that the fight to exercise cultural self-determination and the sovereign authority of a political group is never easy and never ends. Tribes and native peoples have to remain ever vigilant and always ready to defend and to exercise their cultural practices and to teach them to their children and grandchildren if the traditions are to survive. This chapter examines the Makah whaling issue to study how a tribe can revive a dormant cultural practice after seventy years and how it can exert cultural self-determination and sovereignty to exercise that culture. The Makah demonstrate that a tribe or native group has to struggle continually to keep its own culture and traditions alive even within its own cultural and political system, and it must then often fight vigorously against outside interests to exercise these sovereign rights in a traditional manner.

Makah Whaling Culture

Culture is defined as the "pattern of human knowledge, belief, and behavior that depends upon man's capacity for learning and transmitting knowledge to succeeding generations[,] the customary beliefs, social forms, and material traits of a racial, religious or social group."[3] An influential Dutch sociologist defined culture as "the collective programming of the mind which distinguishes one human group from another. . . . Culture is to a human collectivity what personality is to an individual."[4]

These definitions describe the Makah situation perfectly because the tribe, as a racial, social, and political group, wants to preserve and pass on a pattern of knowledge, beliefs, and behaviors to future Makah generations. Furthermore, it is important to the tribe to stay separate and distinguishable from the Anglo-American society that tried so hard to destroy Makah culture and assimilate it into the American melting pot.[5] The Makah have shown that they will fight to keep their own "personality" as a people, so that they can pass on this culture to their children, and so that they can maintain their sovereign authority as a government to make decisions regarding cultural matters for the whole tribe.

It is a testament to the sanctity of American Indian cultures that they still survive today as separate groups. The experience of most minority or conquered cultures has been just the opposite; the conquering, dominant society's language and culture usually take over, and the indigenous culture and language die out. Native Americans, however, have fought for almost four hundred years to keep their governments, cultures, languages, and religions alive and separate from those of the European-American society. Amazingly, tribes have been moderately successful in this endeavor.

Equally surprising is that the Makah have kept alive the desire to preserve and practice whaling after a seventy-year hiatus and that they have the will and strength to fight to exercise their culture and the internal will and strength to preserve and restore this cultural aspect. The Makah effort demonstrates to other peoples that if they want to maintain their separate and distinct cultures, they must continue to practice their culture and pass it on to succeeding generations. If this effort is not maintained, the Makah and other distinct groups will not remain sovereign peoples and societies separate and distinct from American society.

Cultural Self-Determination

As already indicated, "cultural self-determination" is the right of a separate political entity or an identifiable and separate group of people to set the standards of their culture and state and to determine the practices and religion they will follow as a people. Obviously cultural and political conflicts will arise when a group determines its own culture and the practice of that culture affects the interests of other groups or states. Thus issues of sovereignty and relations with other political states arise when a political body—a tribe, for example—exercises cultural rights.

Cultural self-determination is also closely related to the existence of the political sovereignty of any tribe or native group. This is evident because sovereignty is the exercise of power and control over a political body—a group of people and a defined territory, for example—by independent states or political authorities. If a tribe or native group does not control and practice its culture, then it seems clear that the group is not exercising sovereignty or power over its population, territory, and internal affairs. The decision of the Makah tribal government to pursue its ancient whaling custom is an excellent example of a distinct group or a separate political entity defining and practicing its culture and thus exercising cultural self-determination and sovereignty.

Makah Whaling

The Makah Indian Tribe is located on its reservation on the northwestern tip of Washington State at Cape Flattery. The reservation is bordered by the Pacific Ocean to the west and to the north by the Strait of Juan de Fuca, which separates the United States from Canada. The tribe has been on this land for thousands of years and has primarily looked to the ocean as its "land" and as the source of its food, tools, and clothing.[6] The Makah were first and foremost "a seafaring people" who lived close to the shore, were expert at sailing their canoes on the open sea, and took their livelihood from the ocean.[7] In fact, whales were their primary food source. In 1865 a federal agent noted: "What the buffalo is to the Indians on the plains, the whale is to the Makah."[8]

The Makah lived in large permanent wooden houses up to thirty-five feet wide and one hundred feet long. Loosely related family groups of more than forty people lived in these longhouses. The houses were full of whaling implements and other evidence of the importance of whaling to the Makah. The marine environment around the Makah lands was rich, and the tribe became wealthy and prominent while living a comfortable life harvesting the plenty of the ocean.[9] They procured a great surplus of marine items to trade to other tribes for other types of food and goods. The Makah made and used stone and mussel shell tools, animal horn fishhooks, elk antler harpoon barbs, and whalebone clubs and knives.

The importance of whaling to the Makah culture, religion, economy, and way of life for over fifteen hundred years cannot be overstated. Whaling was the preeminent Makah activity, and a successful whaler commanded the highest social status and prestige a Makah could attain. Whales and whaling played the major role in the culture and religious beliefs of the tribe.[10]

WHALING METHODS AND TRADE

The Makah hunted many types of whales, but the California gray whale, the same species captured in May 1999, was the whale they most commonly harvested. They hunted with eight-man crews in specialized forty-foot cedar canoes. A crew consisted of six paddlers, one harpooner, and one steersman; and they would venture up to forty miles out to sea or more. They used fourteen- to eighteen-foot harpoons with razor-sharp mussel shell tips barbed with elk antler and attached to the harpoon with whale sinew. The harpoons were ingeniously designed to facilitate delivering the harpoon tip and the attached floats securely into the whale. The Makah used floats, made of seal skins turned inside out and inflated, attached to the harpoons to follow a whale and to impede and tire it so that the killing blow could be administered. One crewman would dive overboard and sew the whale's mouth closed so that the animal would not fill with water and sink. The crew was then faced with the long tow back to shore, which could last for days.

The whale would be beached on the nearest shore and the entire village would treat the whale like an honored guest by ritually decorating it and singing songs of welcome. The butchering was performed in a traditional manner and was accompanied by dancing, singing, and feasting. The meat and blubber were distributed by traditional rules; the first to strike the whale had the primary meat distribution rights. The Makah utilized almost the entire whale for food or tools, including the sinew to make harpoon ropes, the bones for tools and weapons, and the intestines and stomach to hold oil. It has been discovered that at least at the Makah village of Ozette, large whale bones were even used to retain mud banks and channel rain runoff.

It is unclear how many whales the Makah took each year. Estimates are that they landed five or more a year and also used any other whales that washed up on the beach.[11] The Makah mainly whaled in the spring during the gray whales' northern migration, when the seas were calmer, instead of during the late fall and winter when the grays migrated south.

The Makah were well-known traders in the Pacific Northwest, and whale products helped to make them wealthy. Their primary trade items were whale oil, marine mammals, fish, and shellfish. Whale oil was a prized commodity and the Makah traded it extensively from California to Alaska and inland to Washington, Idaho, and Colorado; it may even "have functioned as a type of currency on the Northwest coast."[12] The Makah traded enormous amounts of whale oil, up to thirty thousand gallons a year, to other tribes and to European and American ships that called at Neah Bay, the main village on Makah land. The tribe made a comfortable living and became prosperous by trading whale oil.[13]

The incursion of European and American commercial whalers into the Pacific Northwest and into Makah waters beginning in the 1840s soon had an adverse impact on the Makah. These "foreign" whalers discovered the calving grounds of the gray whale and soon decimated the gray whale stock.[14] American observers detected a marked decrease in gray whale activity near Makah as early as the 1860s. The near destruction of the stocks by the commercial European and American whaling industries rendered whaling impossible for the Makahs. The last Makah whale hunt is reported to have occurred in 1928.[15]

WHALING CULTURE AND WAY OF LIFE

Whaling formed an integral part of the worldview, heritage, and identity of the Makah. In their culture whalers were the wealthiest and most honored and respected tribal members, and whaling was the core of the tribe's culture. The importance of whales and the marine environment to the tribe is demonstrated by the Makah naming the constellations after whales, fish, and sharks. Many of the months and the moons are named after whaling events, including one month named for the arrival of the gray whale in Makah waters. The tribe also celebrated a first whale of the season ceremony, which is similar to how many fishing tribes celebrate the first salmon.

Whale oil, blubber, and meat were the primary food of the Makah, constituting up to 80 percent of their diet.[16] The Makah used whale oil like butter or gravy. The most prized pieces of whale meat were saved to be served at feasts and ceremonies. The Makah also demonstrated their high esteem of whale meat and oil by giving it as gifts at holidays and celebrations.

Whaling rituals and ceremonialism played a large role in everyday Makah life and had a deep spiritual meaning for the people. The entire community was involved in the hunt in one way or another. The longhouses were filled with whaling equipment and whale oil in seal skins hung from the rafters. The Makah world was full of art depicting whales and marine mammals and utilizing whale bones and body parts. Whale bones were even reassembled into complete skeletons beside houses in the Makah village of Ozette. Most of the art was used for cultural, religious, or hunting ceremonies. Whaling families passed down hunting skills and traditions to their children, and children often played at whaling in small canoes in the ocean surf; actually they were practicing whaling skills, which in turn demonstrates the central role of whaling in Makah life.

Moreover, numerous whaling songs on a variety of subjects—the whales to be taken, how to use the oil, how to turn a harpooned whale toward the shore, and songs to praise the whale—always played a large role in the tribal festivals, celebrations, and feasts. Whaling songs were also used as part of the ritualistic preparation of fasting, bathing, and praying before going whaling. As one would expect, the tribe has many legends regarding whaling. In fact the tribal symbol, a Thunderbird holding a whale in its talons, represents one of these legends. The tribal story is that beached whales came from the Thunderbird sweeping down out of the mountains, capturing a whale, and leaving it on the beach for the Makah.

The enormity of the task of taking whales and the religious and spiritual feelings about the hunt also manifested themselves in tribal celebrations. The whole village would come out to sing and dance to welcome a landed whale and to treat it like an honored guest who had favored the tribe by coming ashore so that the Makah could sustain themselves. The successful hunter would always give a celebratory feast, and the most desirable morsel of whale meat was saved for the special feast held five days after landing a whale. At these feasts, the whalers sang special songs and used special rattles to express their joy and wonder at catching a whale.

Whales also figured prominently in the Makah cultural celebration of the potlatch. The potlatch is the most important cultural ceremonial event in Northwest Coast native cultures and consisted of an individual or a family gifting away an enormous amount of their possessions. Such events often celebrated naming ceremonies or the assumption of chiefly duties and other important occasions in Makah life. Once one gained wealth, it was given away at potlatches to increase one's status and standing in the tribe and to gain "the dignity of a chief."[17] In the Makah world it was primarily the whaling families who were wealthy enough to hold numerous and elaborate potlatches. These families would demonstrate their wealth by pouring valuable whale oil over their guests or into the fire to impress others with their success.

Significantly, whaling also played a role in marriage and family in the Makah Tribe. Wedding proposals were often delivered using a pantomime of whaling. The prospective bridegroom would be carried in a canoe to the home of his intended by an eight-man whaling crew with others mimicking a whale swimming before the canoe. During a marriage proposal there appear to have been required feats of strength related to whaling, in which the bridegroom had to be strong enough to split a board with his harpoon. This would demonstrate his whaling prowess and ability to support his new bride and family. After some weddings, the new bride would be carried to her husband's house in a whaling canoe. Whaling customs also played a part in Makah life from childbirth, as newborn infants were welcomed into the world by having a sliver of whale blubber placed in their mouths, and Makah children teethed on whale meat. Clearly all of these varied and rich aspects of Makah tradition and culture demonstrate the central and important role whales played in their society.

WHALING SPIRITUALITY

Makah whaling was also steeped in spiritual, religious, and ritualistic beliefs, and whalers would undertake months of ritual and physical preparation.[18] The Makah thought the really important part of whaling was the proper observance of various ceremonies to procure the help of the spirits. The ritual or spiritual nature of whaling is based on the belief that humans are too puny to capture such enormous and powerful creatures if the whale does not want to be taken or does not cooperate in its capture. Ritual, religious preparation for months prior to whaling was meant to ensure that the Makah whaler would be pure in heart and deserving of taking a whale and that a whale would voluntarily give itself to the hunter. The Makah whalers believed that the spiritual preparation and customs were as important as the whaling equipment and methods they used.[19]

Makah whalers were also especially interested in gaining spiritual assistance and sought a *tumano* or animal spirit helper to gain the strength and power needed to take whales. The Makah would practice religious rituals in private with the goal of securing the aid of an intermediary spirit or tumano because these beings guarded the destinies of individuals. Whalers would take ritual baths in hidden forest lakes and in the ocean and would swim imitating a whale swimming, spouting water from their mouths. They practiced severe discipline by scourging and purifying themselves with nettles or hemlock branches, by months of special prayers and songs, the use of charms and amulets, fasting, and sexual abstinence.

There were also taboos or traditions that the shore-based Makahs had to follow while whalers were at sea. People would talk quietly and respectfully and move gently about because whales liked to come to quiet, orderly villages. The wives of whalers would stay at home and lie down in the dark to show respect for the whale and to assist the hunt. It is obvious that whales were such an important food source that they deserved the respect of the whole tribe.

Once a whale was struck, the Makah used spiritually powerful songs to turn a harpooned whale toward shore and not toward the open sea. They would pray to the whale and sing to it, begging its spirit to turn toward the shore where the people "stood ready to give it praise" and to honor it with ceremonies and rituals that would last for days. It was only the power of the whalers' tumano that overcame the whale's strength and flattered and cajoled the whale spirit to the beach. Thus the role of spirituality and ritual in capturing whales was clear to the ancient and the modern Makah people, and the centrality of whales to Makah life and culture is clear to us today.

Makah Treaty

The Makah treaty of January 31, 1855, is the only Indian treaty with the United States in which a tribe expressly reserved to itself the right to whale. The tribal government wisely protected their whaling rights in their treaty, and this fact is crucial, because it is the primary reason the federal government supported the tribe's application to revive its hunting of gray whales. An understanding of the treaty is therefore significant in any discussion of Makah whaling rights.

Indian treaties are part of federal law, and the Constitution states that they are the supreme law of the United States.[20] The U.S. Supreme Court has stated that treaties between the United States and a tribe are binding contracts. Many people misunderstand Indian treaties and think the United States was making gifts or giving "special rights" to tribes. This is completely false. Treaties were not gifts to tribes but instead were a negotiated trade of various rights between sovereign governments; they were "not a grant of rights to the Indians, but a grant of rights from them—a reservation of those not granted."[21] Thus those rights that a tribe did not sell to the United States were retained as part of its preexisting sovereign right. In actuality Indian treaty making almost always came about because the United States sought out a tribe and asked the tribe to enter treaties to sell land and various property rights, for which the United States would make various payments and promises of support, protection, education, and health care. Accordingly, in its treaty with the United States, the Makah Tribe agreed to sell some land to the United States for payments, but the tribe expressly bargained for and retained its cultural, traditional, economic, and religious rights and interests in the ocean around its lands and its right to whale. The Makah treaty retained for the tribe "the right of taking fish and of whaling or sealing at usual and accustomed grounds and stations."[22]

The United States initiated treaty negotiations with the Makah Tribe in Neah Bay in January 1855. The U.S. representative at the treaty negotiation and signing was the Washington Territory governor and superintendent of Indian affairs Issac I. Stevens. On January 30, the Makahs met with Stevens and he told them that the Great White Father wanted to buy some of their land for a fair price.[23]

The Makah chiefs explained to Stevens that their land was not fit for cultivation. Hence, the amount of land Stevens proposed to buy for the United States and the amount he proposed leaving for a Makah reservation appeared adequate to the chiefs because they looked to the ocean and the whale for their livelihood and therefore were not overly concerned about the land. Stevens expressly stated, the Makah had prospered by catching vast quantities of fish and whale oil for market, such that few white communities had as much wealth per capita and as evenly distributed as did the Makah.[24]

The tribe's representatives stated plainly the most important negotiating point for the Makah as regards any land cession: "The Indians expressed concern that they would be forced to abandon their fishing grounds and become farmers. Stevens assured them that he would provide fishing equipment and asked only that they share the whale fishery with whites."[25] The Makah governmental representatives made abundantly clear the importance to them of retaining the tribal whaling and fishing rights they already owned. One Makah chief, Kal-chote, said "he ought to have the right to fish, and take whales, and get food where he liked."[26] Two other chiefs expressed agreement with that statement and added that they "did not want to leave the salt water."[27] A fourth chief and a fifth spoke up to reemphasize the importance to the Makah of ensuring that they reserved the right to continue whaling and sealing, to take any whales that washed up on the beach, and to live off the ocean as they had always done.[28] Essentially the tribal representatives made it clear that they were retaining all the rights to the sea and to whaling that they had ever possessed. Stevens heard the chiefs' concerns and agreed that the tribe could retain its whaling, fishing, and sealing rights. Once the Makah chiefs were assured that they had preserved their whaling and ocean rights, they agreed to sell much of the tribe's interior land.

In fact Governor Stevens did far more than just assure the Makah that they could keep their whaling and fishing rights. He clearly promised that the United States would support them in those endeavors, protect their interests, and even assist the Makah in promoting their whaling and fishery industries by providing them with newer, modern equipment to become more effective.[29] Governor Stevens explained that instead of wanting "to stop their fisheries, [the President] wished to send them oil-kettles and fishing apparatus."[30] The Great White Father knew "what whalers [the Makah] are, how far you go to sea to take whales. He will send you barrels in which to put your oil, kettles to try it out, lines and implements to fish with."[31] After hearing these promises, forty-one tribal members signed the treaty on behalf of the tribal government, and Stevens signed on behalf of the United States.

U.S. Policies to Destroy Makah Culture

The United States has officially enacted and enforced many variations of federal Indian policy over the past two centuries. Many of these polices have been purposely designed to destroy Indian cultures and tribes. These policies affected the Makah Tribe to varying degrees. In addition the United States and its employees on the Makah reservation have taken many direct actions that have had a detrimental effect on the Makah culture and were undertaken with the exact purpose of harming or destroying it.

Allotment and Assimilation Era

The era of allotment and assimilation was an official federal Indian policy that was in effect roughly from 1871 to the early 1930s. This federal policy was designed to bring Indians into the American melting pot by destroying their tribal governments and tribal ways of life and assimilating them into mainstream society. The policy had the goals of breaking up tribal ownership of land, opening reservations for settlement, and ending tribal existence.[32]

The government also tried to assimilate Indians forcibly into American life. Even various Christian and liberal groups, the so-called friends of the Indian, were in favor of this attempt to civilize and Christianize Indians, turn them into farmers, and "do away with Indianness and tribal relations."[33] The Bureau of Indian Affairs (BIA) was used during this time to attempt to take absolute control of Indian life and to squeeze out Indian government, religion, and culture.[34] The federal government used a network of off- and on-reservation boarding schools where Indian children were placed in an attempt "to inculcate Indian children with the values of Western civilization and to eliminate any traces of the children's native heritage."[35]

Termination Era

From about 1945 to 1961, the goal of official U.S. policy was again to end the federal-tribal relationship and to destroy tribal governments and treaty rights. In this policy, called the termination era, Congress actively sought to end the authority and legal existence of tribal governments. Once again, assimilation was part of federal policy as Congress sought to "protect" Indians by integrating them into the general American population and exposing them to some state and federal laws for the first time.

Congress took other steps to limit its involvement in Indian affairs and to increase state power over reservations. In 1953, Congress enacted Public Law 280, which ultimately extended some state civil and criminal jurisdiction into Indian country. Also in the 1950s, Congress transferred many of its educational responsibilities for tribes to the states and transferred Indian health duties from the BIA to the Department of Health, Education and Welfare.[36] The BIA actively relocated Indians from the reservations to big cities so that federal responsibilities toward Indians could cease.

Federal Cultural Oppression and Assimilation of the Makah

The Anglo-American view of property, culture, and religion differs significantly from Native American viewpoints. Not surprisingly, the culture of the United States clashed with Makah culture. The Makah suffered through overt cultural oppression under the guise of the various federal Indian policies already discussed briefly and through other policies that were specifically aimed at the Makah. In the first instance, the extent of the Makah territory and sovereign rights was limited during the federal policy of treaty making. The tribe claims to this day that the treaty set the reservation boundaries incorrectly and that the tribe lost more land than was intended to be sold. Furthermore, in the treaty, the tribe agreed to stop trading with persons from Vancouver Island and other areas of Canada and to end its centuries-old practice of owning slaves. In addition, under the federal policy of assimilation, the Makah suffered an active campaign directed at destroying their culture, religion, and families, because those were the goals of the United States in the allotment and termination eras.

Finally, the Makah suffered specific attacks by the federal Indian agents located on their reservation. Agents actively tried to destroy the tribe's government and its cultural, tribal, economic, and family life.[37] These types of federal actions were a serious and common problem throughout Indian country. For example, only in the 1930s did the federal government and the BIA rescind regulations prohibiting reservation Indians, who supposedly were living on their own lands, from wearing long hair and performing their religious ceremonies. In essence the federal government did not recognize that or act as though Indian tribes were sovereign entities and people living on their own lands and according to their own cultures and religions; the United States acted more as if Indians were in prisons where the government could control every aspect of their lives.

CULTURAL AND RELIGIOUS OPPRESSION

For over one hundred years, the federal government purposely tried to alter every aspect of the Makah culture. The ultimate goal of the U.S. Indian Service "was the complete assimilation of the . . . Makahs into American society in as short a time as possible."[38] The government wanted to substitute its way of life for the Makah culture. The annual reports of the commissioners of Indian affairs demonstrated that the U.S. policy was to extinguish the "Indianness" of all Indians and to destroy their way of life by teaching them "civilized" ways.[39] As an example, notwithstanding Governor Stevens's promise to assist the Makah in their whaling and fishing economy, the federal government ultimately brought pressure on the Makah to abandon fishing and whaling to become farmers.

The federal government tried to "save" the Makah Tribe by taking its culture, its religion, and its traditions. In a concerted and calculated strategy the federal agents stationed at the Neah Bay Indian Agency on the reservation tried to wipe out the Makah language and tribal religious ceremonies. The agents also tried to withdraw the children from their culture and raise them as "white" children. Agents did this by teaching the children English and insisting on its use to the exclusion of the Makah language, by prohibiting children from practicing tribal customs and manners, by isolating youngsters from their parents and grandparents, and by indoctrinating them with American culture.[40]

The federal agents worked to change completely even the most basic parts of Makah life. They discouraged the longhouse style of communal living and helped Makahs build single family homes and tear down the longhouses. They would visit Makahs in their homes to see how the people were living and to correct perceived deficiencies; they encouraged the Makah to dress like white citizens. The agents truly tried to control every single aspect of Makah life, right down to setting standards for Makah sexual life and punishing violators. Furthermore, the American legal system of courts, judges, and police was imposed on the tribe. Federal agents interfered with the tribe's internal class and governmental systems by selecting the men who would serve as chiefs. They tried to alter the Makah property rights system concerning coastal fishing sites. Even traditional healing methods were banned by the agents, and Makah doctors were threatened with imprisonment.

The government suppressed other Makah cultural activities such as the Cloqually dances because the agents considered them heathenish and barbarous. The government tried to end the primary tradition of potlatches in which wealthy families or chiefs gave away their accumulated goods to demonstrate their success, to gain honor and prestige, and to benefit the entire community. The Indian agents viewed this practice negatively because it was foreign to their cultural experience, and they misunderstood the economic value of the potlatch. "Activities of a ceremonial or ritual nature were discouraged or prohibited. . . . Potlatches, gambling games, the performance of Indian dances were usually forbidden. The ceremonies of the secret religious and curing societies were . . . banned altogether."[41]

In Washington state in the 1880s, the United States made a special attempt to civilize and Americanize Indians by banning traditional native practices and public gatherings, including dancing, gambling, and spiritual activities, and by requiring reservation Indians to carry identification cards. The Makah resisted the denial of their political, religious, and First Amendment rights by going underground with some potlatch, cultural, and spiritual traditions and by reorganizing their traditional ceremonies around American holidays like Christmas and birthday parties or by incorporating them into Christian beliefs and practices.[42] Threats of imprisonment notwithstanding, the Makah also traveled to Tatoosh Island, just off the tip of Cape Flattery, to hold ceremonies.

ATTACKS ON MAKAH FAMILIES

The federal government tried specifically to destroy Makah family life as part of its attempt to alter Makah culture and assimilate the people into white society. The Indian agents at Neah Bay wanted to segregate tribal members over fifty-five from the rest of the people because, as they reported, younger Indians would not learn "civilized" ways if they continued to associate with and be influenced and taught by their elders. The agents realized that tribal members did not want their children going to school and being taught only English and only white man's ways. Makah parents correctly foresaw what would happen to their children. At the Neah Bay school, children were punished for speaking Makah and were actively taught to ridicule and to be ashamed of their elders and their own families, culture, and language.

Boarding schools were an excellent strategy to separate Indian children from their families and cultures. Such schools were used at Makah from roughly 1870 to 1940, as in the rest of Indian country, to teach Indian children civilized ways and to eradicate Indian culture. Makah families were forced to send their children to the boarding school at Neah Bay or the parents would be arrested. Ultimately the boarding school was not considered effective enough at eradicating parental and cultural influence because many Makah families moved to Neah Bay to be near their children at the school. The movement of families to be near their children at the school at Neah Bay was the main reason other Makah villages came to be abandoned. In 1874, because many families had moved to Neah Bay, the boarding school was purposely relocated farther away with the specific intent of preventing the home influence of Makah culture on the children and to take the children "entirely out of barbarous surroundings and put them in the midst of a civilized Christian home."[43] Makah children were then forced to live at the school and to attend classes from age seven to fourteen; school was usually conducted year-round, with only a few hours a week at home. These deliberate attacks on Makah family life and children succeeded somewhat in weakening Makah culture, alienating several generations of children to some extent from their culture and families.[44]

U.S. Trust Responsibility to Assit Indian Tribes

In stark contrast to the despicable history of United States oppression of tribal cultures, the federal government instead owes a trust responsibility to American Indian and Alaska Native tribes and individual tribal citizens. The United States voluntarily took on this duty by entering into treaties with tribes in which the United States, in exchange for vast tracts of tribal lands, promised to protect the welfare, the remaining homelands, and the existence of tribes, and promised educational, medical, and financial support for tribal members.[45] The U.S. Supreme Court has interpreted the trust responsibility to be a fiduciary relationship like that "of a ward to his guardian," in which Indian tribes and peoples are dependent on the United States for protection and support.[46]

A federal trust responsibility also arises from the plenary or absolute power over tribes that Congress has been determined to possess in Indian affairs.[47] This authority comes from the Indian treaties and the Indian Commerce Clause in the Constitution, which gives Congress the power "to regulate Commerce with foreign Nations, and among the several States, and with the Indian Tribes."[48] The Supreme Court has held that in exercising its broad authority in Indian affairs, Congress and the Executive Branch are charged with the responsibilities of a guardian to act on the behalf of the dependent tribes and individual Indians.[49]

The impact of the trust doctrine and the fiduciary/guardian relationship that the United States has with Indian tribes is extremely important to understanding U.S. interactions with tribes. In fact, in Indian affairs, the United States has "charged itself with moral obligations of the highest responsibility and trust" and the conduct of the United States toward tribes is "judged by the most exacting fiduciary standards."[50] The United States has repeatedly recognized these obligations and has acted in various ways to enhance and strengthen the authority of tribal governments and their practical ability to govern effectively. The federal government, through recognition of government-to-government relations with tribes and through many statutes that protect and support tribal governments, is pursuing a modern official Indian policy of "fostering tribal self-government."[51] In this modern era of federal Indian policy, called the self-determination era, the United States trust and fiduciary responsibilities toward tribes and Indians plays a major role in the latitude the federal government gives tribes to operate and the support it gives to tribal initiatives. Undeniably, the federal trust and fiduciary duties played an important role in the U.S. decision to support the Makah's cultural right to hunt gray whales.[52]

Modern Federal Support for Native American Cultures

In keeping with the trust responsibility owed to tribes and individual Indians, the United States has strongly supported many tribal cultural, religious, and governmental issues in recent years. This is not to suggest that the federal government has fixed all its problems with tribes or that the initiatives discussed in later sections of this chapter have settled the cultural issues they attempt to address. They are highlighted, however, to demonstrate the modern support that the federal government has begun to give to tribal and Indian issues, thus making more understandable the federal support for Makah whaling.

In fulfilling its trust responsibility, Congress and the Executive Branch have taken several major steps to benefit and maintain tribal and individual Indians' cultural practices. The most important aspect of maintaining a separate culture would seem to be the very preservation of the population of that culture. Congress recognized this point in enacting the Indian Child Welfare Act of 1978 (ICWA), when it decided to protect Indian children, their cultures, and the tribal interest in keeping these children in their cultures.[53] The ICWA is arguably the most significant and perhaps the most surprising federal action of any taken to protect tribal cultures and governments. The ICWA is a federal attempt to protect Indian children from the wholesale adoptions and foster care placements outside their culture that Indian children had been suffering for many years at the hands of state agencies. The ICWA was a significant attempt by Congress to protect tribes from losing the crucial membership and citizens they need to survive. In essence, the ICWA is a strong statement by Congress that it will attempt to fulfill its trust responsibility to tribes and Indians to protect their families and cultures.

Probably the second most important issue in maintaining a separate culture is the preservation of the distinct language of the culture. In 1990 Congress, recognizing the importance of preserving tribal languages as an integral part of the survival of tribal cultures, histories, religions, and identities, enacted the Native American Languages Act and recognized its "responsibility to act together with Native Americans to ensure the survival of these unique cultures and languages."[54] Congress reaffirmed the special status of tribes in the

United States, which "recognizes [their] distinct cultural and political rights, including the right to continue separate identities."[55] The act emphasizes the importance of tribal languages to their cultures and to the very survival of Native American cultures.[56] Regrettably, Congress has never appropriated sufficient funding to support this act and truly to work to preserve tribal languages.

In 1996 President Clinton issued an executive order concerning tribal colleges in which he reaffirmed the federal responsibility to "promote the preservation and the revitalization of American Indian and Alaska Native languages and cultural traditions."[57] Again in 1998 President Clinton addressed the unique "educational and culturally related academic needs of American Indian and Alaska Native students" and created a task force to "evaluate the role of native language and culture in the development of educational strategies . . . [and to] assist tribal governments in meeting . . . the need to preserve, revitalize, and use native languages and cultural traditions."[58]

The federal government has undertaken several other attempts to preserve and strengthen Native American cultures. In the Native Arts and Crafts Act, for example, Congress made illegal the counterfeiting of trademarks for authentic Indian-made handicrafts or the misrepresentation of crafts or goods as Indian-made products.[59] In 1990 Congress addressed questions regarding the possession and ownership of Native American human remains and funerary and sacred objects held by federally supported museums or institutions.[60] Congress has also recently funded the construction of the Museum of the American Indian on the mall in Washington DC.

Modern Federal Support for Native American Religions

"Religion is the foundation of Indian life. It is the glue that holds tribes together, and if you strip away legal protections, you are threatening the very survival of tribes in the United States."[61] Thus it seems apparent to state that tribal religions are not viewed as something separate from culture; instead, religion is viewed as a way of life that permeates everything an Indian person does. Every aspect, then, of a tribe's traditions has both religious and cultural components. Consequently, since religion is part of culture in Indian societies, preservation of Indian religions and religious practices is also a cultural survival issue.[62]

In recent years Congress and the Executive Branch have taken several steps to attempt to benefit tribal and individual Indians' religious practices. The National Park Service, for example, has struggled with ways to impose a ban on rock climbing at a traditional Indian religious site in Wyoming when religious ceremonies are being conducted. The National Park Service is currently being sued for trying to restrict tourist access to the Rainbow Bridge, a site that is sacred to the Navajo people.

In a rather stunning display of accommodation for tribal religions, especially in light of the "war on drugs," federal agencies and Congress have extended federal protection to the possession and use of peyote, an otherwise federally controlled substance, for American Indian religious purposes.[63] Congress has also recognized and provided for the tribal religious use of eagle feathers and parts in the Bald and Golden Eagle Protection Act by providing a permit system for Indians to take, possess, and transport eagles and eagle parts for the religious purposes of Indian tribes.

Indian religious practices are often site-specific; that is, the ceremony or practice must be conducted at a specific sacred site. The natural environment actually becomes a fundamental ingredient of these religious rituals, much like an altar or church, because certain powers can only be acquired by worship and ceremonies conducted at certain sites. Indian peoples have had great problems, however, in ensuring their access to these sites and in protecting these sites when they are on private, state, or federal lands. In 1996 "in furtherance of Federal treaties, and in order to protect and preserve Indian religious practices," President Clinton issued an Executive Order that requires Executive Branch agencies to manage federal lands to accommodate access to, ceremonial use of, and preservation of Indian sacred sites.[64] Earlier, in 1978, Congress also addressed Indian religious practices and access to sacred sites by enacting the American Indian Religious Freedom Act.[65] This act, however, has been totally ineffective in assisting tribes to protect their sacred sites.

These few examples demonstrate some of the steps Congress and the Executive Branch have taken in the modern self-determination era of federal Indian policy to support tribal cultural and religious issues. They illustrate some of the positive actions the federal government has taken for tribal governments and cultures, foreshadowing the support the United States gave the Makah in resuming whaling.

The Makah Reestablish Their Whaling Culture

The Makah ceased whaling in the 1920s because of the depletion of whales in their waters by the non-Indian commercial whaling industry. California gray whales, the primary species in the Makah harvest, were seriously endangered due to overhunting. In fact the condition of whale stocks around the world led fifteen nations to meet in Washington DC, in 1946 to sign the International Convention for the Regulation of Whaling (ICRW).

The ICRW was not enacted to stop whaling; instead it was intended to provide for the proper conservation of whale stocks so that future harvesting of whales could continue. The rules and regulations to be developed under the ICRW were to consider the interests of the consumers of whale products and the whaling industry. The gray whale, however, was almost completely protected by the ICRW from its inception in 1946 due to the gray whales' precarious situation. Grays could be taken only by aborigines and had to be used exclusively for local consumption. The United States took an additional step in 1970 to protect the gray whale by listing it as endangered under the Endangered Species Conservation Act, the predecessor to the Endangered Species Act.

The California gray whales of the Eastern Pacific are probably the best known whales because of their incredible annual migration of nearly thirteen thousand miles along the west coast of North America from Baja California to the Bering and Chukchi seas and especially their habit of swimming so close to shore. Grays are probably the most "whale watched" of all whales. They were estimated to number between 15,000 and 24,000 when their winter calving grounds in Baja California were discovered in 1857. Intensive hunting decimated the stock to about 4,000 by 1875. Commercial hunting then ceased because the stock was so drastically diminished that it was uneconomical to continue hunting them. The cessation of commercial hunting and the protection provided by the ICRW and United States law greatly aided a gray whale comeback. The stock made a good recovery to number about 15,000 to 20,000 by 1980, despite the fact that Russia was taking 163 gray whales a year for Siberian natives in 1957–80. The gray whale stock continued to recover, was removed from the United States endangered species list in 1994, and today is thought to have reached its highest population numbers in history.

Throughout the years, the Makah never forgot their whaling culture. Despite a seventy-year hiatus, whaling remained a crucial and important part of the tribe's culture in the 1990s. Whaling was still at the heart of the Makah culture. For example, whaling images decorated buildings, boats, costumes, drums, and the tribal high school and were the backdrop for many traditional dances; whaling stories were still described in detail. Obviously, then, the tribe watched the gray whale recovery with great interest. The moment the gray whale was taken off the U.S. endangered species list in 1994, the tribal government began working toward the resumption of its treaty whaling rights.

Gray Whale Quota Application and Approval

When the United States delisted the gray whale from the Endangered Species Act list, the Makah Tribe immediately turned its attention to resuming its ancient tradition. The tribe approached the United States to represent it in securing a quota of gray whales from the International Whaling Commission (IWC), and in 1995 the United States agreed to help the tribe. Federal law, however, required the United States to secure the permission of the IWC before the Makah could hunt whales. There was not enough time to prepare a formal application for a Makah quota for the May 1995 annual IWC meeting, but the United States informed the IWC at that meeting that it would in the future present a formal proposal requesting a gray whale quota for the Makah. The IWC consists of a representative from every country that is a party to the international whaling convention. Every year the IWC meets to set catch quotas and to consider and decide other issues concerning whales. The IWC has long allowed quotas for Alaskan, Canadian, Siberian, Greenlandic, and Caribbean natives to take hundreds of whales each year.

In early 1996 the federal agencies involved decided to support the Makah application, and the National Oceanic and Atmospheric Administration (NOAA) entered into an agreement with the tribal government for the Makah to prepare a statement of need and for the U.S. IWC commissioner to propose a quota for the tribe. This agreement required the tribe to adopt a management plan and regulations to govern the hunt and required NOAA to revise its regulations to allow and monitor the hunt. Subsequently, in June 1996, the United States presented the proposal for a Makah quota at the IWC annual meeting. The proposal was withdrawn after it turned controversial and when the United States thought it did not have the required vote of IWC commissioners to approve the quota.

Before the October 1997 annual IWC meeting, the United States arranged with Russia to make a joint proposal for a gray whale quota, which would include both Siberian Natives—the Chukotkas, who were renewing their five-year gray whale quota—and the Makah. This joint proposal was submitted to the IWC for 620 gray whales to be taken in the five-year period 1998–2002. Even though the hunt now included both the Makah and Chukotka peoples, the United States and Russia requested a lower quota than the previous five-year gray whale quota. The new proposal included a quota of twenty gray whales for the Makah over the five-year period.

As expected, the IWC engaged in a vigorous debate over another native group taking part of the quota for the Eastern Pacific stock of gray whales.

After extensive deliberations and on and off the record discussions, the IWC approved the Russian–United States joint gray whale quota by a voice consensus; no recorded vote was taken.[66] Some commentators allege that the approval of the new gray whale quota does not in itself specifically authorize Makah whaling but was only intended to be a quota for the Russian Siberian natives. Notwithstanding this strained interpretation of the quota language, there is no question that the IWC commissioners reached a unanimous consensus approving the five-year quota of 620 Eastern Pacific stock gray whales and that they were all fully aware that twenty of the gray whales were to be taken by the Makah.

Spring Whale Hunts, 1999 and 2000

The Makah immediately began their ritual and cultural preparations for the gray whale hunt. The tribe used the eighteen months between the IWC approval of the quota and their first hunt in spring 1999 to train a crew and to prepare both physically and spiritually.[67] Several protest groups were on the scene during this time, but the major environmental groups, including Greenpeace, did not oppose the Makah hunt. Apparently environmental groups thought this was not an environmental or animal conservation issue as gray whales are at a record high number.

The protestors of the Makah whale hunt filed a federal law suit contending that the U.S. government erred in supporting the Makah quota. On November 1, 1998, four protestors were arrested when a physical confrontation occurred as a result of the protestors trespassing on tribal land. The Makah whale hunt in 1999 proved highly controversial and included litigation, several arrests, months of protests, and assaults on the Makah whaling crew. Ironically, several protest boats hit and possibly injured whales.

The tribe used a crew including members of several different Makah whaling families in its initial 1999 spring hunts. The eight-man canoe crew prepared according to many of the old traditions and customs, ritually purifying themselves and physically preparing for the hunt. On the fourth day of whaling, May 17, 1999, the crew killed and landed a thirty-foot, three-year-old female gray whale. At the insistence of the United States, the crew utilized a high-powered rifle to administer a killing shot to ensure a humane kill and a motorized tow boat to ensure an efficient hunt. The celebration that followed was joyous on the tribal and Indian side, but the opposition was angry and ugly. Racist acts and multiple death threats against Makah people followed, and Indian school children of another Washington state tribe received a bomb threat. Before and after the hunt, protestors near the reservation and elsewhere displayed slogans that read "Save a Whale, Harpoon a Makah." The media and worldwide attention surprised many people.

The tribe rejoiced in the revival of its culture. A traditional posthunt feast was attended by thousands of Makah, other tribal people, and other supporters from across the nation. All the whale meat and blubber were distributed and used according to the tribe's ancient customs.

In the spring of 2000 the Makah returned to their tradition of individual families training and preparing for the hunt and whaling in their own family canoes. The Makah did not strike or land a whale in the 2000 hunts. A much smaller group of protestors made its presence felt.

Ninth Circuit Decisions, 2000 and 2002

On June 9, 2000, a federal appellate court decision raised some questions about the future of Makah whale hunting.[68] The U.S. Court of Appeals for the Ninth Circuit invalidated the Environmental Assessment (EA) of the hunt performed by the National Marine Fisheries Service (NMFS) on the basis that the federal agencies had already agreed and contractually bound themselves to support the Makah whaling proposal before the agencies had performed the required environmental reviews. This is true; however, it ignores the fact that the United States has a fiduciary and trust duty toward tribes and has to consult with tribes about their needs and issues, such as their fishing and whaling treaty rights, for the U.S. to determine what its duty is in different situations. The Ninth Circuit's analysis of when the federal decision to support the Makah proposal occurred and when an EA had to be prepared makes it almost impossible for a federal agency to deal with a tribe in this type of situation. Despite that point, the court thought the EA was untimely, was not objective, and violated National Environmental Policy Act requirements. The court ordered the federal government to perform another EA. This raised the interesting question of how the government could perform another EA without again being accused of having prejudged the situation.

The government did issue a new EA in July 2001. It was no surprise when the NMFS and NOAA approved a final EA that allowed the Makah gray whale hunt to resume.[69] The new EA allowed for an expanded gray whale hunt because it removed some of the time and place restrictions on whaling contained in the first EA.

Needless to say, the hunt protestors were not pleased. They sued again to invalidate the 2001 EA. They again raised the question already mentioned:

how could the federal agencies have conducted an unbiased EA when they had already consulted with and contracted to support the Makah quota proposal, in essence having prejudged the situation, before they ever conducted an EA? In December of 2002, the Ninth Circuit court of appeals again agreed with the protestors and invalidated the second EA.[70] The court went further than in its 2000 decision and now ordered the federal government to prepare a much more detailed and time-consuming Environmental Impact Statement, instead of the simpler EAs previously prepared. In addition, the court held that both the federal agencies and the tribe had not satisfied the Marine Mammal Protection Act permit and waiver requirements and would have to meet these requirements in the future before another hunt could occur.[71] It is uncertain at the time of writing what decision will result from an EIS prepared by the federal government and how the tribe and the United States will comply with the Marine Mammal Protection Act.

Conclusion

The Makah Tribe has long fought to preserve its separate and distinct sovereign government, culture, religion, and way of life. It has been successful in this endeavor and has also been successful, in the short term and against great odds, in reviving its whaling culture that had lain dormant for over seventy years. As such, the tribe has set an excellent example for other tribes in how to exercise cultural self-determination and sovereign power and influence, and how to preserve and practice culture according to traditional tribal ways. It is a testament to the Makah as a people and as a government that they kept their tradition alive even when they could not whale for decades and that they had the will to exercise governmental and cultural prerogatives to restore this tradition within the tribe and then the strength to make it happen even with virulent outside opposition.

Despite an active and aggressive federal program to eradicate the Makah culture and government, both persist and thrive today. The Makah people continue to exist as a sovereign government and as a society with traditional cultural aspects separate from those of the dominant American society, even after more than 150 years of forced assimilation. The 1999 and 2000 whale hunts will play a large part in helping the Makah to continue to preserve their existence, their culture, their traditions, and their government as a separate people. For example, the skeleton of the whale landed in 1999 is being reassembled and hung in the tribal museum by tribal high school students, and the hunt itself is helping Makah children to learn about and to take pride in their culture. This community-wide whaling activity has strengthened the bonds of the community and Makah families. This principle is well demonstrated by the results from the Makah hunts themselves and by the whaling cultures of other native peoples around the world.

The importance of whaling in the lives and culture of the Makah is evident from the themes in their songs, legends, art, dance, geographic names, and thoughts. The importance is also self-evident when one considers the great physical risks and enormous effort needed to hunt whales. The Makah clearly demonstrated the importance to their culture of whaling by the efforts they put forth as a government and as a people to regain the opportunity itself. The entire community was involved in that effort, which demonstrates the importance of whaling in assisting the Makah to stay a cohesive, separate society and in preserving their culture. The Makah hunt demonstrates that hunting, distributing, and sharing whale meat is a cultural tradition that is far more important than the sustenance of the food itself, because the hunt reinforces their culture, provides continuity and community, and reaffirms traditional roles in their native society.

The whale hunt also reinforces and supports tribal family units because the whaling is performed by family crews. The cooperation and shared work helps to keep families and the community together. Respect for Makah elders is engendered as the young learn to rely on the knowledge and experience of their parents and elders.

A whaling culture is indeed something special and distinct in today's world. The Makah rituals and customs involving whales reflect the essential elements of a distinctive and respected culture. The tribe's rationale for renewing whaling, as stated by then tribal chair Ben Johnson, was that: "the whale hunt will not only bring the community together, but it enriches our culture."[72] The federal government itself recognizes that the Makah's "subsistence hunting includes far more than physical survival. It is a way of life that includes historical practices and is the cultural 'glue' that holds the Tribe together."[73]

Such positive and beneficial results for their government, culture, families, and tribe demonstrate that the Makah were wise as a people to preserve their whaling traditions and to revive this cultural tradition by pursuing the resumption of whaling. Not surprisingly, there were some dissenting voices within the tribe about resuming whaling, and there were dissenting voices in the international community. For the most part though, the resumption of Makah whaling has drawn protests from only a very small minority. The resumption of Makah whaling is not an issue of animal conservation because it is not about hunting a threatened or endangered species. Gray whales are considered to be at the highest numbers they have ever been and are dying of natural causes in the largest numbers in the past twenty-four years of record keeping, perhaps because they have exceeded the carrying capacity of their food supply.

The Makah hunt, then, is solidly based on legal and moral rights; rights the Makah have always held and which they and their tribal government carefully and wisely preserved in 1855 in their treaty with the United States. The Makah have also wisely kept alive the love of their traditions and culture within their society and the desire to revive that culture by whaling. The tribal government has exercised its sovereign powers and its political relationship with the United States wisely by carefully maneuvering itself and using the cooperation and support of the United States to gain recognition on the international stage that it deserves and needs to exercise its treaty and cultural right to hunt whales. The tribe has handled itself well in the storm of international press coverage and in the face of provocation by protestors. In essence, the tribe has done what was necessary governmentally and traditionally to keep its culture alive and to restore and preserve it. The tribe has exercised its sovereignty and its right of cultural self-determination and has taken on all comers and overcome all obstacles to do so. The Makahs, then, are an excellent example of how tribal governments and native peoples can work to preserve and restore their cultural practices and to engage in these in their own traditional ways and methods. The Makah have demonstrated how to exercise sovereignty and how to practice cultural self-determination.

Notes

1. See for example, Robert J. Miller, "Speaking with Forked Tongues: Indian Treaties, Salmon, and the Endangered Species Act," *Oregon Law Review* 70 (1991): 543 ff., especially 551–63, addressing seventy years of federal litigation about tribal fishing rights in the Pacific Northwest.

2. Robert J. Miller, "Exercising Cultural Self-Determination: The Makah Indian Tribe Goes Whaling," *American Indian Law Review* 25 (2002): 206.

3. *Webster's Ninth New Collegiate Dictionary* (1985), 314. See also V. Robin Fox, "The Cultural Animal," in *Issues in Cultural Anthropology: Selected Readings*, ed. David W. McCurdy and James P. Spradley (Boston: Little, Brown, 1979): "Culture . . . refers to traditional modes of behaving and thinking that are passed from one generation to another by social learning of one kind or another" (17).

4. Geert Hofstede, *Culture's Consequences: International Differences in Work-Related Values* (Beverly Hills: Sage Publications, 1980), 25.

5. Elizabeth Colson, *The Makah Indians: A Study of an Indian Tribe in Modern American Society* (Minneapolis: University of Minnesota Press, 1953), 11.

6. *United States v. State of Washington*, 730 F.2d 1314, 1315 (9th Cir. 1984), quoting a Makah chief at the 1855 treaty negotiation that "he wanted the sea—that was his country"; *United States v. Washington*, 384 F.Supp. 312, 363 (W.D. Wash. 1974), *aff'd*, 520 F.2d 676 (9th Cir. 1975), *cert.*

denied, 423 U.S. (1976). The Makah were primarily a seafaring people who spent their lives on the water or close to the shore; most of their subsistence came from the sea as fish, whales, and seals.

7. James G. Swan, *The Indians of Cape Flattery*, Smithsonian Contributions to Knowledge 14 (Washington DC: Smithsonian Institution Press, 1870), 4; Carroll Riley, "The Makah Indians: A Study Of Political And Economic Organization," *Ethnohistory* 15 (1968): 57.

8. Riley, "The Makah Indians," 71.

9. Swan, *Indians of Cape Flattery*, 22–30; *United States v. Washington*, 384 F.Supp. 312, 363 (W.D. Wash. 1974), *aff'd*, 520 F.2d 676 (9th Cir. 1975), *cert. denied*, 423 U.S. (1976). Makah wealth, power, and culture were achieved by a thriving commercial maritime economy.

10. Ruth Kirk, *Hunters of the Whale: An Adventure of Northwest Coast Archaeology* (New York: William Morrow Publishers, 1974), 20; Ann M. Renker and Erna Guinther, "Makah," in *Handbook of North American Indians: Northwest Coast*, ed. William C. Sturtevant (Washington DC: Smithsonian Institution Press, 1990), 422. The Makah have been whaling for over fifteen hundred years.

11. Frances Densmore, *Nootka and Quileute Music*, Bulletin, Bureau of American Ethnology, Smithsonian Institution (Washington DC: US Government Printing Office, 1939), 63; James G. Swan, *Almost Out of the World: Scenes from Washington Territory* (Tacoma WA: Pacific Northwest Books, 1971), 77.

12. Beth Laura O'Leary, "Aboriginal Whaling from the Aleutian Islands to Washington State," in *The Gray Whale:* Eschrichtius robustus, ed. Mary Lou Jones, Steven Swartz, and Stephen Leatherwood (London: Academic Press, 1984): "Whale oil was the most prized commodity among these Northwest groups" (95). See also *Indian America: A Gift From the Past*, video (Washington DC: Media Resource Associates, 1994): The Makah traded whale parts from southern California to Alaska and into the interior as far as Idaho and Colorado. Riley, "The Makah Indians," 59, 61, 63: Numerous Spanish, English, French, Russian, and American ships traded with the Makah from the 1770s forward.

13. O'Leary, "Aboriginal Whaling," 93: Makah were reported to have sold $8,000 worth of whale oil in 1856. Herbert C. Taylor, Jr., "Anthropological Investigation of the Makah Indians," in *Coast Salish and Western Washington Indians* (2nd ed.), ed. David Agee Horr (New York: Garland Publishing, 1974), 67–68: Makah were major traders with other tribes, Europeans, and the Hudson's Bay Company at Victoria, Canada and by 1850 were trading 30,000 gallons of whale oil annually. See also James G. McCurdy, *Indian Days at Neah Bay* (2nd. ed.), ed. Gordon Newell (Lynwood WA: Working Press, 1981), 108. Densmore, *Nootka and Quileute Music*, 10: Makah engaged in a great amount of trade with Chinooks at the Columbia River and north into Canada. George Gibbs, "Tribes of Western Washington and Northwest Oregon," *Contributions to North American Ethnology* 25 (1877): 2: Makah traded oil and whale meat inland and southward, 30,000 gallons of oil in a single season (see also *Indian America: A Gift From the Past*). *United States v. Washington*, 384 F.Supp. 312, 364 (W.D. Wash. 1974), *aff'd*, 520 F.2d 676 (9th Cir. 1975), *cert. denied*, 423 U.S. (1976): "The Makah enjoyed a high standard of living as a result of their marine resources and extensive marine trade [and] maintained from time immemorial a thriving economy based on commerce."

14. Charles M. Scammon, *The Marine Mammals of the North-western Coast of North America: Described and Illustrated, Together With an Account of the American Whale-Fishery* (New York: Dover Publications, 1968): By 1938, gray whales "had become economically extinct" (33).

15. Robert H. Busch, *Gray Whales: Wandering Giants* (Custer WA: Orca Book Publishers, 1998), 75.

16. Wayne Shuttles, ed., *Handbook of North American Indians: Northwest Coast* (Washington DC:

Smithsonian Institution Press, 1990), 391–97; Densmore, *Nootka and Quileute Music*, 13; Timothy Egan, "Makah Tribe Seeks Return to Tradition of Whaling," *Seattle Times*, 4 June 1995, sec. A1, quoting Hubert Markishtum, tribal chairman.

17. Swan, *Indians of Cape Flattery*, 13.

18. *Indian America: A Gift From the Past*; George Bowechop, Makah Tribal Elder, "Address at Portland State University" (9 March 2000: notes on file with author): "Without the spiritual side the whale hunt means nothing."

19. O'Leary, "Aboriginal Whaling," 91; Bowechop, "Address at Portland State University."

20. The United States Constitution states that "all Treaties made . . . under the Authority of the United States, shall be the supreme Law of the Land . . . ." (U.S. Constitution, art. 6).

21. *United States v. Winans*, 198 U.S. 371, 381 (1905).

22. Treaty with the Makah, Jan. 31, 1855, Art. 4, 12 Stat. 939, 2, in Charles J. Kappler, ed., *Indian Affairs: Laws and Treaties, 1904–1941* (Washington DC: Government Printing Office; reprint, New York: AMS Press, 1971 [1972]), vol. 3, 682.

23. Kent D. Richards, *Isaac I. Stevens: Young Man in a Hurry* (Pullman: Washington State University Press, 1979), 207; I. Hazard Stevens, *The Life of Issac Ingalls Stevens* (Boston: Houghton, Mifflin and Company, 1900), 474.

24. Stevens, *Life of Issac Ingalls Stevens*, 474, 478.

25. Richards, *Isaac I. Stevens*, 207.

26. Stevens, *Life of Issac Ingalls Stevens*, 474; George C. Gibbs, *Ratified Treaty No. 286, Documents Relating to the Negotiation of the Treaty of January 31, 1855, with the Makah Indians*, p. 2 (on file with author).

27. Stevens, *Life of Issac Ingalls Stevens*, 474, 475.

28. Stevens, *Life of Issac Ingalls Stevens*, 475; Gibbs, *Ratified Treaty No. 286*, 2–3.

29. Richards, *Isaac I. Stevens*, 195, 201; Treaty with the Makah, in Kappler, *Indian Affairs*, 682; *United States v. Washington*, 384 F.Supp. 312, 363–64 (W.D. Wash. 1974), *aff'd*, 520 F.2d 676 (9th Cir. 1975), *cert. denied*, 423 U.S. (1976).

30. Stevens, *Life of Issac Ingalls*, 474; Gibbs, *Ratified Treaty No. 286*, 2.

31. Stevens, *Life of Issac Ingalls Stevens*, 476; Gibbs, *Ratified Treaty No. 286*, 4.

32. *Montana v. United States*, 450 U.S. 544, 560 n.9 (1981); David H. Getches, Charles F. Wilkinson, and Robert A. Williams, Jr., eds., *Cases and Materials on Federal Indian Law*, 4th ed. (St. Paul MN: West Information Publishing Group, 1998), 141, 166; Delos S. Otis, *The Dawes Act and the Allotment of Indian Lands* (Norman: University of Oklahoma Press, 1973); Hearings on H.R. 7902 Before the House Comm. on Indian Affairs, 73d Cong., 2d Sess. pt. 9, at 434 (1934); *Winters v. United States*, 207 U.S. 564 (1908).

33. Francis Paul Prucha, *The Great Father: The United States Government and the American Indians* (Lincoln: University of Nebraska Press, 1995), 609–30, 643–52; *Winters v. United States*, 207 U.S. 564, 576–77 (1908); Raymond Cross, "American Indian Education: The Terror of History and the Nations' Debt to the Indian Peoples," *Little Rock Law Review* (University of Arkansas) 21 (1999): 941, 948, 951.

34. Robert J. Miller, "Correcting Supreme Court Errors: American Indian Responses to *Lyng v. Northwest* Indian Cemetery Protective Association," *Environmental Law* 20 (1990): 1037, 1039; Getches et al., *Federal Indian Law*, 184–85.

35. John E. Silverman, "The Miner's Canary: Tribal Control of American Indian Education and the First Amendment," *Fordham Urban Law Journal* 19 (1992): 1019, 1022.

36. Robert J. Miller and Maril Hazlett, "The 'Drunken Indian': Myth Distilled into Reality through Federal Indian Alcohol Policy," *Arizona State Law Journal* 28 (1996): 223, 262, 264–66; Prucha, *The Great Father*, 1023–24, 1060–84.

37. Colson, *The Makah Indians*, 9, 11; Riley, "The Makah Indians," 65 and n.5.

38. Colson, *The Makah Indians*, 2, 11.

39. Colson, *The Makah Indians*, 12; *Indian America: A Gift From the Past.*

40. Colson, *The Makah Indians*, 11, 13; Linda J. Goodman, "Traditional Music in Makah Life," in *A Time of Gathering: Native Heritage in Washington State*, ed. Robin K. Wright (Seattle: University of Washington Press, 1991), 223, 233 n.1.

41. Colson, *The Makah Indians*, 14, 16.

42. Ruth Kirk, *Tradition and Change on the Northwest Coast: The Makah, Nuu-chah-nulth, Southern Kwakiutl and Nuxalk* (Seattle: University of Washington Press, 1986), 236, 245; Colson, *The Makah Indians*, 17–18; McCurdy, *Indian Days at Neah Bay*, 73 n.4.

43. Colson, *The Makah Indians*, 19; Alix Jane Gillis, "History of the Neah Bay Agency," in *Coast Salish and Western Washington Indians* (2nd ed.), ed. David Agee Horr (New York: Garland University Press, 1974), 106.

44. Colson, *The Makah Indians*, 127, 129.

45. *United States v. Kagama*, 118 U.S. 375, 384–85 (1886).

46. *Cherokee Nation v. Georgia*, 30 U.S. (5 Pet.) 1, 17 (1831); *United States v. Kagama*, 118 U.S. 375, 384–85 (1886); *United States v. Sandoval*, 231 U.S. 28 (1913).

47. *Cherokee Nation v. Georgia*, 30 U.S. (5 Pet.) 1, 17 (1831); Felix S. Cohen, *Felix S. Cohen's Handbook on Federal Indian Law* (Dayton OH: Lexis Law Publications, 1982), 207–57; *United States v. Mitchell*, 463 U.S. 206, 225 (1983).

48. U.S. Constitution, art.1, sec. 8, clause 3.

49. *United States v. Mitchell*, 463 U.S. 206, 224–26 (1983); *Cherokee Nation*, 30 U.S. (5 Pet.) at 17.

50. *Seminole Nation v. United States*, 316 U.S. 286, 297 (1942).

51. *Merrion v. Jicarilla Apache Tribe*, 455 U.S. 130, 138 n.5 (1982); *Morton v. Mancari*, 417 U.S. 535, 551 (1974).

52. National Marine Fisheries Service, *Environmental Assessment of the Makah Tribes Harvest of Up to Five Gray Whales per Year for Cultural and Subsistence Use* (Washington DC: U.S. Department of Commerce,1997), 14–15.

53. U.S.C. § 1901(2), (3), (5).

54. U.S.C. §§ 2901–2906, 2901(1).

55. U.S.C. § 2901(2).

56. U.S.C. § 2901(3) & (9).

57. *Tribal Colleges and Universities*, Exec. Order No. 13,021, 61 Fed. Reg. 54,329 (1996).

58. *American Indian and Alaska Native Education*, Exec. Order No. 13,096, 63 Fed. Reg. 4268 (1998).

59. U.S.C. §§ 1158, 1159.

60. The Native American Graves Protection and Repatriation Act of 1990, 25 U.S.C. §§ 3001–3013.

61. Kevin McCullen and Scripps Howard, "Preserving Indian Culture: Bill Would Shield Ceremonial Peyote Use, Sacred Sites," *Arizona Republic*, 18 January 1993, sec. B3), quoting Walter EchoHawk.

62. American Indian Religious Freedom Act, 42 U.S.C. § 1996 ("the religious practices of the

American Indian . . . are an integral part of their culture, tradition and heritage, such practices forming the basis of Indian identity and value systems").

63. C.F.R. § 1307.31 (1990); 42 U.S.C. § 1996a (1994).

64. *Indian Sacred Sites*, Exec. Order No. 13,007, 61 Fed. Reg. 26,771 (1996).

65. U.S.C. § 1996.

66. International Whaling Commission, 49th *Annual Meeting, Extracts from the Verbatim Record*, Monaco, 20–24 October 1997 (Cambridge, U.K.: International Whaling Commission, 1997), 16; International Whaling Commission, *Forth-Eighth Report of the International Whaling Commission*, ed. G. P. Donovan (Cambridge, U.K.: International Whaling Commission, 1998), 30, 51; *Whaling Provisions; Aboriginal Subsistence Whaling Quotas*, 63 Fed. Reg. 16701, 16703 (6 April 1998); E-mail communications from Dr. Ray Gambell, IWC Secretary, 7 March 2000 and 24 March 2000 (hard copy on file with author).

67. Bowechop, "Address at Portland State University": the whalers trained for thousands of hours for the 1999 hunt, both physically and to study weather, tides, and ocean conditions.

68. *Metcalf v. Daley*, 214 F.3d 1135 (9th Cir. 2000).

69. U.S. Department of Commerce, *Environmental Assessment on Allocating Gray Whales to the Makah Tribe for the Years 2001 and 2002*, 66 Fed. Reg. 37641 (19 July 2001).

70. *Anderson v. Evans*, 314 F.3d 1006, 1021–22 (9th Cir. 2002).

71. *Anderson v. Evans*, 1029–30.

72. Richard Blow, "The Great American Whale Hunt," *Mother Jones*, 1 September 1998 (WestLaw computer service WL 10365177). See also Bowechop, "Address at Portland State University": "The great reward was seeing people come together and tribes coming together supporting the Makah."

73. Blow, "Great American Whale Hunt": statement of the National Oceanic and Atmospheric Administration.

Kilipaka Kawaihonu Nahili Pae Ontai (Native Hawaiian)

A Spiritual Definition of Sovereignty from a Kanaka Maoli Perspective

Na kanaka maoli, indigenous people of the Hawaiian archipelago, are struggling to find a definition of sovereignty. Because so much of their past has been lost since the 1898 annexation, most natives have known no other form of sovereignty other than that experienced as citizens of the United States. As a result, na kanaka maoli struggle to define a native form of self-determination, but they reach for sovereignty models that are rooted in Western traditions instead of in their own spiritual/cultural experience. This struggle for an appropriate definition is compounded by over a hundred years of a material-based economy shaped around the concepts of individualism and private property ownership. That the *po'e* (people) are responsible for the care of the gods' *hemolele* (perfect) creation of land and sea and everything in it has been diminished as the high spiritual value underscores the magnitude of cultural confusion that exists within the native community. At least three generations have inured themselves to a material ethos and have in the process, for most natives, largely beclouded their own native spiritual identity and history. This obsession with owning "stuff" and being responsible only to one's self continues to divorce many natives from their *ho'omana* (native spiritual beliefs).

The indigenous peoples' struggle to find a pliable definition based on their past and agreeable in Western terms has met with confusion and strident polarization within the community. Not knowing enough about their own past produces a vacuum that welcomes a Western definition by default. Having rejected their own traditional faith long ago in favor of Christianity only augments their spiritual distance from the past. Fear of being labeled heathens creates a psychological barrier and keeps many natives from straying too far from Western thought. But many natives need to be taught the positive spiritual values of the traditional past in order to gain a better understanding of native self-determination. Trying to merge native tradition with Eurocentricity will be challenging. This approach may be harmful to a reconstituted Hawaiian Nation.

Indeed this approach may prove to be culturally self-destructive and may contradict what it means to be *kanaka maoli* (true native). The struggle for a native definition begins by defining sovereignty on its own native terms. Sovereignty can be defined by the epochal journey of its native people over a millennium of spiritual, historical, and cultural landmarks. How do the underlying spiritual and cultural experiences of kanaka maoli differ from the Western experience? Why the West found its way to the islands and how its religious, political, and economic institutions dominate native life are equations that need to be explored in order to understand the complexities of a native search for a definition of sovereignty that feels *pono* (good) in their *na'au* (stomach). If na kanaka maoli are to remain unique, it is because they do have a very different worldview from the West and it is *pono* (right) for them to define their own concept of sovereignty that reaches into their fifteen-hundred-year history.

Ke Ea O Ka 'Aina: Life of the Land

Mary Kawena Pukui, a native scholar, copublished a seminal edition of the *Hawaiian Dictionary*. Pukui spent years of meticulous research studying native words and their meaning. Finding English equivalency was difficult if not impossible with some words. Words that described certain native experiences had no English equivalents. Uniformity of some words was not consistent throughout the islands. The work was a monumental effort fraught with controversy. The formula used in determining a common definition involved how often a word was used throughout the various native communities and incorporated repeated use and common patterns.

Pukui selected the native word *ea* to describe the newly introduced Euro-American word *sovereignty*. In describing the word, she combined the Euro-American definition and the traditional definition. She gives the traditional definition as meaning "Life, breath . . . Spirit."[1] In the Euro-American definition she uses "Sovereignty, rule, independence." The juxtaposition of the two is revealing and indicative of the controversy embedded in the state motto *Ua mau ke ea o ka 'aina i ka pono*. Mo'i Kauikeaouli (King Kamehameha III) uttered these words to describe his feelings upon the return of national sovereignty by British Admiral Sir Richard Thomas when Thomas rescinded British claims to the kingdom. The motto can be translated as "The life/sovereignty of the land is preserved in righteousness," where *ea* can have either traditional or Euro usage.

Pukui used the traditional definition in setting an example for usage of the word within the native context. In this sense, she introduces the concept of using native definitions when related to native experience. She chooses *life* in this example. Her choice is significant because the word *life* epitomizes the native sense of appropriateness as expressed by the *mo'i* (king) upon return of the sacred land (*'aina*). For natives, the return of the control of land was important because of the traditional caretaker concept of land assigned to their rulers to ensure a way life as practiced for more than a thousand years. The shock of a foreign (*haole*) caretaker of the 'aina had a universal and immediate impact on the native population. Who was this foreign warrior who did not look like them, did not speak their language, and did not practice their religion (*ho'omana*)? By what *mana* (divine power) and inheritance did this *haole* claim to be supreme caretaker over the gods' lands? The life of the land, its breath and spirit, is in every grain of sand, in every rock, in every tree, in every *kanaka* (person), as it has been since the time of darkness and light.[2] In this sense, natives where expressing their version of sovereignty, their sense of independence and self-rule.

These questions posed a dilemma for the ruling class, the traditional divine caretakers of the land, who practiced and honored their traditional responsibility as spiritual and secular rulers on behalf of the gods. Mo'i Kauikeaouli had to make a pivotal decision as a traditional ruler: was he to continue his role as a divine ruler and representative of the gods and his peoples' traditions, or was he to become a secular ruler and embrace the foreigner's ways? To become a follower of the foreigner's ways and their religion implied a denial of his own divine status and the rejection of his ancestral inheritance. It implied the acceptance of a new way of life and governance. He had already succumbed to enormous pressures to give up his hopes to marry his divine sister, an ancient practice to ensure that divine *mana* was retained for his progeny.[3] More and more of his traditional sacred rights were being stripped from his role as divine caretaker of the land and its people. The king drew inward and was often depressed.[4] Native rulers of the nineteenth century would all face this challenge to their traditional roles as divine caretakers. Natives would follow their rulers with confusion and apprehension and would eventually abandon them out of a sense of hopelessness, unable to comprehend the inability of their rulers to control the behavior of foreigners and their strange way of thinking.

Native rulers' inability to curb alien ideas introduced by the British and Americans marked the introduction of the Euro-American version of sovereignty, one not based on the concept of spiritual caretakers of the land for the common good but on individuals owning land as private property. For natives this concept of owning their gods and ancestors was inconceivable and repugnant.[5]

Papa and Wakea: In the Beginning

For as long as can be remembered, na kanaka have been told that they are divine, children of the gods.[6] They are descendants of passionate and loving ancestor god-parents—Papa, Earth Mother, and Wakea, Sky Father, who in turn are the progeny of 'Io, the supreme creator of Po, the time before light.[7] From this holy union, na kanaka are taught that the first born was Haloa, their eldest brother, who was stillborn but was reborn as *kalo*, the taro plant.[8] And as long as Haloa was with them, being cultivated and nurtured, their ancestral divine mother, father, and big brother would take care of them till the end of time, providing the staples of life and all manner of daily comforts and protections needed to live in a world blessed with immense beauty and abundance. *Haloa*, which means eternal breath of life, was cultivated and nurtured in every household farming plot. In precolonial times, vast lands of Haloa were farmed with loving care and with deep ritual respect.[9] The waters of Wakea were intricately woven within each *ahupua'a* (native land planning district) to provide Haloa with the living waters of Lono-a-Wakea. The nurturing womb of Papa provided sustenance for growth. In this broad *ohana* (extended family), life flourished in harmony and in balance with heaven and earth. Food was abundant.[10] This was the cosmic and spiritual belief structure of na kanaka. This was the foundation of their religion, their *ho'omana*. Winter months would be devoted to harvesting, celebrations, games, song and dance, and most of all prayers of gratitude to the gods.[11]

In this theology, native people saw their own creation as closely connected with all the natural world around them, and this connection was divinely connected to the beginning of creation.[12] While Haloa represented their eldest brother in human form, he also took the form of a plant. He presented himself in this form, or *kinolau*, and natives knew that Haloa reproduced new children by simply replanting the corm. Thus kalo, taro, was a direct living representation of their elder brother with an unbroken chain of descendants. His *Ha* (sacred breath) passed down from generation to generation. Na kanaka saw themselves as part of the spiritual world of their gods, manifested by everyday spirit objects surrounding their lives. The earth represented their ancestral grandmother. The sky represented their grandfather. Kalo represented their older brother. All objects in nature represented a spirit force (*mana*), some with more, some with less mana.

Na kanaka buried their loved ones in the womb of Papa. Returning the sacred bones (*iwi*) to the earth or hiding them in the mouth of Mother Earth (a cave) was a sacred rite honoring the ancestral gods and their elder brother. The iwi of great chiefs were hidden or enshrined in temples (*hei'au*) of the sacred grounds of their ancestral gods.[13] Sacred Papa, Mother Earth, received all her children. Cremation was sacrilege. The *po'e* (people) did not own mother earth; rather they returned to grandmother earth. The *iwi kupuna* (ancestral bones) were buried everywhere. Today ancestral bones are often desecrated by urban development projects, a continuing source of great pain and anguish for native descendants.[14]

In this tradition the concept of land and its resources was a function of divine allowance and nurturing from the ancestral gods, who in turn expected *haipule* (piety) and *aloha* (devotion) from the living. In this extended na kanaka family of gods and spirits, all things were divine, from the divine, returning to the divine. The gods fed them, housed them, clothed them. Their rulers, divine themselves, were the earth representatives and caretakers of these spiritual gifts. Land and its resources were personified in the ancestor gods and rulers. They were one in the same, a blend of spirit and material coexistence, with no boundaries. No one owned what was divine and sacred. No one owned the sky, the earth, the wind or stars.

Ali'i: Divine Caretakers

"The Land is a Chief, to whom people are a consecrating sacrifice" is from the Hawaiian book of proverbs.[15] Considered by ordinary natives to be living demigods and deities on earth, the *ali'i* (rulers) represented order, authority, spiritual guideposts, representatives of their spirit ancestors, and temporal and spiritual guardians of the forces that brought food, shelter, comfort, and well-being to everyone.[16] As a theocracy, the native people did not question the spiritual mandate of their ali'i, for the *mana* (power) of the ali'i was divine with the power of life and death over ordinary people. The ali'i, in turn, held the responsibility of maintaining a social and spiritual contract with the common people over whom they ruled. This contract was to include continuous communications with the gods to ensure abundance from the land and sea and to ensure peace and tranquility. This was a trusting relationship, in which commoners depended on their rulers to bring sustenance, comfort, and predictability to their world.

The ali'i set the standards for the arts, architecture, farming, fishing, healing arts, and so forth and, most important, for the spiritual rituals to guide all manner of society. The spiritual *kahuna* (priests) of highest ranks, themselves often of ali'i bloodlines, ruled alongside the ali'i as spiritual advisors. At times they ruled in both roles, carrying out their social and spiritual contract. Law, as defined by native society then, was ruled by divine decree, and all manner of life was regulated and ordered through the *kapu* system established by the ali'i and spiritual kahuna. The kapu system, a system of laws steeped in history and tradition, also governed the relationship between men and women, placing ordinary women below the spiritual ladder of men, except for the highest-born women of powerful bloodlines. But even for these most powerful women, there were ritual restrictions that placed them below their male peers.

Such was the order of kanaka society for at least seven hundred years after the arrival of the Tahitian high priest-king Pa'ao, who revised the ancient ho'omana.[17] Ordinary na kanaka obeyed their god-rulers, piously worshiped their *'aumakua* (ancestor spirits), and remained devoted to the numerous natural spirits that surrounded their everyday lives. For as long as can be remembered, kanaka maoli society functioned well under this order. There were more times of peace than of conflict. The arts, dance, games, astronomy, navigation, agriculture, aquaculture, engineering, building, and much more flourished. Starvation was rare, for the *'aina* (land) and the *kai* (sea) provided sufficient protein, vegetables, and minerals and a healthy environment for the population. The ali'i and spiritual kahuna gave divine assurance of such abundance through their kapu laws and governance. In modern times, most na kanaka still consciously practice kapu toward the 'aina and kai.

Kapu 'Aina: Inviolate Grounds

The native people held certain places on each island to be sacred, places where their gods were most honored, where divine acts and events manifested their presence, and where earthly communications took place between kanaka (people) and *akua* (gods). The sanctity of these places was inviolate. These were the holy grounds of the gods. The kahuna priests/warriors of various orders were expected to be caretakers of these sacred grounds. No one, high-born or commoner, could rule over these grounds.

Kualoa

When kapu chief Kahahana became ruling chief of O'ahu in the latter part of the eighteenth century, he was asked by his stepfather Kahekili, ruling chief of Maui, to give him a gift of appreciation for rearing Kahahana during his childhood. Kahekili asked for the *'ahupua'a* land called Kualoa, sacred ahupua'a, home to the gods of O'ahu. Such a gift would have granted Kahekili the right of divine caretaker of this most sacred of all of O'ahu Island. Baffled by such a request, Kahahana consulted with the high kahuna Ka'opulupulu. The priest advised him that such a request would mean the loss of his divine authority over the Island Kingdom of O'ahu and as a ruler, for in Kualoa were the sacred waters and hill of his god-ancestors, *hei'au* (temples) to the sacred drums (Kapahuulu), and source of the divine ivory (whale tooth) required to mediate offerings to the gods.[18] A chief could not own this venerable site; it belonged to the gods.

Kualoa represents the concept of a sacred land infused with *mana* (divine spirit) of the highest order; a ruling dynasty would be without divine authority if this were in another's hands. Whoever worshiped and made offerings on these sacred grounds had the divine right to rule.

Any high chief could govern over a distant land as long as such a ruler was the caretaker of its holy grounds and *hei'au*. Stewardship over these sacred sites gave divine powers (*mana*) to the chief and the right to rule over its subjects on behalf of their ancestor gods. A defeated chief meant that the new ruler was given the mandate of caretaker. In the eyes of the commoners, a new ruler was ordained by divine will. In the na kanaka world, no ruling chief was legitimate without a genealogical line that testified to *mana*-infused divine blood and that carried land stewardship as a responsibility.

Pu'uhonua

A sacred mound of earth, a place of sanctity in the name of a god or a living god-ruler, was where anyone, high-born or commoner, could seek refuge and not be harmed.[19] This piece of sacred land, enclosed with high stone walls and with its "mouth" forever open, was universally recognized as a place of peace, where men, women, children, the old and infirm, and evil-doers as well as the pious were welcome and assured safety from harm or threats. Its sanctity was inviolate even to a ruling *mo'i*. This was a place where the *Ha* (breath of life) was assured to anyone who entered its grounds, where sins were forgiven, where vengeance was left outside, where temporal rule had no authority, and where the sacred grounds were sovereign only to the god spirit. This was enforced by the kahuna-warrior priests who guarded and celebrated the ancient rituals associated with the god. Sacred *pu'uhonua*, land, was cared for by the kahuna and the ali'i, each having responsibility to nurture the ancient practices and rituals devoted to the gods and ancestors.

'Ahupua'a

The gods provided na kanaka with land and sea from which sustenance was obtained.[20] The god-rulers were responsible for the kapu laws to sustain life (*kalana ola*); the ruler's *konohiki* (land managers) were responsible for land use planning and for the organization of labor.[21] The *'ahupua'a* (system of land division) was the basic land organization system used to maximize agricultural and aquacultural productivity while making efficient use of water and other forces of nature. This sustainable system worked for hundreds of generations, assuring po'e a quality of life free from starvation. Early Europeans were astonished at the productivity of these lands.[22] The abundance of agricultural and animal produce attracted European and American traders to these remote lands to replenish their food stock on long sea journeys.

For na kanaka, this abundance was due to the pious relationship among their gods, embodied through and in the *'aina*; their god-rulers, divine caretakers of the god-*'aina*; and commoners, who obeyed and worshiped both. In their world this system worked, a process of divinely inspired land planning and community organizing where everyone, children and adults alike, had a responsibility and role in carrying out food production on behalf of the entire community. Anyone who was not part of this communal life was ostracized and lived precariously.

Kamehameha's Vision

When the thirteen English colonies were rebelling against their king in the late 1700s, the warrior Kamehameha embarked on uniting all eight major islands of the archipelago, a feat never accomplished in native history. Early chiefs had attempted to do this but failed. During his time all the islands were ruled by four hereditary ruling families, all related by sacred marriages. Kamehameha's vision of uniting the islands was motivated by his desire to bring all the squabbling ruling families together under one rule, to bring *lokahi* (harmony) to the sacred bloodlines, to bring peace to the *maka'ainana* (common folks) and the sacred *'aina* (land).

Having been exposed to European military weapons and tactics as a young man, Kamehameha succeeded in overpowering his cousins who ruled over the other three ancient kingdoms of the island chain. He was adept in the use of European weapons and was impressed with Western technology of the time. His willingness to shape his new dynasty substantially after the English monarchy even lead him to offer his new kingdom to King George as a protectorate state. The offer was politely ignored. He saw the political threat of European technological and military prowess, an insight he had gleaned twenty years earlier upon boarding Captain Cook's *Voyager*. Kamehameha's goal was to unite the islands under one sacred rule, to strengthen his ability to maintain the *ea* (life) of the land against what he saw as a growing foreign threat against his people's sacred way of life.

European explorers, on the other hand, were canvassing the vast Pacific Ocean with the objective of colonizing indigenous people and their lands, either by diplomacy or by military force when diplomacy failed. Their motive was shaped by the concept of mercantilism, a political-economic system based on exploiting indigenous people and their lands for the purpose of enriching and empowering the ruling families of Europe. Kamehameha sensed this external threat and fashioned his policies and governance to offset these forces by establishing international diplomacy with European powers and allowing for trade, commerce, exchange of ideas, and limited foreign citizenship.[23] He brought into his council of advisors foreigners as well as ruling chiefs.

His rule was peaceful, but he encouraged trade and commerce with the outside world, from which came goods and products that amazed chiefs and natives. Silk and cotton, metal tools, and ornate furniture appealed greatly to the chiefs, who desired more and more. Radical ideas and foreign behavior patterns began to appear as well. These ideas filled natives with anxiety, for foreigners often broke kapu but did not bring down the anger of the gods.

Their blatant ways were observed to conflict and contrast with traditional native beliefs. This was especially noticed by women of high rank, who by custom feared the wrath of the gods if they ate publicly with their male peers, yet nothing happened when they ate with foreigners. The *'aikapu* (sacred eating) symbolized the divine nature of the ruling class. To break it meant death even to a chiefly woman. But after his death Kamehameha's two wives, Ka'ahumanu and Keopuolani, would take on a powerful role in overturning this ancient symbol of rule by divine ali'i.

It is ironic that at about the same time Adam Smith would introduce a radical new political-economic theory, one that would be adopted by the new republic of the United States. Smith's theory would become the economic bedrock for the American economy and body politic. Under this model, growth and the creation of wealth would be achieved through private property ownership and a greatly reduced role of government (having rejected King George). Church and government would be separated, and ordinary people would choose their leaders.

Thus the seeds of an inherent clash in spirituality, beliefs, traditions, and governance would divide natives and foreigners in the years to come and would prove to be an inevitable catastrophe for the native people.

Ho'opau: Self-Destruction

If Kamehameha had designs of fashioning a new kingdom based on native spiritual traditions and British monarchical governance, he did not envision his powerful co-ruler to lead the charge in the opposite direction with respect to divine rule. No more than a year after his death, his widow Ka'ahumanu forced his young son and heir Kamehameha II to denounce the eating kapu between men and women and to decree the end of traditional spirituality, ordering the destruction of all sacred sites, hei'au, and kahuna castes.[24] She directly defied tradition by ordering the cremation of the iwi, the ancestral bones of sacred chiefs—the abandonment of a thousand-year-old belief structure deeply interwoven with the concept of divine sovereignty and piety to one's ancestors. This effort did not go forward without strong opposition and rebellion. In the battle of Kuamo'o, all organized resistance came to an end with the defeat of the king's brother.[25] Years later, she would convert to Christianity (strict Calvinist) and order her people to do the same. Hence, from this time on, na kanaka would no longer view their rulers as demigods, divine representatives of ancestral gods, caretakers of sacred Papa and Haloa. Natives would no longer worship their 'aumakua, spirits (sacred *kupuna*), or ask for daily guidance. Their pious nature sought desperately for a god in this imposed vacuum. Arriving a year later in 1820, American Calvinists would fill this vacuum for the next fifty years and, at the same time, introduce a new concept of divine sovereignty to natives and their rulers, one not based on stewardship of the 'aina and worshiping Papa and Wakea. The new spirituality would be centered around Christianity.

Ha'ole Mo'i: Foreign Monarchs

Native rulers could understand the nature of European monarchies. There were many similarities in governance, social structure, ceremony, rituals, customs, and traditions. European divine right to rule was beatified by popes and bishops, who used familiar royal liturgies. Native rulers were born divine and held absolute powers over their people. However, the concept of commoners participating in government was a radical idea introduced by the British parliamentary system of two houses: the House of Nobles and the House of Commoners, with the *mo'i* (king) as the final arbiter of government. Thus when Kamehameha III introduced a constitutional monarchy form of government, he was willing to share his absolute sovereign powers with chiefs and commoners alike to demonstrate to the European powers that his kingdom was a civilized nation.[26] This act further weakened the ruling chief's image as a divine ruler, for it demonstrated that a king could trust commoners to be good caretakers of the land too.

But this evolving governance was necessary if the vision of Kamehameha I was to be realized: that external political threats could be offset by imitating the powerful countries of the time. This approach worked for most of the nineteenth century. By 1839, the ruling dynasty would face its first test of independence. In a dispute over the introduction of Catholicism to Hawai'i, the French king Louis Philippe sent the warship *Artemise* to force Kamehameha III to allow French priests to proselytize, along with the Calvinists.[27] Louis Philippe acknowledged the sovereignty of the Hawaiian king, a royal peer, and did not go any further than this demand. However, the impact on the mo'i was to marginalize further his divine role as sovereign ruler over his people, for now even a foreign king could impose divinity over the native people.

The second test would come shortly afterward in 1843. In this episode, again Kamehameha III's divine right to rule would be challenged, this time by wayward British subjects seeking to annex the islands to the British throne, only to be returned to native rule by order of Queen Victoria, who recognized the sovereignty of the Hawaiian Kingdom since her father's time.[28] In both episodes, monarchs recognized the legitimacy of other royal families out of need to preserve the old order against the growing populist movement toward republicanism.

But even constitutional monarchy would prove fatal by the end of the nineteenth century with the emergence of a strong American community in the islands. They would directly conspire to end a thousand-year history of divine caretakers of the land. These descendants of earlier Christian missionaries would deride native spirituality and betray native trust and *aloha*.

Amelika: The Final Divide

By late 1800s America (Amelika) had become a vast industrial powerhouse, outproducing the combined output of all Europe. It was becoming apparent to business and government leaders that America's industrial abundance could not be totally absorbed by its own domestic market. By 1898 the United States experienced its first industrial revolution recession, a crisis in overproduction—more supply than demand. Congress responded to this crisis by calling for greater overseas trade expansion and protection of its own industries from foreign competition. This was to be done by diplomacy and military force—a policy that would launch America into colonial imperialism and lead her to Hawai'i. Americans would introduce another form of sovereignty based on laissez-faire and a form of government composed of ordinary citizens whose right to vote depended upon proof of land ownership. American republicanism and its religious and economic institutions would alter the concept of sovereignty, divine caretakers of the 'aina, for the next hundred years. The clash in worldviews would be traumatic for natives and would endure to this day. But for many natives of this generation, the spiritual connection to land and sea and the instinct to protect it remains strong and ingrained in their psychic nature; it is part of their ancestral blood (*mana*).

Most na kanaka know the history of the American-led coup d'état of 1893 and the unlawful annexation of Hawai'i to the United States. This conspiracy is well documented.[29] But today as natives examine what sovereignty and self-determination mean within the context of a relationship with America, more questions are being raised in terms of compatibility with traditional values and beliefs and the role of ancestral spirituality.

Pehea I Ka 'Aina: What Is This Land?

History offers many examples of divine rule. Some exist today that are benevolent, and others are harsh. Genealogy alone cannot always produce benign and gifted rulers. Our own history demonstrates the carnage of the four kingdoms of late eighteenth-century rule. But it also includes the inspiring rule of the nineteenth-century monarchies, with our last queen exemplifying the best of native rule: as caretaker of the land and its people. All natives living today can trace their genealogy to some chiefly bloodline. And so they hold the *kuleana* (responsibility) to *malama* (care for) the 'aina. Natives want an assurance that good governance can prevail, that some form of sovereignty can guarantee the continued nurturing of the land and its people.

After more than one hundred years of representative democracy, na kanaka have become accustomed to the notion of ordinary citizens having a voice in governance, a voice in selecting their leaders. This right was given by Mo'i Kauikeaouli and advanced by America. This heritage will be America's contribution to na kanaka. Some form of democracy will prevail. However, natives will choose leaders who demonstrate traditional spiritual values with respect to the land, the 'aina. Strong leadership toward *malama 'aina* (caring for the land) and *aloha 'aina* (love for the land), will be a popular criterion for leadership. Whatever form a reestablished government takes, it will likely be made up of leaders who embody these traditional beliefs and who are trusted by the native citizenry to protect the iwi (often used to symbolize the land) of their ancestors.

How much a new government and native citizenry choose to reach back into the past to incorporate the values and beliefs of their ancestors time will tell, but a strong effort will be made that combines today's modern science and technology with the best of native traditional values and spiritual beliefs. This is the legacy of Kamehameha Ekahi (the first) and Mo'i Kalakaua. Native sovereignty would be possible only if the 'aina were returned to the native people, for the 'aina is at the heart and soul of native sovereignty.

Economics: Together or Separately

Hawai'i today is a modern state with a modern infrastructure and connected to the global economy. Only a fifth of its population is kanaka maoli. Yet its native people suffer from health problems, high unemployment, low household incomes, and many other social challenges. They are a community without unity and consistency. Cultural assimilation and a hundred years of suppressed identity have contributed to this malaise. Their once brilliant culture is largely reduced to remnants now on display in the Bishop Museum as curios to visitors as well as natives. Fortunately, *na halau* (native hula schools) have saved a wealth of ancient secrets hidden in dance and song. Disease, loss of self-determination, and the trauma of political and cultural diffusion have vitiated the will of most natives. The relative swiftness with which these events occurred has left five generations bewildered and culturally adrift. But most of all, the loss of land and of the ability to practice their traditional beliefs as caretakers of the land has been a powerful blow to the psychic and spiritual well-being of natives.

The challenge for a new nation will be to define sovereignty in terms of traditional land values and spirituality—to bring back a vibrant native society. Its meaning must come from the *na'au* (gut) as well as the intellect. Does a new nation return to a policy where land and resources are owned for the common good? Ancestral rulers governed with the mandate of family gods to malama the 'aina for the good of all. The land and sea were protected and preserved, yet the system was skillfully organized to provide sustenance for all, with everyone contributing to maintain this order. The spirits of primeval forests, the purity of mountain waters, the life-giving powers of the ocean, the healing powers of native flora, and the ancestral voices of native fauna were all part of native sovereignty. Should not these resources be protected, given *pu'uhonua*? These resources should be protected for all generations to come. These were the practices and beliefs that formed the foundations for a healthy and vibrant native society that prevailed for over a thousand years.

Will the new leaders embrace the political economy of America and a market economy based on global trade? What role does private property ownership play in a new native nation? Can there be a better way to create capital in this modern economy through community intercourse instead of private initiatives? Is the *mana* of kanaka maoli different from that of *haole po'e* (non-natives)? Are natives motivated by communal or individualistic interest? Can the new *kapu* (capitalism) allow for both in order to be a part of the twenty-first-century global economy? Native history is full of innovation and adaptation. Kanaka maoli will find a productive base that embraces its spiritual traditions, yet will find mechanisms for holding onto the past with new tools, unique to its history and culture.

Are there limits of physical growth on an island state? How does a growing population and its economic principles work with limited land? How do they accommodate growth without imperiling the limited resources and capacity of an island state? Modern Hawai'i cannot sustain itself with unlimited population growth. Nor can it sustain a globalized economy with unlimited expansion. Hawai'i does not have the land mass for large-scale productivity, nor can it compete against cheaper labor beyond its shores. Its beautiful beaches cannot forever remain attractive under the assault of millions of tourists. As long as America needs Hawai'i for its forward defense operations to protect its economic interests in the Pacific basin, Hawai'i will continue to receive federal dollars and resources, and it will benefit from technological and intellectual advancements. But how much do na kanaka maoli sacrifice to maintain this relationship? How much of an American way of life do na kanaka maoli give up in order to keep their traditions?

Native ancestors were successful farmers and fishermen whose daily life flowed with the rhythm of nature and stayed within its resources and boundaries. Taking from the 'aina was followed by giving back. The new nation will find a model that provides for growth while embracing sustainability and replenishment. The Kumulipo, the ancient creation chant, describes the world as a constant evolution of life forms adapting since the beginning of time. It expresses the intimate connection between life and the 'aina. The 'aina should not be abused; it should not be exploited by individual interests at the expense of the common good. As global warming causes sea level to rise, how will resources be efficiently managed to meet the challenge? The new sovereign economy should be attuned to nature and to Papa and Wakea.

Will the new leaders embrace traditional values to preserve and nurture the 'aina on behalf of the people for generations to come? Will they protect the iwi of the ancestors? Will they deserve the mandate of Kualoa, the sacred land? Or is it too late? Is the chasm unbridgeable between the present and the past? Are native people ready to *kuleana* (take responsibility) for the Kualoa that America now holds?

The new sovereignty must find a form of governance that embraces the traditional role as sacred caretakers (*malama 'aina*) of the land and that satisfies the ancient mandate: assuring the people of the sustenance and productivity promised by ancestral gods. In defeating High Priest Kekuaokalani at the battle of Kuamo'o, *na kaula* (traditional seers) foresaw the great suffering that would befall the ali'i and natives for the next four generations.[30] It is said that this *'ana'ana* (curse) will end in this current generation. If this is so, na kanaka maoli will be given a second chance to define sovereignty with the blessings of the *'aumakua* (family spirits). They must place the life of the land, *ea*, at the core of a native definition.

Notes

1. Mary K. Pukui and Samuel H. Ebert, *Hawaiian Dictionary* (Honolulu: University of Hawai'i Press, 1957), 34.

2. Martha W. Beckwith, *The Kumulipo* (Chicago: University of Chicago Press, 1951), 7.

3. Marjorie Sinclair, *Nahi'ena'ena, Sacred Daughter of Hawai'i* (Honolulu: Mutual Publishing Press, 1995), 146.

4. Sinclair, *Nahi'ena'ena*, 141.

5. Lilikala Kame'eleihiwa, *Native Land and Foreign Desires* (Honolulu: Bishop Museum Press, 1992), 33.

6. David Malo, *Hawaiian Antiquities* (Honolulu: Bishop Museum Press, 1951), 52.

7. June Gutmanis, *Na Pule Kahiko* (Honolulu: Editions Limited Press, 1983), 3; Beckwith, *The Kumulipo*, 160.

8. Malo, *Hawaiian Antiquities*, 244.

9. Malo, *Hawaiian Antiquities*, 206.

10. Malo, *Hawaiian Antiquities*, 63.

11. Samual M. Kamakau, *Ruling Chiefs* (Honolulu: Kamehameha Schools–Bishop Estate Press, 1964), 19.

12. Beckwith, *The Kumulipo*, 7.

13. Malo, *Hawaiian Antiquities*, 105.

14. "Ancestor's Remains Laid to Rest," *Honolulu Advertiser*, January 14, 2002, Sec. A, p. 2.

15. Kame'eleihiwa, *Native Land and Foreign Desires*, 341.

16. Malo, *Hawaiian Antiquities*, 53.

17. Malo, *Hawaiian Antiquities*, 6.

18. Kamakau, *Ruling Chiefs*, 129.

19. Kamakau, *Ruling Chiefs*, 312.

20. Beckwith, *The Kumulipo*, 55.

21. Kamakau, *Ruling Chiefs*, 79.

22. Gaven Daws, *Shoal of Time* (Honolulu: University of Hawai'i Press, 1974), 45.

23. John Papa Ii, *Fragments of Hawaiian History* (Honolulu: Bishop Museum Press, 1959), 106.

24. Kamakau, *Ruling Chiefs*, 222.

25. His Hawaiian Majesty David Kalakaua, *The Legends and Myths of Hawai'i* (Honolulu: Mutual Publishing Press, 1990), 446.

26. Daws, *Shoal of Times*, 107.

27. Kamakau, *Ruling Chiefs*, 331.

28. Kamakau, *Ruling Chiefs*, 366.

29. Michael Dougherty, *To Steal a Kingdom* (Honolulu: Island Style Press, 1992), 165.

30. *Mo'olelo*, an oral history, handed down by *kupuna*, native elders, from the South Kona District of the Big Island of Hawai'i.

Michael P. Perez (Chamorro)

Chamorro Resistance and Prospects for Sovereignty in Guam

Being Chamorro yet born and raised in Southern California, I have had questions raised about my identity throughout my life. Our notions of Chamorroness were often manifested in Chamorro household decorations and wood carvings from Guam (often made elsewhere), and the planting of boonie peppers and banana trees in our yard.[1] I vividly remember a painting that was a gift to my father from a Chamorro artist; a painting he displayed with pride in our home. The painting was of a Spanish bridge in Agat, Guam, with a panoramic hilly landscape in the background.

During this period in a suburban public school in Los Angeles County, my fifth grade teacher assigned an art project in celebration of the U.S. melting pot. We were required to paint a picture of ourselves to symbolize our cultural heritage. I recall my classmates painting images of themselves as London soldiers, leprechauns, and mariachis. Others drew themselves wearing ethnic dress like kimonos and shawls. Most students had some notion of cultural identity that made sense within U.S. culture. I remember feeling ambivalent. I was not sure what to paint. But the image of the Chamorro artist's painting came to mind. So I replicated the painting and positioned myself in the background as a distant stick figure flying a kite on that hilly landscape. I painted with pride because the image in the painting gave me a sense of who I was in relation to a historical landmark in Guam, our family homeland. At the time, I was unsure why I chose to put the land at the center of the image and place myself in the background. In retrospect, perhaps it was because my notion of self was tied to a land base about which my father often told stories with pride, and a *place* to which we returned throughout my life.

In contrast, all my classmates painted images of themselves in which they were at the center, surrounded by cultural symbols in the background. I was the only one who deviated. As I turned in my assignment, my teacher reacted in a hostile manner, scolding me in the presence of the entire class, "What is this! . . . Where are you in the painting? . . . This is wrong!" With my head bowed down, I was embarrassed, ashamed, confused, and silenced out; not just because I had initially felt good about my work of art but because a schoolwide parade through the classrooms to view the displayed paintings was to follow. But Mrs. Reeves was *right*. She was the *authority* figure. Her words were *legitimate*. She determined the parameters of the project. Or was I right since I derived my image from my self, my family, my homeland, my heart?

Issues of sovereignty are entangled in a complex web of legitimacy, not unlike my grade school experience. Sovereignty is politically constructed and relative. Whether my fifth grade painting was right or wrong depends on where one is standing. But it may also depend on where one is ordered to stand.

With the passing years I now recognize my multiple levels of marginality as a Chamorro born and raised in the United States who remains professionally and personally tied to life on Guam.[2] At one level I find myself at the edge of political and cultural life on Guam as an insider without, observing my people from my remote academic position in Southern California. On another level the mainland is a place where Pacific Islanders tend to be socially invisible as native islanders, yet socially visible as homogenized U.S. minorities assumed to fit under umbrella categories such as Hispanic and Asian Pacific. As with our ancient ancestors who navigated vast stretches of ocean to and from our islands to return and re-return with more seafaring knowledge, what provides insights is precisely my personal and academic marginality and transnationality as a diasporic Chamorro at the edges of life on Guam, U.S. minority relations, and academia. This standpoint as an insider without and an outsider within serves as a lens of analysis.

As this anthology attests, sovereignty struggles and their inherent obscurity are manifested nowhere more vividly than within the experiences of indigenous people throughout the globe. In light of the "New World Order" entangled in neocolonial backlash, globalization, geopolitics, and transnationalism, contemporary prospects of resistance and sovereignty are located in an increasingly complex terrain. Guam and the Chamorros represent a critical juncture of prospective forms of sovereignty in an increasingly messy neocolonial and territorial arena. Being among the first Pacific territories to be colonized but with a native population who have yet to exercise their right of self-determination, Guam has been bombarded with successive waves of colonization by the Spanish, Japanese, and the United States. Chamorros of Guam have displayed ongoing forms of resistance, and issues of Chamorro sovereignty and political status continue to be challenged.

However, in light of the colonial paradox embedded in Guam's history, we find ourselves at a crossroads, having been absorbed into a contradictory U.S. discourse of plenary power, constitutionality, and rights that has long promoted equality on the basis of inequality. Therefore sovereignty issues are especially complex and ambiguous in colonies like Guam. In this essay, I explore Chamorro political resistance in the larger context of indigenous sovereignty. In so doing, as a Chamorro scholar I discuss manifestations of sovereignty in the evolution of Chamorro resistance and prospects for sovereignty in Guam.

Contesting Sovereignty in a Postcolonial Context

To examine Chamorro resistance and sovereignty, I find it necessary to describe some theoretical context in which issues of identity politics and sovereignty are debated, trajectories in which indigenous people have positioned their academic and political voices. With the proliferation of multidisciplinary postmodernist, cultural, postcolonialist, and indigenous canons, identity and sovereignty are reconceptualized with renewed vitality. Whether one rejects or subscribes to these "alternative perspectives," analyses of identity politics and sovereignty seem insufficient without consideration of them. I proceed with an affirmative view of postmodernism and postcoloniality in order to outline the theoretical, political, and cultural contours of the current landscape in which identity politics and sovereignty are entangled.

Postmodernist as well as postcolonial conceptions of identity and sovereignty contrast sharply with static modernist notions. Modernist perspectives tend to fall into traps of colonial discourse by conceptualizing identity and sovereignty as fixed entities epiphenomenally determined by dominant epistemologies, ideologies, and institutions. Rather, identities are fragmented, fragile, and unstable as a consequence of decline of some unitary self, largely resulting from challenges to and crises in modernism.[3] Similarly, notions of sovereignty need not be constrained within the binary parameters of the nation-state. As John Hoffman states, "postmodernists focus in particular upon what they call 'logocentrism'—the presentation of conceptual categories in an exclusionary and divisive way so that one 'side' is right, the other must be wrong. No space is allowed for compromise, ambiguity or toleration . . . logocentrism as a theoretical expression of modernity fits the practice of the state like a glove. For states only exist because the claim they make to exercise a monopoly of legitimate force is contested."[4]

Likewise, there need not be a hierarchy of knowledges and sovereign authority with a fixed center, hence opening a legitimate window for the articulation of indigenous voices. In other words, the legitimacy of identity and sovereignty can emanate from their authenticity, multiplicity, and fluidity, rather than their legitimacy as politically constructed by those who wield legitimate authority. Therefore counterhegemonic prospects of indigenous sovereignty and voice are conceivable.

However, deconstructing colonial legitimacy is easier said than done, for the romantic ideals of U.S. sovereignty rooted in constitutional discourse that has long promoted equality on the basis of inequality are rather seductive, while cloaking the inherent contradictions rooted in the evolution of "sovereignty." But deconstructing and transcending U.S. sovereignty is precisely what needs to be done if meaningful space is to be carved by and for indigenous peoples. As Hoffman further suggests, this is an important point because if the sovereign state is identified solely with "modernity, then it follows that states in the premodern past were not sovereign, and there might be states in a postmodern future which are not sovereign. The need to look beyond the state itself is called into question."[5]

Indeed Guam, "Where America's Day Begins," is located in a perplexed political position. As a U.S. territory, Guam has a political status that remains ambiguous, while Chamorro sovereignty persists as a contentious issue. Chamorro resistance manifests itself in a variety of ways ranging from political reform to Chamorro nationalism. However, discourse surrounding Chamorro sovereignty seems to fall into the traps of static conceptions of modernity. For instance, Chamorro self-determination continues to be attacked on constitutional grounds, while claims to U.S. economic and political benefits are often challenged precisely because Guam is a U.S. territory not a state. Even more contentious is what I call the "you can't have your cake and eat it too" hypothesis, as Chamorros in Guam have been asked by non-Chamorros: "What do you want—this or that?" Therefore it is necessary to transcend these constraining binarisms so that shifting notions of identity and alternative forms of sovereignty can be fathomed and actualized. As Ronald Stade suggests:

> What future for sovereignty then? As I see it, any call for clear-cut, unambiguous concepts and identities implies regulatory measures. Rather than being a way out of the paradox of liberatory regulation, the very idea and reality of sovereignty contains this paradox. When writers like Joseph Fallon demand the exclusion of the territories from the union he fails to hear the voices in Guam and other U.S. possessions that do not want to be excluded. If asked on what side of the fence they want to be they just might answer, "both." Considering that sovereignty is ambiguous, paradoxical, and diffused anyway,

> what would be wrong with adapting one's practice to this fact? What could be wrong with being both on the inside and on the outside of the union; of being Chamorro, Micronesian, Asian, and American at one and the same time; of being both a tourist destination and the host for (a few) military installations; of receiving both private and federal revenues; of being a part of both the Pacific Basin and the Pacific Rim; of combining Old and the New Pacific; of being both *tahdong* [deep, serious, profound] and *adilantao* [progressing, improving]?[6]

In this vein I take stock of Chamorro resistance based on the realization that sovereignty struggles take on a multiplicity of forms. Guam's residents are certainly not homogeneous culturally or politically. So it stands to reason that issues of identity and sovereignty are multidimensional and in flux. Micronesian scholar, Vicente M. Diaz states:

> This twentieth-century cultural crisis makes it even more important to rethink the reigning ideas of culture, politics, and history in places such as Guam. In spite of (or precisely because of) nearly four hundred years of ongoing colonial domination, scholars must scrutinize the historical processes by which the natives have learned to work within and against the grain of such outsider attempts to colonize the Chamorro. We might look at ways that the Chamorro have "localized" nonlocal ideas and practices, how they have sought to convert the dangerous into the pleasurable, the foreign into the local, the tragic into the comic. . . . We might look at ways in which the Chamorros have built a kind of central political organization of resistance around, paradoxically, a polyglottal language and ambivalent discourses of Chamorro culture.[7]

Pursuant to Diaz's suggestion, I explore the prospects for indigenous sovereignty in Guam, as rooted in Chamorro resistance to U.S. Empire.

The Historical Context of Chamorro Sovereignty

Despite the effects of colonialism in the Mariana Islands, Chamorro resistance marks the colonial history of Guam. After European contact Guam was a colony of Spain until 1898. Since the close of the Spanish-American War in 1898, Guam and the Chamorros have been subjugated to U.S. rule. As a foundation of contemporary sovereignty struggles, Chamorros have always resisted colonization. Specifically under U.S. rule, Chamorros localized U.S. politics toward the promotion of Chamorro interests within the U.S. political structure, which Stade refers to as "cacique nationalism."[8] This emergent strategy of political struggle involved the construction of political voice to contest violations of indigenous and civil rights within U.S. colonialist politics. Perhaps most significant to future Chamorro sovereignty was the Chamorro quest for civilian government and U.S. citizenship, which rages on in the present.[9]

By the 1940s most Chamorros converged in their interest in becoming U.S. citizens. Efforts to pressure Washington to grant U.S. citizenship and civil liberties persisted into the late 1940s, despite a long series of denials of citizenship by the U.S. government.[10] With the emergence of new world politics after World War II, the legitimacy of self-determination and indigenous sovereignty was articulated with the creation of the UN Trusteeship Council.[11] In the late 1940s the establishment of the Guam Congress set the tone that later enabled Chamorros to pass laws locally, when the Guam Congress was replaced by the Guam Legislature in 1951. Years of festering animosity by Chamorros toward the colonial practices of the U.S. military ignited in a heated confrontation between the Guam Congress and Governor Charles A. Pownall in 1949, culminating in the removal of naval government from Guam.[12] President Harry S. Truman formally transferred administrative control of Guam from the navy to the Department of the Interior and appointed the first civilian governor of Guam—Carlton S. Skinner. Civilian election of the governor eventually replaced executive appointment, further empowering the people of Guam.

Following years of enduring political resistance, the Chamorro drive for U.S. citizenship and to limit military control was codified with the Organic Act of Guam in 1950. Chamorros achieved a political voice in the context of U.S. sovereignty through the Organic Act, which was perceived as a steppingstone toward indigenous sovereignty claims, self-rule, and decolonization. For Chamorros the Organic Act established U.S. citizenship, balance of power, and a Bill of Rights.

In hindsight the Organic Act led to token instances of political voice for Chamorros, as sovereignty was constructed under the U.S. political framework, rooted in European discourses.[13] Following World War II the Chamorro population split between patriotic Chamorros who supported the United States (largely as a result of the Liberation of Guam from the Japanese by the U.S. military) and a minority of Chamorro rights advocates who remained discontented in spite of the American recapture of Guam. This undercurrent of resistance laid the foundation for a new, more radical wave of Chamorro nationalism that surfaced in the 1970s. Therefore, in spite of the token "victories" of the Organic Act, and although this was perhaps unintended on the part of the U.S. government, the act provided a legitimate platform for indigenous sovereignty (in conjunction with the UN Trusteeship Council and later the UN declaration of human rights) that has been located by Chamorro activists and leaders.

U.S. Sovereignty and Political Reform

Consistent with Stade's notion of cacique nationalism, the initial wave of political contestation spins off from the series of events culminating in the signing of the Organic Act, which congressionally established U.S. citizenship for residents of Guam. These political reform efforts primarily through legislative channels are forms of sovereignty struggle yet within the framework of U.S. political discourse. As noted, these reformist strategies of Chamorro resistance provided a legitimate trajectory for indigenous sovereignty. Upon critical examination, working within the U.S. institutional and ideological frameworks to promote Chamorro interests might be interpreted as a mode for indigenous people to respond adaptively to their colonial situation by appropriating the colonizer's system in ways conducive to their indigeneity. Indeed it was the Organic Act that marked a small yet significant window of opportunity in which Chamorro sovereignty claims would later be articulated.

Following the replacement of military-appointed naval governors with U.S.-appointed civilian governors, the Guam legislature further pressured Washington to establish local election of governors in the early 1960s to increase the local voice. Initiated with the election of Carlos Camacho, the Guam Elective Governor Act was passed in 1968 by Congress, which amended the Organic Act and enabled the people of Guam to elect their governors beginning in 1970. This sparked local control of the executive branch and subsequent alterations of the Organic Act.

Utilizing this newly acquired electoral control of the executive branch, Chamorro rights were politicized, especially during the tenure of Governor Ricardo ("Ricky") Bordallo in the mid-1970s and early 1980s.[14] These political developments of achieving executive and legislative control provided a platform for Chamorro claims to indigenous rights and self-determination.

Indigenous Sovereignty and the Chamorro Movement

In contrast to liberal reformist efforts, alternative strategies to promote indigenous sovereignty emerged with the evolution of indigenous organizations in the 1970s. In contrast to earlier reformist cacique strategies promoted by Guam's elite, the more progressive post–Organic Act movements were multidimensional and involved the intelligentsia and Chamorros of lower socioeconomic status. Since the 1970s Chamorros have been instrumental in staking claim to indigenous sovereignty by taking the United States to task on its own constitutional principles. As Chamorros were faced with new forms of neocolonialism, multiple strategies of resistance toward sovereignty became necessary. In other words, U.S. neocolonialist discourse has effectively advocated romanticized ideals of democracy and human rights while justifying the violation of those very principles, which in turn has distorted the reality of U.S. neocolonialism. As former Chamorro activist scholar Robert A. Underwood states:

> These contradictions are conveniently dealt with in a variety of ways that separate the real issues from the artificial ones. The fake issues are then combined within the unique framework of a consciousness that enables them to ignore the duplicity inherent in their views, their prescriptions for society, and their operations in society. . . . They accept society's prescriptions for life without recognizing them to be false, dehumanizing, or alienating. If the contradictions are at first apparent, a generalized consciousness will inevitably overcome these pangs of uneasiness and thus they will be able to be bought, and sold, as reality in operation.[15]

However, such realities have been exposed by what Underwood refers to as the "maladjusted" (progressive Chamorro nationalists) who are positioned at critical historical junctures of resistance:

> But still the maladjusted continue to argue, to point out, to offer non-cooperation, and to reject the artificial friendship of those who are liberal enough to recognize that there has been injustice. The hidden strength of the people lies with the maladjusted. They have been unable to fend off powerful forces and once they are strong enough to demonstrate not that choices are ours to make, but that others have no right to put boundaries on our choices, the Chamorro people will again be free. Thank God for the maladjusted.[16]

The 1970s elections set the tone for contemporary Chamorro nationalism and indigenous sovereignty, when Chamorro rights became a central campaign issue. In turn the "first island-wide grassroots political organization throughout the villages" was established in the early 1970s.[17] In addition environmental organizations were created in reaction to ongoing attempts by the U.S. government to seize land for military purposes. Chamorro rights activism escalated in reaction to military land acquisition. For instance, the Guam Landowners Association (GLA), was one of the island's first "vernacular" nationalist organizations.[18] In the midst of this increasing tide of Chamorro rights advocacy, the Twelfth Guam Legislature passed the Chamorro Land Trust Act in 1974, which enabled the lease of GovGuam (Government of Guam) land to landless Chamorros.[19] However, this act was not implemented for eighteen years due to the questioning of the bloodlines of the Chamorro people by the U.S. government, similar to blood quantum identity politics in Hawai'i.[20]

Ironically, with their contact with the Europeans, Chamorros were racialized as an inferior race and culture, first with the classification of Chamorros as *indios* by the Spanish and later by U.S. racial politics (i.e., antimiscegenation policies, policies prohibiting local practices such as cohabitation and whistling in public, and the racial undertones of designating Guam as an "unincorporated" territory). Yet in recent decades, as Chamorros advance notions of "indigenous" and "native" to justify their existence, authenticity, and indigenous sovereignty, U.S. racial projects have questioned the "purity" of the "Chamorro race," as with the Miwok in what is now central California.

Nonetheless Chamorro political organizations emerged as major vehicles of indigenous sovereignty. Thus politics and culture became intertwined in Chamorro sovereignty, characteristic of indigenous grassroots movements in general. For instance, in the 1970s a number of Chamorro organizations were created to legitimize native interests and to expose the genocidal consequences of neocolonialism. Among the most active early indigenous Chamorro organizations to emerge was Para' Pada Y Chamorros—"Stop slapping Chamorros."[21]

In 1981 a nationalist organization was formed—the Organization of People for Indigenous Rights (OPI-R).[22] Based on the articulation of indigenous sovereignty within the discourses of the United Nations, the U.S. constitution, and U.S. territorial relations, OPI-R's key exemplars represent the intelligentsia of the Chamorro Movement. As an influential source of consciousness, the OPI-R has played a significant role in protecting Chamorro rights, promoting political and educational campaigns, and advocating Chamorro self-determination. For instance, OPI-R has been instrumental in facilitating the discourse on the "Chamorro inalienable right of self-determination."[23] The OPI-R has "represented Chamorro aspirations and indigenous views in numerous forums including the United Nations Committee Hearings on Decolonization and Non Self-governing Territories."[24] The OPI-R has also contributed to the political articulation of "indigenous Chamorros" despite racial purist backlash. Furthermore, OPI-R members have been key players in protesting indigenous rights violations, such as the destruction of ancient burial grounds by capitalist investors.

In the 1990s another grassroots organization emerged—the Chamoru Nation, which was formed on the basis of establishing a nation to promote the self-sufficiency of Chamorros as an indigenous people. Seven fundamental elements of indigenous people in need of nurturing are identified—language, culture, spiritual matters, water, air, land, and respect—indigenous elements that are threatened by lack of self-determination, by westernization, and by rapid rates of in-migration. The Chamoru Nation further legitimized indigenous sovereignty and participated in numerous protests. However, in contrast to OPI-R, the Chamoru Nation was established by a group of underprivileged Chamorros (*Manakpapa'*) and became the progressive indigenous organization of the early 1990s. As Stade observes: "Since the beginning of the 1990s, OPI-R has lost its position as the most vocal and visible group of political activists on the island. The organization that took over the OPI-R's position was the *Nacion Chamoru* ('Chamorro Nation'). This is the first 'all-vernacular' nationalist group in Guam. It began as a loosely organized association of non-privileged men and women."[25]

Other indigenous organizations, ethnic associations, and cultural foundations have likewise surfaced in recent years. Through such political contestation, the historical issue of Chamorro identity and sovereignty has been articulated in the contemporary context with the ongoing expression of indigenous Chamorro rights.

Indigenous Land Rights

As Chamorro resistance progressed through subsequent waves of identity politics, subsequent projects of Chamorro sovereignty have confronted physical and cultural genocide, citizenship dilemmas, exclusionary electoral politics, and land acquisition. In light of Guam's political (under)development, indigenous rights issues emerged as the centerpiece of contemporary sovereignty struggles for Chamorros. Since indigenous rights claims exist within a turbulent contest for legitimacy, Chamorro rights advocacy continues to confront the task of establishing legitimacy within the U.S. framework.

At the heart of broader Fourth World sovereignty issues surrounding self-determination and human rights, the struggle for land rights remains central among all segments of the Chamorro population.[26] The value of land to contemporary Chamorros is emphasized in the context of ancient Chamorro history, cultural continuity, and the ongoing centrality of land to Chamorro culture.

> Scientists have shown that Chamorros have lived here for more than 4,000 years, sharing a unique and social relationship with the land and sea. Chamorros are commonly referred to as *taotao tano'*, which literally means "people of the land"; it is also a way of indicating that a person is native to these islands. Land is the soul of our culture; it, together with the sea, gives life to the Chamorro. . . . , the value of land to today's Chamorro is nothing less than life-giving (Phillips, 1996, p.3). Therefore, the issue of land persists as an essential component to the survival of the Chamorro people especially in the face of persistent exploitation of land.[27]

According to Michael F. Phillips, "A culture can only survive in a homeland, and ours is seriously threatened."[28]

Political activities and landmark legal events surrounding Chamorro land rights have taken place in recent decades. For instance, in the 1980s and early 1990s, political activism centered on the desecration of ancient Chamorro burial grounds at the hands of capitalist developers.

As part of the effort to ensure self-determination and to provide land to landless Chamorros, the Chamorro Land Trust Act was passed in 1974, patterned after the Hawaiian Homes Commission Act of 1920.[29] The Chamorro Land Trust Act was designed to provide qualified applicants (landless Chamorros) "with the opportunity to lease, for $1 per year, up to one acre of government land for residential occupancy, 20 acres for farming, and 40 acres for grazing."[30] As noted previously, however, the act was not implemented until the 1990s. The unsettled issue of the Chamorro Land Trust Act initiated in 1974 was finally challenged in court in 1992 by the Chamoru Nation and activist Angel L. G. Santos (who later became a democratic senator of the 24th Guam Legislature and gubernatorial candidate in the 1998 elections). Angel Santos and the Chamoru Nation exerted pressure on then governor Joseph F. Ada to implement the act. The result was the ordering of the governor to appoint members to the Chamorro Land Trust Commission, implementation of the Chamorro Land Trust Act, and further articulation of "indigenous" Chamorro identity. The significance of such events lies in the actualization of legitimate space for sovereignty struggle within the legal system.

Indigenous Self-Determination and Political Status

Prompted by decolonization efforts among other U.S. colonies, new strategies emerged in Guam that recognized the need to transform the existing neocolonialist relationship between Guam and the United States. Resulting largely from the advocacy of Ricky Bordallo, there were initial thoughts of reunifying the Chamorros of the Marianas (Northern and Southern islands) by politically unifying Guam with the Northern Mariana Islands (formerly a trust territory), to become a new U.S. entity and then initiate negotiations with Washington toward decolonization. But rapprochement failed to become a reality; the political divergence of the Northern Marianas and Guam remained. Seeking U.S. affiliation, the Commonwealth of the Northern Mariana Islands (CNMI) was codified in 1975. The CNMI achieved U.S. citizenship while obtaining greater local control and financial support than Guam. In light of the seemingly more "successful" decolonization efforts of the Northern Marianas as well as Puerto Rico, Guam's leaders pondered strategies toward decolonization and self-determination such as commonwealth, statehood, independence, or further reform.[31] Despite division among Chamorros regarding the most feasible alternative to pursue toward decolonization, in the 1980s the people of Guam approved the Guam Commonwealth Act (later known as H.R. 100) via plebiscite vote, a step intended to increase the level of self-government while remaining under U.S. sovereignty.[32]

Chamorro activist and former senator of the Guam legislature Hope Alvarez Cristobal analyzes the ongoing Chamorro political status question and quest for self-determination.[33] She details the political and socio-legal history of Guam, first grounding the Chamorro inalienable right to self-determination within the contradictory paternalistic governance of the United States. In spite of the oppressive legacy of political subjugation, Chamorro self-determination and sovereignty are grounded in post–World War II international politics.

> Out of the ashes of World War II, the world was swept by new trends which recognized the sanctity of self-determination and which brought new meaning to the concepts of human rights. Although these ideas have not always prevailed, many of them are embodied in the United Nations Charter, one of the legacies of World War II. Both new nations and the old colonial powers recognized that dependent peoples should no longer be subjected to the whims of the nations which governed them. These new ideas gave birth to the Trusteeship system and the Declaration on Non Self-Governing Territories. Recognizing its responsibility on the matter, the U.S. voluntarily placed Guam on the list of non self-governing territories in 1946.[34]

But irony lies behind action on the part of the U.S. government to facilitate Chamorro self-determination, which is precisely why limited notions of sovereignty need to be transcended. Although it is legally codified, the

Chamorro right of self-determination exists merely in theory. Guam's political status remains obscure, while question marks continue to occupy the minds of Chamorro leaders. Furthermore, appeals to the United Nations regarding Guam's lack of local autonomy took place but to no avail, since Guam was already a strategically valuable U.S. possession. In the years that followed, Guam's status efforts have been an uphill struggle due to the lack of incentive on the part of the U.S. government to decolonize their possession.

In addition, claims to indigenous rights ignited other obstacles. As noted, indigenous Chamorro rights have been challenged by purist rhetoric regarding the blood existence of Chamorros and issues of exclusion of non-Chamorros. Pleas of unconstitutionality also surfaced in reaction to nationalist Chamorro claims, such as the OPI-R's position "that the concept of 'self-determination' belongs to the people who have a special historical relationship to a given area—the Chamorros; and the exclusive Chamorro right to vote in a self-determination plebiscite."[35]

Despite these challenges, indigenous Chamorro rights claims have emerged as a legitimate issue for the Chamorro and non-Chamorro public in Guam, local and federal politicians, the United Nations, and the Fourth World community. Chamorro sovereignty is a central theme of public discourse in Guam, across all social institutions and vehicles of mass media. Likewise, acknowledgment of Chamorro sovereignty is articulated within legal discourse. In reference to the U.S. first annual report to the United Nations in 1946, Cristobal notes that "on the basis of this initial report by the U.S. to the United Nations, it is obvious that the people of Guam being discussed for the purpose of fulfilling the obligation under Article 73 are, in fact, the Chamorro people. The term Guamanian, which was invented after World War II, was and is synonymous with the term Chamorro in this context."[36] Cristobal also underscores the political existence of Chamorros within the Organic Act, which acknowledged the idea of inherent indigenous sovereignty and rights by giving preference to Chamorros in government appointments and promotions.

Benjamin F. Cruz indicates that Chamorro voting rights are constitutionally legitimate and irrefutable based on U.S. constitutional history. He also grounds the legitimacy of Chamorro sovereignty within the "world culture" or "Fourth World" premise of international human rights: "Human Rights is more than an ideological or political concept. The concept of human rights is a concept of world order. It is a proposal for structuring the world so that every individual's human value is realized, every individual's human dignity protected. Human Rights is law. When a nation violates the human rights of a person or a people, it is violating international law."[37]

Ironically, the U.S. government maintains a contradictory ideology that self-righteously advocates human rights yet ignores the reality of its own violation of human rights across the globe. Cruz suggests that such claims often employ a limited conception of human rights by making exclusive reference to more recognized cases of human rights violation as demonized by U.S. discourse, such as "apartheid in South Africa, tyrannical dictatorships in Chile, El Salvador, Korea, Nicaragua, Haiti, and the Marcos regime in the Philippines, or communist invasions into Afghanistan."[38]

To the contrary, the violation of human rights goes beyond monolithic notions; hence the U.S. government has often failed in its "human rights advocacy," especially with respect to self-determination. As many political analysts contend, the recent "War on Terrorism" by the U.S. government is yet another distortion of U.S. human rights violations in the name of national security and the protection of human rights of others. The need to "cause the United States Government to place Human Rights as the primary cornerstone of our foreign policy" is highlighted.[39] Employing a comparative perspective, Cruz draws a parallel between the human rights violations visited upon Chamorros and other Pacific Islanders. He makes reference to the historical violation of the right to self-determination among people of the Federated States of Micronesia, the Marshall Islands, Belau, Bikini, and Enewitok. Specific rights that the U.S. government must be forced to contend with are brought to bear (i.e., return and compensation of surplus lands, signing of Pacific fishing treaties, implementation of compacts of new Pacific nations, and the basic human right of self-determination).

In light of the ongoing sovereignty question in Guam and token efforts to establish self-governance by the U.S. government, the status quest has raged on as manifested in a series of efforts toward self-determination. For instance, steps taken by the government of Guam to facilitate legal recognition of the right to self-determination include the establishment of the Political Status Commission, research on the status question, numerous proposals and resolutions, appropriation of funds, and elections aimed at establishing a cohesive vision of Guam's potential status.

Major strides have also been made at the grassroots level. Among these efforts are protests, monitoring of commission meetings, and education campaigns. These combined efforts have resulted in a number of consciousness-raising gains, such as reducing ambiguity regarding political status and self-determination.

Such efforts continue to face seemingly insurmountable conditions, since the process occurs within the larger U.S. political framework and will remain subject to it as long as Guam's ambivalent colonial status persists. "A fiduciary relationship exists between the dependent people and the administering authority. The dependent people of Guam need the cooperation of the U.S. to exercise their inalienable right to self-determination. It is unrealistic, and a violation of the obligations outlined under Article 73, to expect a dependent people to unilaterally engage in self-determination without the support of their administering power. Yet this is precisely the situation on Guam."[40]

In the midst of existing barriers, Cristobal outlines windows of opportunity at the grassroots level in accordance with OPI-R's vision. First, within the parameters of U.S. political and legal institutions, the significance of Chamorro rights and the political status process needs to emanate from treaty obligations and provisions—"by being a signator to the United Nations in accordance with U.S. Congressional plenary power over the territories as outlined in the U.S. Constitution."[41] Second, in light of the ambiguity and confusion resulting from the failure of the U.S. government to clarify the issues of political status and self-determination, educational campaigns must continue. Finally, in the face of the historical record and documentation of the Chamorros' sovereign right to self-determination, pressure needs to be exerted on the U.S. government to ensure "that all binding plebiscites and referenda relative to the question of Guam's ultimate political status must recognize that it is the Chamorro people who have not yet engaged in self-determination and it is only they who shall be allowed to participate."[42]

Cristobal further indicates that the OPI-R and commission members have been instrumental in the draft of the Guam Commonwealth Act. Commonwealth was proposed as an interim step in the direction of full self-determination while remaining under U.S. sovereignty. Outlining specific articles of the proposed Commonwealth Act, Joe T. San Agustin reveals its potential and significance to the future of Guam: "Overall, the proposed Commonwealth Act is a blue print of the desires of the people of Guam and a reflection of the level of political maturing the people have achieved despite decades of colonial rule. Each article implies a stirring consciousness toward the island's deserved autonomy and further definition of the island's place in the regional and global political map."[43]

However, Washington's reluctance and the resurgence of intra- and interethnic antagonism regarding political status have further obscured the issue. At the intragroup level, the Chamorro Movement has been splintering. For instance, there is a discourse of resistance concerning the insufficient representation of indigenous Chamorro rights within the Commonwealth proposal. At the intergroup level, many non-Chamorros oppose Chamorro nationalism for its exclusionary connotations. Moreover, migrants tend to oppose Commonwealth on the grounds that it would shut off immigration by politically locating Guam outside the United States. The constitutional legitimacy of the Commonwealth proposal has also been questioned on the basis of "mutual consent" and "local control over immigration."[44] Thus the Commonwealth quest as a major manifestation of sovereignty struggle in Guam has been difficult in light of these diverse perspectives and interests.

On October 29, 1997, the Guam Commonwealth Act finally obtained a long-awaited congressional hearing—only the second hearing on the act within a ten-year span. After pleas and testimonies from numerous Chamorro leaders and advocates, Deputy Secretary of Interior John Garamendi, President Clinton's representative for Guam Commonwealth negotiations, indicated that the administration was not willing to agree to the three core areas of the act—mutual consent, immigration control, and Chamorro self-determination. Therefore, as then congressman Robert Underwood noted: "The most significant outcome of the hearing was the clarification of the executive branch's official position on the draft Act." The future of Guam's political status quest therefore remains uncertain. Some of Guam's leaders discussed several options in a number of posthearing public forums. As Underwood asked: "Where do we go from here? It is clear that the people of Guam must decide whether or not to negotiate with the Congress . . . determine whether the spirit to continue is still there, and decide whether we have the will and the energy to negotiate. Negotiations should continue with both Congress and the Administration, but a time-line should be set."[45]

In light of sovereignty struggles in places like the Commonwealth of the Northern Marianas and Puerto Rico, sovereignty in Guam is currently at a critical crossroads. Likewise new waves of nationalist sentiment toward independence exist among Chamorro activists who oppose Commonwealth. More recently there has been discussion of a "Chamorro-only" plebiscite vote to determine future directions in the status effort, such as independence, statehood, or free association, and whether Chamorros in the United States should be allowed to vote.

Concluding Remarks: Prospects for Sovereignty in Guam

As a diasporic Chamorro scholar on the edge of political life in Guam, I have provided an overview of Chamorro sovereignty struggles from my transnational standpoints. By positioning sovereignty struggles in Guam within a Fourth World context, my intention is to locate prospects for Chamorro sovereignty within a larger transnational arena. Cristobal similarly expresses this sentiment in terms of indigenous sovereignty: "One of the strongest movements in recent times is the recognition of the inherent and moral rights of indigenous people particularly those who are non-self governing. The Chamorro people fit this category on all counts and should be allowed the opportunity to decide their fate."[46]

Similarly, Stade posits sovereignty struggles in Guam within a larger "world culture" and transnational political arena involving parallel conditions of colonialism, human rights violations, and nationalism: "What is the fight for indigenous rights other than an appeal, on the one hand, to a global logic of 'peoples' and nations, and, on the other, to a national or international state structure that should ensure a number of rights?"[47] Indeed the Chamorro Movement parallels sovereignty struggles throughout Native America, Latin America, the Caribbean, and the Pacific Islands.

In the particular context of U.S. territorial relations there are places like Guam, such as the Commonwealth of the Northern Mariana Islands, Puerto Rico, American Samoa, and the Virgin Islands.[48] Their respective sovereignty struggles in terms of their territorial status are painfully similar to that of the Chamorros. These territories continue to struggle in the face of cultural erosion, land acquisition, and ambiguous political status. Self-determination in the form of self-government remains the cornerstone of their parallel sovereignty movements. In light of Guam's latest chapter in the status quest, there is much to gain in discussing prospects for sovereignty in Guam in comparison to the CNMI, Puerto Rico, and Hawai'i. Ongoing obstacles in these three places suggest illusions of sovereignty as the U.S. government maintains plenary power and its paternalistic grasp.[49]

Native Hawaiian sovereignty struggles represent a critical case of comparison, Hawai'i having transitioned from territorial status to statehood. What prospects of U.S. sovereignty toward statehood lie in the wake of indigenous resistance in Guam and Puerto Rico? On the one hand, Hawai'i as a state seemingly enjoys a level of U.S. sovereignty that can hardly be fathomed in Guam and Puerto Rico. On the other hand, ongoing neocolonial conditions mark the experiences of Native Hawaiians in spite of the incorporation of Hawai'i into the union.[50] Native life is apparently not so wonderful in paradise under U.S. sovereignty. In analyzing the role of identity politics and blood quantum in the U.S. Supreme court ruling in *Rice v. Cayetano*, J. Kehaulani Kauanui observes: "Although the relationship is typically not recognized as such, the United States retains a colonial relationship with the Hawaiian people—not despite the fact that Hawai'i is a state but perhaps because of it. It is precisely this misrecognition of the colonial correlation that perpetuates that same relationship."[51] Given the ongoing processes of neocolonialism in Hawai'i because of its statehood, obstacles remain for Chamorros of Guam.

Nonetheless, as this anthology underscores, Chamorro experiences in Guam (and those of indigenous peoples in general) need not be conceptualized in narrow discursive terms. As postmodern and postcolonial perspectives suggest, indigenous peoples can reshape their assaulted identities vis-à-vis political resistance and cultural sovereignty. This is precisely the cultural terrain in which Chamorro sovereignty might be conceptualized. As Diaz asserts:

> Yet Guam's history does not have to be understood as the definitive Euro-Americanization of the Chamorro people at the tragic expense of indigenous culture. Nor does Chamorro culture need to be understood in terms of an immutably bounded, neatly contained thing that was once upon a time characterized by essential qualities, pure untainted, as Chamorro culture has (a)historically been conceived and represented. History and culture—and historiography and ethnography—can be conceptualized in different ways. They can be viewed as contested sites on which identities and communities are built and destroyed, rebuilt and destroyed in highly charged ways.[52]

In other words, the notion of "indigenous" does not necessarily entail racial, ancestral, linguistic, or cultural continuity in itself—nor does "self-determination" need to be legitimized by the very colonial structures that native peoples resist. Rather, the fact that emergent antithetical notions of indigeneity emanate in response to colonial and neocolonial conditions marks our progress toward indigenous and cultural sovereignties. These fluid emergent notions of identity are indigenous precisely because they draw upon an indigenous worldview despite geographical remoteness and are positioned within a contemporary political, economic, and cultural landscape within a territory historically settled by indigenous people.

Notes

1. This essay is a revised reprint of Michael P. Perez, "Contested Sites: Pacific Resistance in Guam to U.S. Empire," *Amerasia Journal* 27, no. 1 (2001): 97–115, originally presented at the Sovereignty 2000: Locations of Contestation and Possibility conference at the University of California, Santa Cruz, May 2000.

2. Born, raised and educated in Southern California, I returned to Guam in the 1990s to conduct field research and complete my Ph.D. dissertation. I consequently landed my first full-

time academic position at the University of Guam, prior to accepting a position at California State University, Fullerton. My travels to and from Guam as well as my ongoing involvement in Guam are both academic and personal, as I remain tied to family, friends, and colleagues on the island. This is the basis of my diasporic and transnational identities.

3. David Harvey, *The Condition of Postmodernity* (Cambridge MA: Blackwell, 1990); Douglas Kellner, *Media Culture: Cultural Studies, Identity and Politics between the Modern and the Postmodern* (New York: Routledge, 1995); Steven Seidman, *The Postmodern Turn: New Perspectives on Social Theory* (Cambridge: Cambridge University Press, 1995).

4. John Hoffman, *Sovereignty* (Minneapolis: University of Minnesota Press, 1998), 6–7.

5. Hoffman, *Sovereignty*, 3–4.

6. Ronald Stade, "What Future for Sovereignty? Guam in the New Pacific and the New Pacific in Guam," paper presented at the Third Conference of the European Society of Oceanists, Pacific Peoples in the Pacific Century: Society, Culture, Nature, Copenhagen, 13–15 December 1996, 12.

7. Vicente M. Diaz, "Simply Chamorro: Tales of Demise and Survival in Guam," *Contemporary Pacific* 6, no. 1 (1994): 53.

8. Stade, "What Future for Sovereignty?"

9. Ben Blaz, "Chamorros Yearn for Freedom," in *Liberation: Guam Remembers* (Agana, Guam: Golden Salute Committee 1994), 92–94.

10. Don A. Farrel, *The Pictorial History of Guam: The Sacrifice 1919–1943* (San Jose, Tinian, Commonwealth of the Northern Mariana Islands: Micronesian Productions, 1991). Jonathan Friedman, *Cultural Identity and Global Process* (London: Sage Publications, 1994).

11. Hope Alvarez Cristobal, "The Organization of People for Indigenous Rights: A Commitment towards Self-Determination," in *Hale'-ta Hinasso': Tinige' Put Chamorro/Insights: The Chamorro Identity* (Agana, Guam: Political Status Education Coordinating Committee, 1993), 137–53.

12. Robert R. Rogers, *Destiny's Landfall: A History of Guam* (Honolulu: University of Hawai'i Press, 1995).

13. See Joanne Barker, "For Whom Sovereignty Matters," this anthology.

14. Stade, "What Future for Sovereignty?"

15. Robert A. Underwood, "The Consciousness of Guam and the Maladjusted People," in *Chamorro Self-Determination*, ed. Laura Souder-Jaffery and Robert A. Underwood (Agana, Guam: Chamorro Studies Association, 1990), 9. I find it important to distinguish the earlier career of Robert Underwood as an activist scholar from his recent position as Guam's nonvoting delegate in the House of Representatives and more recently as a gubernatorial candidate in Guam. This particular piece was written during his first career wave as an activist scholar. Nonetheless, as a political leader in office, Underwood remained steadfast in his commitment to Chamorro self-determination.

16. Underwood, "Consciousness of Guam and the Maladjusted People," 18.

17. Robert Rogers, *Destiny's Landfill: A History of Guam* (Honolulu: University of Hawai'i Press, 1995), 244.

18. Stade, "What Future for Sovereignty?" 176.

19. Robert A. Underwood, *American Education and the Acculturation of the Chamorros of Guam* (Ph.D. diss., University of Southern California, School of Education, 1987).

20. See J. Kehaulani Kauanui, "The Politics of Hawaiian Blood and Sovereignty in *Rice v. Cayetano*," this volume.

21. Rogers, *Destiny's Landfill*, 263.

22. Cristobal, "Organization of People," 137.

23. Cristobal, "Organization of People," 149. See also Laura Marie Torres Souder, *Daughters of the Island: Contemporary Chamorro Women Organizers on Guam*, 2nd ed. (New York: University Press of America, 1992).

24. Souder, *Daughters of the Island*, 250.

25. Stade, "What Future for Sovereignty?" 188.

26. Michael F. Phillips, "Land," in *Kinalamten Pulitikat: Sinenten I Chamorro/Issues in Guam's Political Development: The Chamorro Perspective* (Agana, Guam: Political Status Education Coordinating Commission, 1996), 2–16.

27. Phillips, "Land," 3.

28. Phillips, "Land," 15.

29. Rogers, *Destiny's Landfill*, 249; Kauanui, "Politics of Sovereignty," this volume.

30. Phillips, "Land," 11.

31. Cristobal, "Organization of People," 146–50.

32. Robert Rogers, *Guam's Commonwealth Effort 1987–1988* (Mangilao, Guam: Micronesian Area Research Center, University of Guam, 1988); Joe T. San Agustin, "The Quest for Commonwealth: A New Chapter in Guam's History," in *Kinalamten Pulitikat: Sinenten I Chamorro/Issues in Guam's Political Development: The Chamorro Perspective* (Agana, Guam: Political Status Education Coordinating Commission, 1996), 119–24.

33. Cristobal, "Organization of People," 144–50.

34. Cristobal, "Organization of People," 140.

35. Cristobal, "Organization of People," 143.

36. Cristobal, "Organization of People," 141.

37. Benjamin F. Cruz, "Chamorro Voting Rights," in *Kinalamten Pulitikat: Sinenten I Chamorro/Issues in Guam's Political Development: The Chamorro Perspective* (Agana, Guam: Political Status Education Coordinating Commission, 1996), 78–82.

38. Cruz, "Chamorro Voting Rights," 128.

39. Cristobal, "Organization of People," 150.

40. Cristobal, "Organization of People," 153.

41. Cristobal, "Organization of People," 153

42. Cristobal, "Organization of People," 153.

43. San Agustin, "Quest for Commonwealth," 122.

44. Robert E. Statham, Jr., "U.S. Citizenship Policy in the Territory of Guam: The Making of One Out of Many, or Many Out of One?" Paper presented at the International Political Science Association 17th World Congress, Seoul, Korea (1997), 26.

45. Robert A. Underwood, "Commonwealth at a Crossroad," in Asun ton Kongresu: News from Congressman Robert A. Underwood (December 1997) 1–5.

46. Cristobal, "Organization of People," 138.

47. Ronald Stade, *Pacific Passages: World Culture and Local Politics in Guam* (Sweden: Stockholm Studies in Social Anthropology, 1997), 48.

48. Arnold Liebowitz, *Defining Status: A Comprehensive Analysis of United States Territorial Relations* (Norwell MA: Kluwer Law International, 1989).

49. See Déborah Berman Santana, "Indigenous Identity and the Struggle for Independence in Puerto Rico," and Kauanui, "Politics of Sovereignty," this volume. See also Ronald Fernandez, *The*

Disenchanted Island: Puerto Rico and the United States in the Twentieth Century, 2nd ed. (Westport CT: Praeger, 1996).

50. Haunani-Kay Trask, *From a Native Daughter: Colonialism and Sovereignty in Hawai'i* (Honolulu: University of Hawaii Press, 1999).

51. See Kauanui, "Politics of Sovereignty."

52. Diaz, "Simply Chamorro," 31.

Leonie Pihama (Maori)

Asserting Indigenous Theories of Change

Maori society has its own distinctive knowledge base. This knowledge base has its origins in the metaphysical realm and emanates as a *Kaupapa Maori*, a "body of knowledge" accumulated by experiences through history of the Maori people. This Kaupapa Maori knowledge is the systematic organization of beliefs, experiences, understandings, and interpretations of the interactions of Maori people upon Maori people and Maori people upon their world.[1]

Introduction

In Aotearoa–New Zealand there is a growing literature about Kaupapa Maori theory. The development of Kaupapa Maori theory has grown from Maori struggles for *tino rangatiratanga* and *mana motuhake*.[2] As a part of the wider struggle against colonialism Maori people have engaged multiple forms of intervention and resistance. Our histories remind us of many acts of resistance to colonial imperialism and struggles of resistance against the forced cultural genocide imposed in our lands. In the history of Taranaki, where my own tribal links hold firmly, we have many examples of the approaches taken by our *tupuna*, our ancestors, in the struggle against the confiscation of our land, the imprisonment and death of many of our people, and the denial of our language, culture, and knowledge bases. As such our people have always been theorists. We have for generations engaged with our world and constructed theories as a part of our own knowledge and ways of understanding our experiences. The denial of our knowledge and theorizing has been an integral part of the colonizing agenda.

For many Maori who have actively sought theoretical explanations for our experiences, Kaupapa Maori theory provides a culturally defined theoretical space. There is resistance from many sectors of the university and from some educationalists. Asserting a right to argue Kaupapa Maori theory has been an ongoing struggle. The historical dominance of Western theorizing is being challenged at a very fundamental level; that is, at the level of relevance to the Indigenous people of this land. For many Pakeha academics this challenge is viewed as a threat. The possibility of Maori taking control of our own theoretical frameworks is a threat to the survival of many of those Pakeha academics who have spent the best part of their academic lives theorizing "about" and "on" Maori. However, in spite of these things, Kaupapa Maori theory continues to thrive. Kaupapa Maori theory is presented as an Indigenous theoretical framework that challenges the oppressive social order within which Maori people are currently located and does so from a distinctive Maori cultural base.

The drive for tino rangatiratanga and mana motuhake in this country is based within historical and cultural precedents set by many of our tupuna.[3] In my own tribal area of Taranaki the struggle against colonial imperialism is one that was multifaceted; the message, however, was consistently that of Taranaki people maintaining our own autonomy and sovereignty over all things.[4] The commitment of our people to philosophies of resistance against colonial power acts, for me, as an example of the expectations of our people to regain our fundamental rights as people of the land. The affirmation of being Maori is central to our struggles. That affirmation is also central to Kaupapa Maori theory.

Whereas the theoretical assertion of Kaupapa Maori theory is relatively new, Kaupapa Maori is not. Kaupapa Maori is extremely old, ancient in fact. It predates any and all of us in living years and is embedded in our cultural being. The naming of Kaupapa Maori theory indicates an explicit acknowledgment of the theoretical approach being undertaken. The multiple layers of meaning within *te reo Maori* means that the term *Kaupapa* has many possibilities.[5] Kaupapa relates to notions of foundation; plan; philosophy and strategies. Kaupapa Maori, therefore, indicates a Maori view of those things. It relates to Maori philosophies of the world, to Maori understandings upon which our beliefs and values are based, Maori worldviews and ways of operating.

Tuakana Nepe emphasizes that Kaupapa Maori knowledge is distinctive to Maori society and has its origins in the metaphysical.[6] Kaupapa Maori, she states, is a *body of knowledge accumulated by the experiences through history, of the Maori people.*[7] For her, this knowledge form is distinctive to Maori in that it derives fundamentally from Maori epistemologies that include complex relationships and ways of organizing society. She argues that this distinctive nature of Kaupapa Maori is seen in the ways in which Maori conceptualize relationships: "The concept of the relationship between the living and the dead; life and death; the Maori concept of time, history and development; the relationships between male and female; individual and group; and the implication of such relationships for social power relations. These knowledge types and their functions are the content and product of the interconnection of the purely Maori metaphysical base and Maori societal relationships."[8]

Tracing further the origins of Kaupapa Maori knowledge Tuakana places its origins in Rangiatea, which she states makes it exclusively Maori. Rangiatea is the first known Whare Wananga located in Te Toi-o-nga-Rangi, the home of Io-Matua-Kore, the creator.[9] What is clear in her writing is that Kaupapa Maori is grounded in Maori knowledge. Knowledge has always had a central place within Maori society and the complexities of knowledge and knowledge transmission recognized in the structures of the Whare Wananga. Kaupapa Maori, Tuakana argues, is the conceptualization of Maori knowledge transmitted through te reo Maori.[10] Kaupapa Maori underpins Kaupapa Maori theory and therefore informs our theoretical analysis and understandings. It is the development of a distinctly Maori theoretical framework as a means of informing our understandings.

Kaupapa Maori is a transformative power. To think and act in terms of Kaupapa Maori while experiencing colonization is to resist dominance. This is not something that Maori alone are engaging. It is the experience of vast numbers of Indigenous Peoples across the world. Native woman writer Rayna Green, reflecting on Indian notions of leadership in their communities writes: "In Indian country, maybe the most radical change we will ever have is a return to tradition."[11] Being grounded in Maori knowledge, Kaupapa Maori cannot be understood without a knowledge of *matauranga Maori* and the ways in which we as Maori engage knowledge and forms of knowing.[12] Te Ahukaramu Charles Royal outlines matauranga Maori as theory and *whakapapa* as research methodology.[13] In posing a number of possibilities in what he refers to as theory in "embryonic" form, Te Ahukaramu gives the following working definition:

> He mea hanga te matauranga Maori na te Maori. E hangaia ana tenei matauranga i roto i te whare o Te Ao Marama, i runga ano hoki i nga whakaaturanga o te whakapapa kia marama ai te tangata ki tona Ao. Matauranga Maori is created by Maori humans according to a worldview entitled "Te Ao Marama" and by the employment of methodologies derived from this worldview to explain the Maori experience of the world.[14]

Matauranga Maori is created by the use of whakapapa. Whakapapa is regarded an analytical tool that has been employed by our people as a means by which to understand our world and relationships. In such a framework it appears that whakapapa is both vehicle and expression of matauranga Maori. The assertion through whakapapa of the origins of matauranga Maori returns us to Papatuanuku, earth mother, and Ranginui, sky parent.[15] Rapata Wiri also locates matauranga Maori as essential to the construction of what he refers to as a Mana Maori model. Matauranga Maori provides a distinct Maori epistemology and ways of knowing and draws upon a range of both verbal and nonverbal forms for its expression. Rapata highlights the complexity of definitions of *matauranga Maori* and its multiple elements as follows: "Maori epistemology; the Maori way; the Maori worldview; the Maori style of thought; Maori ideology; Maori knowledge base; Maori perspective; to understand or to be acquainted with the Maori world; to be knowledgeable in things Maori; to be a graduate of the Maori schools of learning; Maori tradition and history; Maori experience of history; Maori enlightenment; Maori scholarship; Maori intellectual tradition."[16]

Defining Theory and Its Place in Indigenous Movements

The appending of the term theory to Kaupapa Maori may for some be literally a contradiction in terms. Kaupapa Maori is conceptually based within Maori cultural and philosophical traditions. Theory, however, may be said to be conceptually based within European philosophical traditions. To query the relationships between Maori traditions and Western traditions is not unfamiliar to Maori. Linda Tuhiwai Smith has recently given an in-depth analysis of the impact of Western research forms on Indigenous Peoples.[17] In *Decolonizing Methodologies: Indigenous Peoples and Research* she argues that Western research has been instrumental in the marginalization of Indigenous Peoples' knowledge and as such has contributed in key ways to the maintenance and perpetuation of colonization.

Theory, like research, has rarely been "Maori friendly." In fact theory often provided the justification for the ongoing perpetuation of violence on Maori. Theories of racial inferiority, deficiencies, and cultural disadvantage have been key in denying Maori people access to our land, language, and culture.[18] It is clear that theories can be used both for and against Maori. Graham Hingangaroa Smith maintains that Maori, as a subordinate group, must critically engage theory as a site of struggle.[19] As a tool theory is not inherently oppressive, just as it is not inherently transformative. As African American intellectual bell hooks writes, "Theory is not inherently healing, liberatory or revolutionary. It fulfils this function only when we ask that it do so and direct our theorizing towards this end."[20] All theories are socially constructed, and therefore the worldviews and philosophies of those who participate in their construction inform all theories. In terms of Kaupapa Maori theory, Graham Smith argues that the deliberate co-optation of the term *theory* has been an attempt to challenge dominant Pakeha notions of theory and to provide "counter-hegemonic practice and understandings" in terms of how theory is constructed, defined, selected, interpreted, and applied.[21]

Thomas J. Ward in his article "Definitions of Theory in Sociology" gives an extensive overview of the use of the term theory by a range of sociologists. The complexities of attempting to provide a definition of theory are highlighted most significantly in Ward's addressing of the question: what is theory? "Using language that reflects at least some areas of consensus, a theory is a logical deductive-inductive system of concepts, more selected aspects of phenomena and from which testable hypotheses can be derived. Theories in sociology are intended to be descriptive, explanatory, and predictive of phenomena of interest to the discipline and to its individual practitioners."[22]

Pamela Abbott and Claire Wallace note that since all people engage in acts of thinking and having ideas, we are all theorists.[23] We are all able to theorize and analyze what is happening around us; in fact we all participate in commonsense notions that are a part of our engaging with processes of theorizing. There is, however, a need to distinguish between commonsense notions and sociological theorizing. Drawing on the work of Stuart Hall they identify that in the social sciences a theory is expected to be "open-ended, open to new evidence, capable of modification and improvement, and clear about the way its concepts are formed."[24] Social theories are expected to be more systematic in their explanations and ideas, trying to take account of the "facts" presented and be coherent in their explanations, and yet be open to refutation. These expectations make social theories quite distinct from commonsense assumptions.

As such, the possibilities of theory are multiple. Theories are not solely descriptive or explanatory or predictive but can be all of these simultaneously. Focusing on the explanatory nature of theory Coxon and colleagues note that theories may be viewed fundamentally as collections of general principles that provide explanations for events and experiences.[25] Theories can provide ways of explaining the world through the use of given understandings. Given the diversity of worldviews, of cultural ways of seeing, understanding, and therefore explaining the world, it is expected that a range of theories may exist simultaneously for any given event or to explain experiences. Theories are, and must be, more.

After looking at some of the literature that presents theory as prescription, description, explanation, and analysis it is clear to me that theory cannot only be about these things but must be rooted in practice. To use a term from the work of Paulo Freire, theory and practice must exist in *dialectical unity*.[26] Dialectical unity acknowledges the interdependence of theory and practice. One cannot act fully without the other, and there is a process of constant reflection and reshaping as each part of the unity informs the other. Theory and practice are not closed entities; they are open to each other and therefore we, in our practice and our theorizing, need to be open to the possibilities that come with such a process of reflection.

The shifting of a definition of theory from the descriptive mode within which it is positioned by Ward to one that is related explicably to practice, and therefore is informed by the politics and social realities within which the practice is located, makes theory worthwhile for Maori. Without the unity of theory with practice, theory has little to offer. The idea of theory as a means of describing and explaining what is happening around and more often than not to us, and its relationship to transformative practice, is explored in some depth by bell hooks in her piece "Theory as Liberatory Practice." Coming to theory, for hooks, was "because I was hurting—the pain within me was so intense that I could not go on living. I came to theory desperate, wanting to comprehend—to grasp what was happening around and within me."[27] bell hooks's exploration of theory as liberatory practice is helpful in that her discussion engages with some issues that are central for African Americans, of which many also have direct relevance for Maori. Where theory has on the whole been imposed upon Maori experiences and events, there has emerged an often deep resentment and dismissal of the idea that theory could be at all transformative. Reflecting on similar responses within her own community, hooks identifies the difficulties that such responses pose for the black intellectual, in particular the ways that dismissal of intellectuals and theory can silence the black academic. The silencing noted by hooks can equally be felt by Maori academics in this country. It is a process that I have felt and seen on many occasions. The dismissal of Maori academics and any notion of theory, through utilizing anti-theory discourses, has become a means of silencing or of capturing ground within a debate.

Barbara Christian, an African American woman literary critic, offers much to this discussion. Christian gives an articulate and powerful critique of the developments in literary theory.[28] A key point of concern is what she considers the "race for theory" and the ways in which new literary criticism is being constructed. While it is important to engage and develop theory, she states, it must be grounded in experiences and practice, without which theory becomes "prescriptive, exclusive, elitist."[29] Further, she challenges the notion that new theoretical developments will make change for black women writers: "These writers did announce their dissatisfaction with some of the cornerstone ideas of their own tradition, a dissatisfaction with which I was born. But in their attempt to change the orientation of Western scholarship, they, as usual, concentrated on themselves and were not in the slightest interested in the worlds they ignored or controlled."[30]

For theory to be invented in ways that have little or no relevance to people's lives because of prescriptive, exclusive, and elitist foundations is of no use to Maori. Any theoretical framework must be located within our experiences and practices. Equally, I would argue that a strong Kaupapa Maori theoretical framework must be cognizant of our historical and cultural realities, in all their complexities.

A further source of rejection of theory is related to accessibility. Many theoretical frameworks that espouse a focus on transformation are themselves inaccessible. If theory is inaccessible because of the language chosen by academics, then the potential for that theory to transform the lived realities of oppressed groups becomes limited. A common complaint by Maori students is regarding the inaccessibility of some theoretical discussions. bell hooks expresses her amazement at the limited number of feminist theoretical texts that actually "speak" to women, men, and children about transforming our lives. By "speak" she is referring to the meanings and theories being accessible. The academy does little to support the development of accessible texts.

Maori academics often speak of being caught in the bind between our communities and the academy. Maori thesis students often voice the position that their work must be able to be read by their *whanau* (extended family of at least three generations) and the wider Maori community; if it cannot, then its potential for offering information and knowledge is, in their minds, diminished.[31] This can create a dilemma for Maori students in that the expectations of the university, and about what constitutes a thesis and theory, can differ significantly from the expectations of the students and their priority audience.

Struggling with and over the notion of theory is a part of Kaupapa Maori theory. The process of decolonizing theory is a crucial element of a Kaupapa Maori theoretical approach. Developing analyses that can both engage the underpinning assumptions of a range of theoretical approaches and provide critique is key to identifying whose interests are served and how power relationships are being constructed. What I am arguing is for a need to be able to "name" the dominant theories that form the basis for much of the analysis of

Indigenous Peoples' experiences and issues. Theory is constructed by groups of people through their own cultural and political understandings. Like other social constructions, theory is both socially and culturally bound. In Aotearoa we have a history of theoretical frameworks imposed upon our people. Assimilation and integration were the focus of early colonial contact, and since then biological and environmental deficit theories that have dominated the ways in which Maori issues are analyzed.[32] Western psychological theories focused on the individual have consistently placed Maori as requiring change.[33] A deficit approach imported from the United States in the 1960s has held currency in most sectors since that time.[34] As such Maori continue to be viewed as "deficient," "culturally disadvantaged," "environmentally lacking," and more recently through a process of biological/genetic reductionism in health issues, Maori are being presented as genetically deficient.[35] However, we should not delude ourselves that only the more conservative theoretical constructions require challenge. There are also more recent theories positing notions that have the potential to disturb and disrupt Maori epistemologies further. Poststructuralism, postmodernism, postcolonialism, and postfeminism have all emerged as "new" forms of analysis that lay claim to "opening the debate" to issues of difference and otherness. There is little acknowledgment that Maori people have struggled to have our voices heard over the past two hundred years of colonial imperialism on our lands. Furthermore, the assumption of the existence of the "Western individual self" as central to analysis acts to marginalize Maori assertions of whakapapa and collective relationships. The imposition of theoretical frameworks that deny Maori knowledge, cultural and societal, merely maintain the dominance of Western theoretical imperialism over Indigenous theories.

As in other areas of our existence in the academy for both teachers and students, the use of theory and how we use theory are sites of contestation. There are ways to present theory in understandable language, and this is something that many Maori academics seek in their own writings. This is especially relevant to Kaupapa Maori theory as its sustainability is dependent on its reproduction by Maori for Maori. To write in ways that deny access to the majority of Maori people is in my opinion bringing closure rather than ensuring ongoing debate and evolution. I agree with Graham Hingangaroa Smith's contention that theory is a central problematic in the development of liberatory processes, which Smith refers to as "transformative action in the interests of subordinated groups."[36]

However the development and assertion of liberatory theory can only derive from a political positioning that acknowledges the existence of injustices and oppression. Without that acknowledgment the need for liberatory theory would not be evident. bell hooks calls for the recognition of the potential for theory to be liberatory, asserting that such recognition is realized through active critical reflection located in an understanding of oppression, of pain, of struggle. Theories that develop from these concrete and known experiences bring possibilities for transformation.[37]

For Graham Smith, theory is a definite site of struggle between interest groups, and the struggle for theoretical space to support Maori in analyzing our experiences critically is a worthwhile struggle. This struggle is about contesting theoretical space. As with all forms of contestation the underpinning power relations require challenge. This is a threat to those who argue the dominance of Western theories. It is also about Maori constituting theory within our own terms. Sheilagh Walker argues that Maori academics engage in theory because of our engagement in the struggle for Kaupapa Maori. In her terms "our struggle becomes our Theory."[38] Furthermore, she suggests that Kaupapa Maori theory is not defined within Western philosophical traditions but through Kaupapa Maori praxis. It is worth outlining this argument more fully by referring directly to a statement made in her research.

> I conclude that Kaupapa Maori is not a Theory in the Western sense; it does not subsume itself within European philosophical endeavours which construct and privilege one Theory over another Theory, one rationality over another rationality, one philosophical paradigm over another paradigm, one knowledge over another knowledge, one World view over another World view of the Other. Kaupapa Maori Theory is rather Kaupapa Maori Praxis. My problematic continues. I deconstruct the title further; what remains is simply Kaupapa Maori.[39]

This raises again the necessity or otherwise of appending the word theory to Kaupapa Maori and dealing with the problematic of the dominant conceptualization of theory in Western terms. I would argue that the use of the term theory, when applied in resistance terms, is one that can serve to validate the underpinning intentions of Kaupapa Maori theory, but as with any concept that derives from a Western base, the issues raised by Sheilagh Walker must be continually present and be central to our ongoing reflection on the terms we choose to use. As both bell hooks and Lee Maracle would say, that would be absurd, as it would deny that there are theories of Western origin that can be of use for oppressed groups.[40] This position is clearly taken by Maori academics such as Linda Tuhiwai Smith, Graham Hingangaroa Smith, Margie Kahukura

Hohepa, Patricia Maringi Johnston, Kuni Jenkins, Ngahuia Te Awekotuku, Kathie Irwin, Mereana Taki, and Cherryl Smith.[41]

Kaupapa Maori Theory

Kaupapa Maori theory is a theoretical framework that ensures a cultural integrity is maintained when analyzing Maori issues. It provides both tools of analysis and ways of understanding the cultural, political, and historical context of Aotearoa. A fundamental premise upon which Kaupapa Maori theory is argued is that in order to understand, explain, and respond to issues for Maori there must be a theoretical foundation that has been built from here, from Papatuanuku, not from the building blocks of imported theories. Kaupapa Maori theory provides such a foundation.

It is necessary to acknowledge that Kaupapa Maori theory is not a theoretical framework that provides answers by following a set recipe. Where there are recognizable elements within Kaupapa Maori theory, as it is presently being defined, these are not seen to be deterministic or exclusive. This is not an attempt to close or define the parameters of Kaupapa Maori theory in a way that would prevent those who draw upon Kaupapa Maori theory having the ability to be flexible and adaptable to the ever changing contexts of Maori collectively and whanau, hapu and iwi, as distinct units. To promote closure would in my mind be the antithesis of what is proposed within Kaupapa Maori theory. The term *theory* itself is multiple in the definitions associated with it, and some exploration of that provides understanding of the need to ensure against a closure of Kaupapa Maori theory.

Much of the strength of Kaupapa Maori theory comes in the ability of many Maori to "see" the relevance of such theoretical engagement and to recognise much of what is said in their own practices. What is also important is the recognition that Kaupapa Maori theory is not set in concrete but is very much a fluid and evolving theoretical framework.[42] In a wider sense this is a part of a recognition that dominance seeks to set cultures in concrete, to hold us in a construction that is static and unchanging and often relentless in its denial of growth and change. We cannot afford for this to be the case. Therefore in developing, drawing upon, and refining Kaupapa Maori theory as Indigenous theory, we need to be part of a process that is accessible and fluid, not something that is controlled by a few or static and unchanging. The evolving of Kaupapa Maori theory is long term and requires intense reflection. The process itself is as important as the outcome, if not more so. It is through the process that we are able to engage more deeply with Maori knowledge, with *te reo Maori me ona tikanga*, in ways that can reveal culturally based frameworks and structures providing a foundation of Indigenous Maori analyses.

In identifying the evolving nature of Kaupapa Maori theory it is also important to acknowledge those who have been instrumental in its articulation. Much is owed to the foundational work done by Linda Tuhiwai Smith and Graham Hingangaroa Smith in providing key elements for exploration in terms of what Kaupapa Maori theory might look like.[43] This is also indicated in the area of research, where Kaupapa Maori research has been carefully developed alongside Kaupapa Maori theory.[44] What is most impressive in the works of both these writers is their desire to be part of collective and open development of Kaupapa Maori theory with other Maori academics such as myself. More recent works by a range of Maori writers highlights the expansiveness that is Kaupapa Maori theory.[45]

Kaupapa Maori Theory as an Evolving and Organic Theoretical Development

As a theoretical framework Kaupapa Maori theory is still developing. However, we can be assured that development comes from a philosophical tradition that is as longstanding as any Western philosophical tradition. The idea that Kaupapa Maori theory is still growing is an important aspect to consider as it would be easy to stay with what has been written and not build on, critique, and reshape Kaupapa Maori theory. To ensure the diversities of Maori experiences and an inclusion of whanau, hapu, and iwi knowledge, Kaupapa Maori theory must be reflective, and we as its proponents must remain open to an evolving process. In one of the most in-depth discussions of Kaupapa Maori theory, Graham Hingangaroa Smith establishes Kaupapa Maori theory as an evolving theory of transformation that can be understood through an analysis of Kaupapa Maori intervention initiatives.[46] He locates the genesis of Kaupapa Maori theory securely within the political initiatives driven by Maori. This is critical, as Kaupapa Maori theory is not constructed in the competitive, hierarchical nature that is often the case in the assertion of Western theories. Kaupapa Maori theory is not dualistic or constructed within simplistic binaries. It is not about asserting the superiority of one set of knowledge over another or one worldview over another. It is not about denying the rights of any peoples to their philosophical traditions, culture, or language. It is an assertion of the right for Maori to be Maori on our own terms and to draw from our own base to provide understandings and explanations of the world.

Kaupapa Maori theory is a theoretical movement that has its foundation in

Maori community developments. These developments are epitomized in the Maori education initiatives Te Kohanga Reo and Kura Kaupapa Maori.[47] Both Te Kohanga Reo and Kura Kaupapa Maori are initiatives that originated from Maori communities. They were and are driven primarily by the motivation of Maori for initiatives through which te reo Maori could be regenerated for our people and which would intervene in the crisis of Maori educational underachievement that had been the experience of generations of Maori children and whanau. The development of these initiatives brought a need for Maori people to reflect on and draw upon our own cultural knowledge. Te Kohanga Reo, the first of the Maori education initiatives to develop, is a prime example. The history of the development of Te Kohanga Reo has been well documented by Maori people involved in the movement, as has its role in the revitalization of te reo Maori.[48]

Maori students across the country have been told that it is not sufficient to reference Kaupapa Maori theory as their theoretical framework or to rely solely on the writings of Maori academics when discussing issues regarding Maori education. It is clear that those Pakeha academics, some of whom are supervising Maori students at graduate level, are unable to accept that Kaupapa Maori theory is a valid theoretical framework or that Maori are able to develop theoretical frameworks that have origins in te reo Maori me ona tikanga. This is a particularly ethnocentric notion, yet it continues to pervade the academy in ways that can seriously disadvantage Maori staff and students.

In spite of resistance to the assertion of Kaupapa Maori theory, we continue seeking ways to claim ground in the framing of our own theories. We do this with the knowledge that theory is not in itself transformative, that it is a site of struggle, and that it must be located in direct relationship with practice. Theory is a term that has a tenuous relationship to Maori. It is my hope that Kaupapa Maori theory will bring to the fore the possibility of no longer having to adhere to an idea that theory belongs only to the colonizer; rather, I hope we as Indigenous people can once again acknowledge always having theorized about our world and that our theories, grounded historically on this land, are valid. Kaupapa Maori theory is, I believe, a theoretical framework that is organically Maori.

The organic development and nature of Kaupapa Maori theory is perhaps one of its strongest aspects. Having already noted that the coining of the phrase came within a university context, it is vital that we do not then assume that Kaupapa Maori theory is only about academia, as this is not the case. Kaupapa Maori theory has in very real terms developed from Maori. Given that te reo Maori me ona tikanga is central to Kaupapa Maori theory, we have an established foundation that can be described as nothing other than organic.

Kaupapa Maori theory is part of a wider resurgence for Maori, part of what is often termed the Maori Renaissance. That renaissance is an outcome of the struggles by many Maori to regain the fundamental rights guaranteed under te Tiriti o Waitangi (see Fiona Cram, "Backgrounding Maori Views on Genetic Engineering," this volume). The struggles of groups such as Nga Tamatoa and Te reo Maori association were instrumental in the maintenance of Maori struggles for te reo Maori me ona tikanga. The Wai 11 case to the Waitangi Tribunal, a claim related to the Maori language, has provided an ongoing thrust for Maori who are active in the struggle for the revival and retention of te reo Maori (see Cram, "Backgrounding Maori Views"). From these struggles have emerged the Maori educational initiatives of Te Köhanga Reo, Kura Kaupapa Maori, Whare Kura, and Whare Wananga. The political and historical development of these initiatives has been recorded by those directly involved.[49] It may be stated in more general terms that the development of these initiatives has come about from a basis of the need for Maori to take control of our own educational processes and, in doing so, of our own destinies. Fundamental to this is the revival, maintenance, and development of te reo Maori me ona tikanga for present and future generations of Maori. Discussion surrounding the context within which Te Kohanga Reo emerged highlights these general intentions.

Margie Hohepa describes Te Kohanga Reo as having developed as a part of wider concerns in regard to te reo Maori.[50] Concern for the potential loss of te reo Maori emerged with various movements and petitions of the 1970s.[51] Linda Tuhiwai Smith also identifies the significance of the 1970s in the revitalization of te reo Maori. It was a time when significant actions were being undertaken in regard to land issues, including the 1975 Land March, reoccupation of Bastion Point by Ngati Whaatua, occupation of the Raglan Golf Course by Eva Rickard and her whanau, and establishment of the Waitangi Tribunal.[52] Maori movements of the time were not removed from wider international movements.[53] Ngahuia Te Awekotuku places the American Civil Rights movement of the 1960s as a key influence in Maori politics at the time. The American Indian Movement (AIM) was also gathering momentum struggling for Indigenous rights.[54]

Having derived from organic Maori movements, Kaupapa Maori theory provides us with a theoretical process ensuring that those struggles and the inherent power relationships within those struggles are a conscious part of our analysis. Given the unequal power relations that exist between Maori and the

State, the recognition that the organic developments are the outcome of Maori aspirations and a subsequent struggle for the realization of those aspirations means there is a clearly articulated political agenda that sits alongside cultural aspirations for te reo Maori me ona tikanga. The organic nature of Kaupapa Maori theory also means that there are many ways in which Kaupapa Maori theory can be and is articulated. Kaupapa Maori theory is not singular. Kaupapa Maori theory is, by nature of its development, multiple. There is no set formula that we can use to say, "here, this is what it looks like"; rather, Kaupapa Maori theory has a range of expressions that are influenced by things such as whanau, hapu, iwi, urban experiences, gender, and geography, to name a few. The multiple possibilities of Kaupapa Maori theory also enable a range of potential forms of transformation to occur.

bell hooks reminds us that theory can be liberatory if we seek to use it in that way.[55] Transformation is one of the driving elements of Kaupapa Maori. How that transformation is defined and brought is determined by how the issues are understood, theorized, and engaged. Therefore it is necessary, while avoiding a formulaic development, to indicate what may be considered some specific elements that are inherent within Kaupapa Maori theory and ways in which a range of Maori people are articulating methods of analysis. The transformation or emancipatory intent of Kaupapa Maori theory may be viewed as a decolonization process; however, it is not solely about theorizing for transformation but is also directly related to the development of practical interventions. Again Te Kohanga Reo and Kura Kaupapa Maori are clear examples of the emancipatory intent of Kaupapa Maori theory. Graham Hingangaroa Smith takes this aspect of Kaupapa Maori theory a step forward in drawing upon the theorizing of Jurgen Habermas.[56] Graham argues for a need to include a utopian vision within the development of Kaupapa Maori theory, which serves to highlight the transformative potential of Kaupapa Maori theory.

Summary

This chapter has opened a discussion of Kaupapa Maori theory as an Indigenous theory of change. The key intention was to outline the broader philosophical context within which Kaupapa Maori theory needs to be considered. What is important is the understanding that Kaupapa Maori theory is founded within knowledge that derives from learnings, experiences, understandings, worldviews, values, and beliefs that are ancient. Those forms have been handed down through generations, and although disrupted and disregarded through colonial impositions they have survived to continue to inform how we are in the world. Kaupapa Maori theory is developed from a foundation of Kaupapa Maori and matauranga Maori. Its base is firmly entrenched on Maori land, on Papatuanuku, and that holds Kaupapa Maori theory as a distinctive framework.

Theory is considered to hold possibilities for liberation, but wariness remains in Maori communities as a result of the imposition of theories that have historically worked against our interests. Within the academy Western theories have been privileged. Indigenous Peoples' theoretical voices have rarely been heard, let alone engaged with the same status as those of the West. This is not a surprise to Maori academics, given the ongoing marginalization of Maori knowledge. Maori knowledge has been under attack since the arrival of colonial settlers in our lands. Within the colonial education system Maori knowledge has been through processes that have denied the validity of our own knowledge and worldviews.

I argue that Kaupapa Maori theory provides us with the potential to continue a tradition of thinking about, explaining, and understanding our world in a way that is not the domain of the colonizing forces but has been a part of Indigenous Peoples' worlds since creation. Kaupapa Maori theory is a theoretical framework that is evolving. It is evolving from a base of being Maori, from whanau, hapu, and iwi and from collective Maori movements. As a theoretical framework Kaupapa Maori theory is engaged in a struggle within the academy. It struggles for recognition, validation, and affirmation of our cultural worldviews as Maori. It asserts that we have always been researchers, have always engaged in theorizing our lives, our experiences, our context. The organic and multiple nature of Kaupapa Maori theory is a powerful force for the future creation of a range of Kaupapa Maori theoretical expression. To position ourselves clearly as Kaupapa Maori theorists is to identify ourselves, to place before others where we are coming from, so that there is no guise of neutrality or assumed objectivity.[57] The resurgence of Maori language and culture over the past thirty years and the continued assertion of tino rangatiratanga indicate that as the Indigenous people of Aotearoa, we will continue to struggle for our fundamental rights on our lands. Kaupapa Maori theory provides a theoretical and analytical framework to support those struggles.

Notes

1. Tukana Mate Nepe, "E hao nei e tenei reanga: Te Toi Huarewa Tupuna" (unpublished MA thesis, University of Auckland, 1991), 4.

2. These terms are discussed in more depth later in the chapter; for current reference *tino rangatiratanga* relates to Maori sovereignty as affirmed within Te Tiriti o Waitangi, and *mana motuhake* relates to Maori self-determination and Indigenous autonomy.

3. *Tupuna* relates to ancestors.

4. Taranaki is a geographical area on the west coast of Te Ika a Maui (the North Island) and within the borders are a number of *iwi* (tribal) and *hapu* (subtribal) groupings.

5. *Te reo Maori* relates to the Maori language. Reo refers to language and voice.

6. Nepe, "E hao nei e tenei reanga."

7. Nepe, "E hao nei e tenei reanga," 4.

8. Nepe, "E hao nei e tenei reanga," 5.

9. *Te Toi-o-nga-Rangi* refers to the uppermost domain of the twelve domains that exist in the spiritual realm.

10. Nepe, "E hao nei e tenei reanga."

11. Rayna Green, "American Indian Women: Diverse Leadership for Social Change," in *Bridges of Power: Women's Multicultural Alliances*, ed. L. Albrecht and R. M. Brewer (Philadelphia: New Society Publishers in cooperation with the National Women's Studies Association, 1990).

12. *Matauranga Maori* refers to Maori knowledge.

13. *Whakapapa* refers to Maori genealogical connections that form layers of relationships.

14. T. C. Royal, "Te Ao Marama: A Research Paradigm," pp. 87–86 in *Te Pumanawa Hauora, 1999, Proceedings of Te Oru Rangahau: Naori Research and Development Conference* (Palmerston North: School of Maori Studies, Massey University, 1999), 83.

15. Royal, "Te Ao Marama," 83.

16. R. Wiri, "The Prophecies of the Great Canyon of Toi: A History of Te Whaiti-nui-a-Toi in the Western Urewera Mountains of New Zealand" (unpublished Ph.D. diss., University of Auckland, 2001), 25.

17. Linda Tuhiwai Smith, Decolonizing Methodologies: Research and Indigenous Peoples (London: Zed Books, 1999).

18. Linda Tuhiwai Te Rina Mead, "Nga Aho o te Kakahu Matauranga: The Multiple Layers of Struggle by Maori in Education" (unpublished Ph.D. diss., University of Auckland, 1996).

19. G. H. Smith, "The Development of Kaupapa Maori Theory and Praxis" (unpublished Ph.D. diss., School of Education, University of Auckland, 1997), 132.

20. bell hooks, Teaching to Transgress: Education as the Practice of Freedom (New York: Routledge Press, 1994), 61.

21. Smith, "Development of Kaupapa Maori Theory," 455.

22. Smith, "Development of Kaupapa Maori Theory," 39.

23. Pamela Abbott and Claire Wallace, *Introduction to Sociology: Feminist Perspectives* (London: Routledge Press, 1997).

24. Stuart Hall, cited in Abbott and Wallace, *Introduction to Sociology*, 25.

25. E. Coxon, K. Jenkins, J. Marshall, and L. Massey, eds., *The Politics of Learning and Teaching in Aotearoa—New Zealand* (Palmerston North: Dunmore Press, 1994).

26. Paulo Freire, *The Politics of Education: Culture, Power and Liberation* (Massachusetts: Bergin and Garvey Publishers, 1985).

27. bell hooks, "Theory as Liberatory Practice," in *Teaching to Transgress*, 59. This article is one I use in a graduate course I teach, as it promotes discussion about the possibilities of theory. It has become increasingly obvious to me that many Maori hold a deep distrust for anything that is called "theory." That distrust has been well earned. As Linda Tuhiwai Smith relates in regard to research, Maori have been at the receiving end of being "researched on" and "researched by" the colonizer. As Maori, our experience of theory, like our experience of research, has been as the

object who is studied and theorized about. Our lives, our culture, our language, our entire being has been theorized by Pakeha academics and researchers over the past two hundred years. Our world has been theorized through paradigms that bear no resemblance to the ways in which we would explain and understand ourselves.

28. Barbara Christian, "The Race for Theory," in *This Bridge Called My Back*, ed. Cherrie Moraga and Gloria Anzuldua (New York: Kitchen Table Women of Colour Press, 1983), 335–45.

29. Christian, "The Race for Theory."

30. Christian, "The Race for Theory," 339

31. Mereana Taki, "Kaupapa Maori and Contemporary Iwi Resistance" (unpublished MA thesis, University of Auckland, 1996); Dallas Pahiri, "Me Whakatupu Ki Te Hua O Te Rengarenga, Me Whakapakari Ki Te Hua O Te Kawariki Reclaiming and Contesting Culture: Popular Culture and Maori Youth" (unpublished MA thesis, University of Auckland, 1997).

32. See P. Johnston and Leonie Pihama, "What Counts as Difference and What Differences Count: Gender, Race and the Politics of Difference," in *Toi Wahine: The Worlds of Maori Women*, ed. K. Irwin, I. Ramsden, and I. and R. Kahukiwa (Auckland: Penguin Books, 1995), 75–86; J. Simon, ed., *Nga Kura Maori: The Native Schools System 1867–1969* (Auckland: Auckland University Press, 1998).

33. Margie Hohepa, "Hei Tautoko i Te Reo': Maori Language Regeneration and Whanau Bookreading Practices" (unpublished Ph.D. diss., University of Auckland, 1999); Tereki R. Stewart, "Ka Pu Te Ruha, Ka Hao Te Rangatahi: Contributions to 'Indigenous Psychology' in Aotearoa/New Zealand" (unpublished MS thesis, University of Auckland, 1995).

34. For a critique of deficit theories and a discussion of education programs influenced by American programs such as Head Start, refer to Leoni Pihama, *Tungia te Ururua, Kia Tupu Whakaritorito Te Tupu o te Harakeke: A Critical Analysis of Parents as First Teachers*, RUME Masters Theses Series no. 3 (Auckland: University of Auckland, 1993).

35. See C. W. Smith and P. Reynolds, *Maori, Genes and Genetics: What Maori Should Know about the New Biotechnology* (Whanganui: Whanganui Law Centre, 2000). This publication was adapted from Debra Harry, Stephanie Howard, and Brett Shelton, *Indigenous Peoples, Genes and Genetics: What Indigenous Peoples Should Know about Biocolonialism* (Reno NV: Indigenous Peoples Council on Biocolonialism, 2000).

36. G. H. Smith, "Development of Kaupapa Maori Theory," 131.

37. hooks, "Theory as Liberatory Practice"; Smith, "Development of Kaupapa Maori Theory," 70.

38. S. Walker, "Kia Tau Te Rangimarie: Kaupapa Maori Theory as a Resistance against the Construction of Maori as the 'Other' " (unpublished MA thesis, University of Auckland, 1996), 119.

39. Walker, "Kia Tau Te Rangimarie."

40. hooks, Teaching to Transgress; L. Maracle, I Am a Woman: A Native Perspective on Sociology and Feminism (Vancouver: Press Gang, 1996).

41. L. T. R. Mead, "Nga Aho o te Kakahu Matauranga"; G. H. Smith, "Development of Kaupapa Maori Theory"; P. M. Johnston, "He Aro Rereke: Education Policy and Maori Underachievement: Mechanisms of Power and Difference" (unpublished Ph.D. diss., University of Auckland, 1998); Hohepa, "Hei Tautoko i Te Reo' "; K. E. H. Jenkins, "Te Ihi, Te Mana, Te Wehi O Te Ao, Maori Print Literacy from 1814–1855: Literacy, Power and Colonisation" (unpublished MS thesis, University of Auckland, 1991; Kathie Irwin, "The Politics of Kōhanga Reo," in *New Zealand Education Policy*

Today, ed. S. Middleton, J. Codd, and A. Jones (Wellington: Allen and Unwin, 1990), 110–20; Ngahuia Te Awekotuku, *Mana Wahine Maori: Selected Writings on Maori Women's Art, Culture and Politics* (Auckland: New Women's Press, 1991); Taki, "Kaupapa Maori and Contemporary Iwi Resistance"; C. W. Smith. "Kimihia Te Maramatanga: Colonisation and Iwi Development" (unpublished MA thesis, University of Auckland, 1994); C. W. Smith and M. Taki, "Hoihoi Wahine Pakeha," in *Te Pua* 2 (Auckland: Te Puawaitanga, 1994), 38–42.

42. G. H. Smith, "Development of Kaupapa Maori Theory," 97.

43. Smith, "Development of Kaupapa Maori Theory."

44. L. T. Smith, Decolonizing Methodologies.

45. See notes 45 and 46. See also Nepe, "E hao nei e tenei reanga"; Taina Pohatu, "I Tiipu Ai Taatou I Ngaa Turi O O Tatatau Maatua Tiipuna: Transmission and Acquisition Processes within Kaawai Whakapapa" (unpublished Master of Education thesis, University of Auckland, 1996); Hine Waikere-Ang, "Te Kete, The Briefcase, Te Tuara: The Balancing Act—Maori Women in the Primary Sector" (unpublished Master of Educational Administration thesis, Massey University, Palmerston North, 1999).

46. G. H. Smith, "Development of Kaupapa Maori Theory," 457.

47. In 1979 a gathering of elders at the Waananga kaumatua affirmed te reo Maori "*Ko te reo te mauri o te mana Maori" the language is the life principle of Maori mana*. This was followed in 1981 with a resolution from another hui, Waananga Whakatauira, for the development of bilingual education at preschool level. These were taken further to a proposal for immersion preschool programs. In April 1982 the first Te Kohanga Reo opened at Pukeatua Kokiri Centre Wainuiomata, the overriding goal being the fluency of te reo Maori, which would address the priority concern for the revitalization of te reo; see M. K Hohepa, "Te Kohanga Reo Hei Tikanga Ako I Te Reo Maori" (unpublished MA thesis, University of Auckland, 1990), 7–18.

48. I would urge any reader who is interested in Te Köhanga Reo to refer to the following works: M. K. Hohepa, "Te Kohanga Reo"; Kathie Irwin, "The Politics of Köhanga Reo," in *New Zealand Education Policy Today*, ed. S. Middleton, J. Codd, and A. Jones (Wellington: Allen and Unwin, 1990), 110–20; Arapera Royal-Tangaere, "Te Puawaitanga O Te Reo Ka Hua Te Haa O Te Potiki I Roto I Te Whanau Ko Tenei Te Tahuhu O Te Köhanga Reo: Transference from Te Köhanga Reo to Home, the Roles of the Child and the Family" (unpublished MA thesis, University of Auckland, 1992); Tania Ka'ai, "Te Hiringa Taketake: Mai i te Kohanga Reo: Maori Pedagogy, Te Köhanga Reo and the Transition to School" (unpublished MA thesis, University of Auckland, 1990); Mere Ngautauta Skerrett White, "Te Wero—Te Uru Whakatupu Ake Te Uru o Matawhaura: Language Scaffolding in a Köhanga Reo" (unpublished Master of Philosophy in Education thesis, University of Auckland, 1995).

49. Refer to Hohepa, "Te Kohanga Reo"; Nepe, "E hao nei e tenei reanga"; L. T. Smith, "Maori Education: A Reassertion," in *Puna Wairere: Essays by Maori* (Wellington: New Zealand Planning Council, 1990), 62–70; G. H. Smith, "Kura Kaupapa Maori: Innovation and Policy Development," *Access* 8 (1989): 26–28 (Journal of the Policy Studies Group, Education Department, University of Auckland); G. H. Smith, "Development of Kaupapa Maori Theory." For a bibliography refer to M. Hohepa and R. Ratapu, *He Kete kupu korero: A Bibliography of Readings on Te Köhanga Reo and Kura Kaupapa Maori* (Auckland: Research Unit for Maori Education, University of Auckland, 1992); K. Jenkins with T. Ka'ai, "Maori Education: A Cultural Experience and Dilemma for the State—A New Direction for Maori Society" in *The Politics of Learning and Teaching in Aotearoa—New Zealand*, ed. E. Coxon, K. Jenins, J. Marshall, and L. Massey et al. (Palmerston North: Dunmore Press, 1994),

148–79; H. M. Mead, "The Development of Wananga: Politics and Vision," sound recording, University in the 21st Century Winter Lecture Series, University of Auckland, 1998.

50. Hohepa, "Te Kohanga Reo."

51. A. Brown and J. Carlin, eds., "Hana Te Hemara," in em Mana Wahine: Women Who Show the Way (Auckland: Reed Publishing, 1994), 51. In this publication Hana discusses the instigation of the Maori Language petition in 1970, which was instrumental in the resistance movements that have seen the growth of Maori Language initiatives in Aotearoa. The petition was presented to parliament on 14 September 1972 and bore 44,000 signatures.

52. For reflections on Bastion Point refer to S. Hawke, ed., *Takaparawhau, The People's Story: 1998 Bastion Point 20 year Commemoration Book* (Auckland: Ngati Whaatua ki Orakei and Moko Productions, 1990).

53. For discussion of the occupation at Whaingaroa refer to A. Greensill, A. Sykes, and L. Pihama, eds., *Nga Puna Roimata: Tuaiwa Hautai Kereopa Rickard, 1925–1997* (Whaingaroa, New Zealand: Tuaiwa Hautai Kereopa Whanau & Moko Productions, 1998).

54. L. T. R. Mead, "Nga Aho o te Kakahu Matauranga."

55. hooks, Teaching to Transgress.

56. G. H. Smith, "Development of Kaupapa Maori Theory."

57. L. T. Smith, Decolonizing Methodologies.

Déborah Berman Santana (Puerto Rican/Boricua)

Indigenous Identity and the Struggle for Independence in Puerto Rico

In recent years the Taíno (indigenous Caribbean) movement has begun to challenge the official doctrine of their extinction over four hundred years ago. Puerto Ricans—particularly in the U.S. diaspora—show increasing interest in efforts to document Taíno survival. Meanwhile, a number of organizations are reviving Taíno beliefs and practices and pursuing official tribal recognition in the United States, Puerto Rico, and internationally.

At the same time, growing numbers of Puerto Ricans are demanding proper recognition and respect for African heritage, which has long been denied or minimized. Some express concern about DNA testing in Puerto Rico to attempt to distinguish indigenous from African ancestry as well as about the emphasis placed by some Taíno activists on "Taíno physical appearance" (i.e., not Black); accordingly, they question whether the Taíno revival is yet another attempt to de-Africanize Puerto Ricans. Other critics challenge the authenticity of Taíno survival, after so many centuries of presumed nonexistence. Debates about biological or cultural bases of identity and recovery of "lost" cultures hold more than merely academic significance, for they may speak to ownership, not only of identity but also of legitimate control over land and other resources—which are the material foundations of "sovereignty" and self-determination.

Without discounting the potentially problematic and divisive elements, it is worth considering how these movements might relate to the ongoing struggle for Puerto Rican independence. For example, how might recovery of indigenous, non-Eurocentric perspectives and practices not only help break Puerto Rico's colonial dependence upon the United States but also form a basis for a noncapitalist and sustainable Puerto Rico? More broadly, how might recovering indigenous values help rescue a people from destructive Western values such as separation from nature, individualism, and pursuit of profit? How might indigenous revival help reconnect people with nature and with one another and promote meaningful self-determination?[1]

Claiming Taíno Identity

Although the peoples inhabiting the Caribbean at the time of the first European invasions probably identified themselves according to their particular home territory, today the term *taíno* (meaning "good" in Arawak) generally refers to the dominant indigenous societies in the larger islands. Similarly, while Borikén is the oldest known name for Puerto Rico, the island is most commonly called by its more familiar Spanish name.[2] Historical accounts depict Spain's genocidal campaign of extermination against the Taínos during the century following Columbus's voyages to the Caribbean. Such accounts, coupled with the disappearance of *indio* as a census category in Puerto Rico after the eighteenth century, form the basis for the dominant view that the Taínos disappeared as a distinct people.[3] This has not, however, prevented the island's cultural institutions from promoting Taíno heritage as part of Puerto Rican identity.[4]

The oldest organized groups dedicated to reviving Taíno culture are about thirty years old; however, the "Taíno revival" went public in 1992 during "500 years of resistance," the anticolonial response to the quincentennial celebration of Columbus's first voyage to the Western Hemisphere. These organizations are dedicated to refuting the dominant view that Taínos ceased to exist centuries ago asserting their continuous existence up to the present—albeit in disjointed and isolated fragments, and until recently only in private. They seek to establish bases for legitimate claims to Taíno ethnic identity; in addition, they work to obtain official recognition by municipal, state, tribal, and federal governments as well as from international bodies.

Taíno organizations have sought to establish their legitimacy through pursuing various attributes of indigenous identity; activities include identifying "authentic" Taíno cultural practices as well as emphasizing particular physical attributes. However, they place special emphasis on authenticating genealogy, developing a sense of community, and claiming rights to specific lands—three "identity markers" that often serve as criteria for official recognition of indigenous groups.[5] By applying these categories to the Taíno movement, we can briefly review its progress and challenges.

Genealogy

Taíno activists believe that indigenous heritage can be established through genetic studies, genealogical research, and a close review of regional history. Recently a biology professor from the University of Puerto Rico at Mayagüez received a $270,000 grant from the National Science Foundation to determine the indigenous ancestry of Puerto Ricans through testing the mitochrondrial DNA inherited through X chromosomes; that is, through maternal lines.[6] Some critics point out that—assuming that indigenous "American" DNA can be distinguished from African or European DNA—biological descent does not necessarily equal cultural affiliation. Indigenous activists have also expressed concern about other agendas that may lie behind funding the collection of their peoples' genetic material.[7] Nonetheless, Taíno activists are hopeful that this study might powerfully refute the extinction thesis and perhaps encourage more Puerto Ricans to identify as Taínos.

Genealogical searches using Puerto Rican archival resources, such as the records of church ceremonies, slave purchases, and town archives, are generally popular among Puerto Ricans, both on the island and in the United States. At least one Taíno organization maintains a genealogical database for its members, while other activists have developed expertise in such research. However, even a well-documented family tree may not definitively indicate the ethnicity of one's ancestors. For example, while a record of Spanish surnames within a family for several hundred years might indicate Spanish ancestry, it could also include *ladino* (hispanicized) indigenous forebears who were adopted—or enslaved—by a Spanish family. People of African descent also carry Spanish surnames: Puerto Rico's first African settlers were free ladinos from Spain, while those held in slavery were baptized with the surnames of their owners.[8] Indians, Africans, and—to the chagrin of church officials—poor whites intermarried and together formed the bulk of the rural population, known as *jíbaros*.[9] In the rural areas people were most often married not by the church but rather by local customs, such as going away together and then setting up housekeeping; in such cases official marriage or birth records would not be helpful in tracing genealogy. Finally, while the island's upper classes have meticulously conserved their family names for generations (thus cementing their claim to land and power), the poorer classes—including slaves, laborers, peónes, and fugitives—frequently changed surnames; such practices cast doubt on the value of most archival records for documenting indigenous descent.[10]

Many Taíno activists also assume that Puerto Ricans with roots in the western mountainous regions are likely to have Taíno ancestry, particularly if those roots stretch back more than two hundred years, as the last Spanish census mentioning indios took place in the region at that time. Conversely, activists are less likely to accept claims of indigenous ancestry from people who come from the coastal sugar cane areas, where African communities predominated. One problem with this assumption is that Indians also hid out from the invaders in the coastal swamplands and nearby islands such as Vieques; meanwhile, Africans also escaped slavery by hiding out in the mountains. Numerous accounts—some written but most documented through oral testimony—tell of the years of *guácaras*, referring to a time before the mid-nineteenth century when thousands of people lived in caves and other inaccessible areas in order to avoid Spanish censuses, taxes, and forced labor.[11] Among other things, these stories indicate that official census records may be of limited value for tracing indigenous descent according to geographic region.

Community

Taíno-identified groups strive to create a sense of community via shared and learned rituals and cultural practices. Their Internet Web sites contain reports of families in the mountainous areas of Puerto Rico and in the diaspora who have consciously (if privately) identified as Taínos for hundreds of years; they claim to have guarded cultural traditions, religious practices, ceremonial regalia, and rare documents and have only recently been making this information public. Regular meetings, retreats, and ceremonies take place, mostly in the United States but also in fairly remote mountain areas of Puerto Rico, where participants are taught elements of Taíno culture such as food, religion, crafts, legends, music, and dance. Current projects include attempts to revive the Taíno (island Arawak) language as part of community building efforts. One organization, the Jatibonicu Taíno Tribe (described in more detail later), examines applications for tribal membership on the basis of a number of criteria, including the individual's own personal ethnic identification, genealogy, family oral history, and willingness to follow tribal regulations. Applicants are also required to submit photographs for tribal leaders to examine. Based on these criteria, applicants may be accepted as either a "blood" or adopted tribal member or may be rejected.

Critics of the Taíno revival point to the difficulty of determining which cultural attributes are indigenous and which are African in origin. They also question the use of phenotypes as proof of indigenousness, which tend to favor lighter skin, straighter hair, and narrower noses over more African features—ignoring the fact that straight hair, for example, could just as easily indicate European heritage. While most Taíno activists are quick to acknowledge that they have African and/or European ancestry, it has long been common in the Caribbean to explain obvious nonwhiteness by claiming Indian rather than African roots. Of course some claims to indigenous ancestry are legitimate—and being a Taíno was assuredly not an advantage under Spanish rule; nonetheless, historic antiblack prejudice may still motivate some people to play down their African heritage. Indeed, although official Puerto Rican cultural policy idealizes and celebrates the presumably "extinct" Taínos through festivals, museums, and cultural preservation, blackness is routinely ignored or minimized.[12]

In the diaspora Puerto Ricans have faced virulent racism in great part because of their African heritage, yet they do not fit culturally or politically into the "white/black" racial construct that dominates U.S. society. Some observers of U.S.-based Taíno groups suggest that identifying themselves as Indians may represent an attempt to resolve their ambiguous racial identity. Ironically, by affirming greater authenticity through claiming direct descent from the first peoples of Borikén, so-called Nuyoricans can also turn the tables on their island-based cousins, who have often disparaged them for not being "real Puerto Ricans."[13] Most writers critical of Taíno activism have focused on the U.S.-based groups, probably because they are more numerous and have put forth the most written materials, especially on the Internet. In fact relatively little information has appeared by or about Puerto Rico–based groups and individuals, apart from announcements of ceremonies and accounts of visits by U.S.-based tribal members. According to some critics, this suggests that it is easier to become accepted as Taíno in the United States than in Puerto Rico.[14] Nonetheless, Taíno-identified activism on the island has benefited from a general interest in indigenous survival and has recently gained some visibility on such issues as environmental and archeological conservation. These groups have not, however, been active in demanding an end to U.S. military occupation and destruction of indigenous sites—most notably in Vieques, where some of the Caribbean's oldest known human remains (over four thousand years old) were discovered.[15]

Land

Two Taíno groups (Jatibonicu and Turabo/Aymaco) identify with and claim direct descent from two of the autonomous divisions that existed in Borikén (Puerto Rico) at the time of the Spanish invasion. The Jatibonicu organization, the leaders of which are based in New Jersey, refers to itself as the tribal government of the island's central mountain region and questions the authenticity of Taíno groups that lack explicit ties to a particular home territory. The New Jersey Band of Jatibonicu Taínos was originally incorporated as the Taíno Intertribal Council, Inc. of New Jersey, a nonprofit educational and cultural organization; it was an associate member of the New Jersey Coalition of American Indians and claimed informal recognition by the state.[16] Since

2001, however, the organization has phased out its identification as an educational/cultural entity and now refers to itself as the United States Regional Taíno Tribal Affairs Office of the Jatibonicu Taíno Tribal Nation of Borikén.[17]

The Turabo/Aymaco leader claims that her family's land in Puerto Rico is part of the original *cacicazgo* (autonomous region) of Turabo. The daughter of Caguax (the last *cacique*, or chief, of Turabo) married a Spaniard who was then given title to much of her land—which has been maintained as part of the family inheritance ever since. As the Turabo/Aymaco leader's claim fits well with official genealogical records, the municipality of Caguas recognized her family as descendants of the Taíno rulers of the Turabo cacicazgo.[18] In accordance with such recognition, the municipality is supposed to consult with them whenever indigenous artifacts or remains are discovered. In fact all Taíno organizations appear greatly concerned with gaining official recognition in all available forums—state, federal, tribal, and international—in order to gain a determining voice regarding the disposition of Taíno material and cultural artifacts. They actively seek representation in native North American and international indigenous initiatives; these include the U.S. National Holiday Petition for Native Americans, the Pan-Tribal Confederacy of Amerindian Tribal Nations, and the campaign calling on the Vatican to revoke the Papal Bull Inter Catera of 1493.[19]

The use of relations to land in affirming indigenous identity leads to the issue of sovereignty claims over that land; such questions inevitably involve political power and the right to determine ownership and use of natural resources. Most Taíno groups prefer to sidestep the issue by stressing that they are more concerned with cultural and spiritual matters and are not political organizations.[20] Nonetheless, references to themselves as the original people of Borikén, as distinct from "settlers of many ethnic origins"—meaning the majority of Puerto Ricans—raises questions as to where they stand regarding the political status of Puerto Rico, a United States colony with an active independence movement.[21] Both critics and more sympathetic observers voice concerns about the potential for divisiveness, particularly since Taíno rhetoric on culture and identity can often appear essentialist and exclusionary. Interestingly, while the Jatibonicu organization is clearly controlled by the New Jersey office, its leaders have recently specified that the "Jatibonicu Taino Tribe of Borikén (Puerto Rico)"—an affiliated group located in Puerto Rico within the historic boundaries of that Taíno cacicazgo—is the official location of the tribe; by contrast, its U.S.-based organizations are merely affiliated "migratory tribal bands." This shift may represent an attempt to meet one of the requirements for federal recognition: "evidence that a substantial portion of the group inhabits a specific area viewed as American Indian and distinct from other populations in the area, and that its members are descendants of a tribe which historically inhabited a specific area."[22]

It is also worth asking if the seemingly greater respect of the Jatibonicu for Washington than for San Juan could be interpreted as supporting U.S. rule over Puerto Rico and as such could be manipulated to the detriment of the anticolonial struggle.[23] Indeed, some leaders have claimed that they are not Puerto Rican but "Taíno Native American"; they have expressed a preference for greater U.S. authority over the island (such as statehood)—possibly in order to gain federal tribal recognition and a tribal reservation in the central island region. Land in Puerto Rico owned or used by people identified as Taínos is often referred to as "sovereign Taíno land," while the Jatibonicu organization calls itself "the government of a sovereign Taíno nation."[24] Such references display vagueness in understanding of the concept of sovereignty, which within the colonial context of Puerto Rico could be quite troubling.

Taíno Survival and History

Undoubtedly there is much to question about the Taíno revival. On the other hand, I would caution against dismissing the entire phenomenon as mere "wannabe-ism." Far too many Puerto Ricans have been told of Indian forebears by their elders for such stories to be easily disregarded. As in the rest of Latin America, the Spanish conquerors of Borikén were nearly all men; with the blessing of the Church, they took Taíno wives and gave them Spanish names. It seems reasonable to assume that those women passed on much of their heritage to their children (as is claimed by the leader of the Turabo group).

Moreover, in Puerto Rico the Cimarrones (elsewhere known as Maroons and as Seminoles) included both Africans and Indians. Together they resisted slavery and colonization and lived outside Spanish control in the more inaccessible mountains and wetlands—including on the island of Vieques, the scene of today's well-known struggle against the U.S. Navy. People of those resistance communities were not counted in the Spanish census, yet they became the ancestors of many Puerto Ricans.[25] As in the case of other peoples such as the Garifuna and Miskitu, we may find more instances of survival in Puerto Rico of indigenous knowledge, customs, and perspectives by looking at the most African communities, especially those with a history of resistance. Thus one unfortunate consequence of privileging nonblackness may be to limit the amount of recoverable Taíno culture and knowledge.

The Spanish census included the category indio until the beginning of the nineteenth century, when all nonwhite free persons were simply lumped together as "free people of color."[26] Various Taíno organizations consider it proof of indigenous survival that immediately after the United States invasion in 1898, sixty-three Puerto Rican youths were sent to the Carlisle Indian School in Pennsylvania, where their "tribe" was listed as "Porto Rican."[27] Yet according to eyewitness accounts they voluntarily enrolled in the hope of studying English and academic subjects (the latter were not offered at this vocational school). Moreover, the accounts made clear that the youths identified themselves as Puerto Ricans and were separated from the Indian students—who had not enrolled voluntarily.[28] Another indication that the Puerto Ricans' attendance at the Carlisle School does not "prove" their Indian identity is that Filipino youths—who were called indios by both Spanish and U.S. colonizers—also attended the Carlisle School. Nonetheless, history appears to point not to the Taínos' extinction but rather to their absorption into what became the Puerto Rican nation. Specific cultural elements may sometimes be traceable to the island's pre-Columbian indigenous societies; more often, however, specifying their origins as indigenous rather than African or European would require considerably more research.

Survival, Sovereignty, and Sustainability

Notwithstanding the concerns raised about the Taíno movement, recovery of indigenous knowledge and perspectives holds tremendous significance for those of us who work for our people's survival and self-determination. The benefits for colonized peoples of reclaiming and affirming a positive, noncolonized identity are well documented; among other things, raising self-esteem is essential for successfully challenging sociopolitical impotence and economic dependence upon the colonizer.[29] Particularly in view of current global ecological and social crises engendered by the prevailing ethics of domination and alienation, recovering the values and practices of indigenous peoples—place-based, community-focused, and oriented toward long-term survival—may be key to our survival. Some writers are convinced that indigenous communities retaining an active link to their place-based knowledge may form the last chain of human defense against the destructive Western principles of alienation of people from land, from other species, and from one another.[30] Moreover, knowledge of and pride in such heritage is a key component of struggles for self-determination, because a positive understanding of their identity may allow people to build enough collective strength to gain control over their future.

The reality of Puerto Rico today is that of a "non-incorporated territory belonging to but not a part of the United States"—in other words, a colony—which is governed largely by statutes that were based on the conquest and subjugation of indigenous "domestic dependent nations" in North America.[31] Puerto Rico's official status as an "associated free state" allows for a limited amount of sovereignty, in deference to its demonstratively distinct identity. Yet whenever its "self-government" conflicts with U.S. governmental or corporate interests, the island's colonial powerlessness and dependence is revealed, often in the most humiliating fashion. Not surprisingly, almost no Puerto Ricans express satisfaction with the current status; however, they remain bitterly divided as to alternatives. At one end of the spectrum are those who argue that full incorporation and inclusion in the United States through statehood will help achieve rights for Puerto Ricans, as part of a racial/ethnic minority; at the other end independence supporters maintain that only complete political independence can satisfy the aspirations of the Puerto Rican nation. Those in the middle—including proponents of an "improved" version of the present status—affirm Puerto Rican national identity but fear the consequences of losing Uncle Sam's "protection." That aspects of this most consuming of all Puerto Rican issues resemble the struggles of Native Americans and Hawaiians (and other indigenous peoples) against being "racialized" out of existence—and for their rights to self-determination as a free people on their own free land—is certainly not coincidental.[32] Seen from this perspective, the efforts of at least some Taíno organizations to win the blessing of the "Great White Father" in order to gain access to the limited "Indian entitlements pot," and perhaps a small reservation back home, could be seen (to quote Taiaiake Alfred) as "agreeing to live as artifacts" in the hope of securing "a limited but perpetual set of rights" that depends on the existing colonial framework.[33]

Fortunately, efforts in Puerto Rico to challenge the dominant and destructive paradigm of alienation and domination—and to recover a more sustainable path based on respect for the land and for one another—are already under way. Nowhere are anticolonial resistance and the search for alternatives more apparent than in the struggle to expel the U.S. military from the Puerto Rican island of Vieques, site of more than four thousand years of continuous human habitation. From 1941 until 2003 the U.S. Navy occupied most of the island; it was also subjected to intensive bombing with conventional explosives and "nonconventional" experimental weapons, such as napalm and "depleted" uranium, with disastrous consequences for the natural environment.[34] Meanwhile, the slightly more than nine thousand inhabitants who remained were enclosed within a long process of economic, social, and environmental strangulation, compounded by rising levels of cancer and other diseases. One might suggest that the navy pursued genocidal policies in order to rid the island of its people, who are the black and brown descendants of Cimarrones and sugar cane workers. The strong attachment of Viequenses to their island is well documented and readily apparent; that this attachment is transmitted through the generations is evidenced by the multigenerational composition of the activism and the commitment of the youth to return permanently to the lands where their ancestors were born.

In 1999 people began to occupy the navy's training range in order to stop the bombing, after a local civilian security guard was killed in a training accident. Two of the leaders of the struggle are brothers from Vieques named Yabureibo and Cacimar: in recognition of the historic continuity of the struggle, the brothers bear the same names as the last Taíno caciques of that island, who lost their lives five hundred years ago fighting Spanish colonialism. Throughout Puerto Rico and in the diaspora Puerto Ricans mobilized to demand justice for Vieques, sending material support for the civil disobedience campaign and joining the Viequenses in continually invading the occupied lands to prevent further bombing. Meanwhile, the Viequenses received technical and legal support without charge from Puerto Rican experts to develop plans for community-controlled and ecologically and socially sustainable rescue and use of the lands that they hope the navy will eventually be forced to clean and return to its rightful inhabitants.

The Vieques struggle has transformed Puerto Rico in profound ways. Threats of arrest and imprisonment—once a fearsomely effective part of the mechanism of colonial control—became badges of honor for the hundreds of Puerto Ricans who served federal court–imposed sentences and thousands more who committed civil disobedience "for the peace of Vieques." In dozens of support groups throughout Puerto Rico, people discussed how to use Vieques as a model for recovering their sense of connection to their own home territories and communities and for throwing off the yoke of dependence. The realization is growing that the struggle against navy occupation was only one chapter in the much longer story and greater challenge of truly liberating Vieques—and Puerto Rico.

We should ask what recovering indigenous identity and consciousness—or, as Chicano/Indigenous writer Roberto Rodríguez puts it, "becoming human"—might contribute toward decolonizing and dewesternizing Puerto Rico.[35] For even if we were to call ourselves Taínos instead of Puerto Ricans, and even if we should gain political independence, such achievements would not necessarily guarantee a sustainable society that properly honored our homeland and one another. We might achieve the outward trappings of recognition and national "sovereignty"; but unless we return to the indigenous values of loving and honoring the earth and our communities—putting their long-term benefit ahead of individual short-term gain—we will not be able to halt the ongoing destruction of our land and our spirit. This is, of course, a tall order, and perhaps not what most Taíno revivalists—nor Puerto Rican independentistas—may have in mind. Yet it is precisely in rising to this challenge that we may begin to realize the possibilities of true sovereignty.

Notes

1. Sources of information for this chapter include Taíno organization Internet Web sites and discussion groups, published books and articles, site visits, and personal conversations with both activists and critics. I am grateful to Joanne Barker and two anonymous reviewers for their helpful comments on an earlier draft.

2. Manuel Aacutelvarez Nazario, *El Influjo Indígena en el Español de Puerto Rico* (Río Piedras: Universidad de Puerto Rico, 1977).

3. Salvador Brau, *Puerto Rico y su Historia*, 2nd ed. (San Juan: Ed. IV Centenario, 1972 [1894]).

4. Arlene Dávila, *Sponsored Identities: Cultural Politics in Puerto Rico* (Philadelphia: Temple University Press, 1997).

5. Various writers have discussed the use of genealogy, community recognition, and relations to land to "define . . . specific tribal populations" (Russell Thornton, "The Demography of Colonialism and "Old" and "New" Native Americans," in *Studying Native America: Problems and Prospects*, ed. Russell Thornton (Madison: University of Wisconsin Press, 1999), 26. Thornton mentions all three criteria (among others), while other writers discuss one or more. See for example M. Annette Jaimes, "Federal Indian Identification Policy: A Usurpation of Indigenous Sovereignty in North America," in *The State of Native America: Genocide, Colonization, and Resistance*, ed. M. Annette Jaimes (Boston: South End Press, 1992) 123–38; Ward Churchill, "The Crucible of American Indian Identity: Native Tradition versus Colonial Imposition in Post-Conquest North America" (*Z Magazine Online*, January 1998, accessed June 2003 at *http://www.zmag.org/ZMag/articles/jan98ward.htm*).

I found these three categories useful for organizing my discussion of efforts by Taíno organizations toward receiving recognition. They were also used by Raymond D. Fogelson in "Perspectives on Native American Identity" (in Thornton, *Studying Native America*, 40–59). However, their use here is not meant as an endorsement of Fogelson's sweeping generalizations about "invented" or "imagined" indigenous identities.

6. Gladys Nieves Ramírez, "Estudia la genética de los boricuas," *El Nuevo Día*, 11 July 1999, reprinted and e-mailed by PRenbreve@aol.com, 11 July 1999; José Fernández Colón, "Estudio podría probar población indígena no fue exterminada," *El Nuevo Día*, 8 January 2000, accessed 8 January 2000 at *http://www.endi.com/ultimahora/jtml/estudio8.html*).

7. Debra Harry, Stephanie Howard, and Brett Lee Sheldon, *Indigenous People, Genes and Genetics: What Indigenous People Should Know about Biocolonialism* (Wadsworth NV: Indigenous Peoples Council on Biocolonialism, 2000).

8. Jalil Sued Badillo, *Puerto Rico Negro* (Río Piedras: Ed. Cultural, 1986).

9. Fernando Picó, *Historia General de Puerto Rico* (Río Piedras: Ed. Huracán, 1986).

10. Juan Manuel Delgado, "Sobrevivencia de los apellidos indígenas según la historia oral de Puerto Rico," *Revista de Genealogía Puertorriqueña* 2, no. 1 (April 2001): 41–80), especially 47–49.

11. Delgado, "Sobrevivencia de los apellidos indígenas," 77.

12. Among many writers who discuss the preference for indigenous Caribbean over African identity, see Gladys Jiménez Muñoz, "The Elusive Signs of African-ness: Race and Representation among Latinas in the United States," *Border/Lines* 29–30 (1993): 9–15); Peter Roberts, "The (Re)construction of the Concept of 'Indio' in the National Identities of Cuba, the Dominican Republic, and Puerto Rico," in *Caribe 2000: Definiciones, Identidades y Culturas Regionales y/o Nacionales*, ed. Lowell Fiet and Janette Becerra (Río Piedras: Universidad de Puerto Rico, 1997), 99–117; Jorge Duany, "Making Indians out of Blacks: The Revitalization of Taíno Identity in Contemporary Puerto Rico," in *Taíno Revival: Critical Perspectives on Puerto Rican Identity and Cultural Politics*, ed. Gabriel Haslip-Viera (New York: Centro de Estudios Puertorriqueños, 1999), 31–55.

13. Miriam Jiménez Román, "The Indians Are Coming! The Indians Are Coming! The Taíno and Puerto Rican Identity," in Haslip-Viera, *Taíno Revival*; Yarimar Bonilla, "The Taíno Native American Movement and the Search for Authenticity," *Boricua*, March–April 2000, 26–31 (accessed April 2000 at http://www.boricua53.com/Tainos/tainos.html).

14. Román, "The Indians Are Coming!" 92.

15. José Javier Pérez, "La Isla Nena: Una frontera arqueológica," *El Nuevo Día*, 14 May 2000.

16. This information comes from Principal Chief Peter Guanikeyu Torres, "Jatibonicu Tribal History," *Taíno Land Review* 1, no. 1 (January 1997, accessed May 2000 at http://www.hartford-hwp.com/taino/revista/revista1–1.html). Interestingly, New Jersey does not recognize all of its own Indians, such as the Ramapough.

17. "New Registration and Tribal Enrollment," letter signed by Peter Guaniel Torres, Director of Tribal Enrollment, dated 3 April 2001. This letter was to be sent to all applicants for enrollment with the Jatibonicu Taíno Tribal Nation of Borikén (Puerto Rico; accessed 15 June 2003 at http://www.taino-tribe.org/enrollment-letter.htm).

18. Oscar Bunker, *Historia de Caguas*, vol. 1 (Caguas: Gobierno Municipal, 1979).

19. For information on the Papal Bulls campaign see the Web site http://bullsburning.itgo.com/Papbull.htm. On the Pan-Tribal Confederacy see http://www.PanTribalConfederacy.com/. On efforts to include Taínos in the petition for a U.S. Native American holiday see http://mytwobeadsworth.freeservers.com/HOLIDAT.html.

20. Arlene Dávila, "Local/Diasporic Taínos: Towards a Cultural Politics of Memory, Reality and Imagery," in Haslip-Viera, *Taíno Revival*, 21.

21. The quoted text is from Peter Guanikeyu Torres, "A letter to the Puerto Rican people: to our good brothers and good friends of Boriken, the letter of November 24, 1970, a vision for the year 2000" (accessed 15 June 2003 at http://www.taino-tribe.org/prl.html).

22. This is one of seven criteria used by the Bureau of Indian Affairs since 1978 as part of its FAP (Federal Acknowledgment Process) to acknowledge that a petitioning entity is an Indian tribe (accessed 15 June 2003 at *Native Net*, http://www.nativenet.uthscsa.edu/archive/nl/9201/0010.html).

23. By contrast, the Turabo/Aymaco leader has criticized such a pro-U.S. statehood stance, and the latter group's Web site does not appear to reject a Puerto Rican identity.

24. "Taíno, the Native American Indians of Borikén (Puerto Rico)," (accessed October 2001 at http://www.500nations.com/Puerto_Rico_Tribes.asp).

25. Jalil Sued Badillo, "Un sueño en Vieques" (Cupey, Puerto Rico, November 1999), unpublished historical essay distributed via e-mail, 17 November 1999.

26. Loída Figueroa, *History of Puerto Rico: From the Beginning to 1892* (New York: Las Americas International Book Center, 1977), 74–75.

27. See Record Group 75 of Carlisle Indian School, Group Record 1327, National Archives, Washington, DC-NARA 75.

28. Luís Muñoz Rivera, "Una visita al Indian School," *Puerto Rican Herald* (New York) 1, no. 10, 14 September 1901; reprinted in *Revista de Genealogía Puertorriqueña* 1, no. 2 (October 2000): 5–7). See also Olga Rodríguez Pérez de Conrad, "Un experimento educacional en nuestra historia," *Revista de Genealogía Puertorriqueña* 1, no. 2 (October 2000): 3–4.

29. The importance of building a positive identity as part of liberation was at the heart of the classic work by Paulo Freire, *The Pedagogy of the Oppressed* (New York: Continuum, 1970). More recent case studies have confirmed his analysis; see for example Laura Pulido, *Environmentalism and Economic Justice: Two Chicano Struggles in the Southwest* (Tucson: University of Arizona Press, 1996).

30. See for example Winona LaDuke, "From Resistance to Regeneration," in *Ecology: Key Concepts in Critical Theory*, ed. Carolyn Merchant (Atlantic Highlands: Humanities Press, 1994), 266–71; Vandana Shiva, *Biopiracy: The Plunder of Nature and Knowledge* (Boston: South End Press, 1997); and Haunani-Kay Trask, *From a Native Daughter: Colonialism and Sovereignty in Hawai'i* (Honolulu: University of Hawai'i Press, 1999), 59.

31. Déborah Berman Santana, "No somos únicos: The status issue from Manila to San Juan," CENTRO 11, no. 1, (Special Issue: 1898–1998): 127–40, see pt. 2, p. 129.

32. Several of the writers in this volume highlight the dangers that portrayal as "minorities" poses to indigenous people; see for example essays by Joanne Barker and J. Kehaulani Kauanui.

33. See Taiaiake Alfred's essay in this volume for a devastating critique of colonial state-sanctioned "sovereignty."

34. Among various articles on the environmental impacts of militarization of Vieques, see Rafael Cruz Pérez, "Contamination Produced by Explosives and Residuals of Explosives in Vieques, Puerto Rico," *Dimensión* (Journal of the Puerto Rican Association of Engineers and Surveyors) 2, no. 8 (January 1988); José Seguinot Barbosa, "Vieques: Ecología de una isla acosada," first published in 1988, reprinted in Seguinot Barbosa, *Geografía, Ecología y Deerecho en Puerto Rico y el Caribe* (San Juan: First Books, 1994).

35. Roberto Rodríguez, *Codex Tamuanchan: On Becoming Human* (Albuquerque: Roberto Rodríguez, 1998).

Contributors

JOANNE BARKER is an enrolled member of the Delaware Tribe of Indians. She earned her Ph.D. in June 2000 from the History of Consciousness Department at the University of California, Santa Cruz, where she specialized in indigenous jurisprudence, women's/gender studies, and cultural studies. She is an assistant professor in the American Indian Studies Department at San Francisco State University. She has been the recipient of the Rockefeller Foundation Humanities Fellowship and the University of California President's Dissertation Year Fellowship. She has published articles in *Inscriptions*, *Wicazo Sa Review*, and *Cultural Studies*.

TAIAIAKE ALFRED (Mohawk) was born in 1964 in the territory of the Mohawk Nation. He was raised in the community of Kahnawà:ke, attended high school in Montréal, and as a young man served in the U.S. Marine Corps infantry. He has a Ph.D. in government from Cornell University and an undergraduate degree in history from Concordia University. He is the author of two books, *Heeding the Voices of Our Ancestors* and *Peace, Power, Righteousness: An Indigenous Manifesto*. Taiaiake is a highly regarded speaker on the history and philosophy of the Iroquois people and is respected as one of Native America's leading scholars. He is a professor in the Faculty of Human and Social Development and the founding director of the Indigenous Governance Program at the University of Victoria. An avid hunter and lacrosse player, he lives in the territory of the Saanich Nation with his wife, Rose.

FIONA CRAM is a Maori (indigenous) woman from Aotearoa–New Zealand. Her tribal affiliations are to Ngati Kahungunu on the east coast of Aotearoa and she is the mother of one son. Fiona has a Ph.D. in social and developmental psychology from the University of Otago and is based within the International Research Institute of Maori and Indigenous Education (IRI) at the University of Auckland. Fiona's research interests are wide-ranging, including Maori health, justice, and education.

GUILLERMO DELGADO-P. is an Andean anthropologist (Oruro, Bolivia) and human rights activist who has written about Indigenous movements in the Americas and about Quechua notions of the sacred. He taught Quechua at the University of Texas, Austin, and has translated Quechua poetry into English. His article "The Internet and Indigenous Texts" is reprinted in P. B. Goodwin's *Global Studies/Latin America* (Guilford CT: Dushkin/McGraw-Hill, 2000). He is the current editor of the *Bolivian Studies Research Review* and is coeditor (with John M. Schechter) of *Quechua Verbal Artistry / Arte Verbal Quechua* (Bonn: Bonner Amerikanistische Studien, 2004). Since 1989, he has taught in the Latin American and Latino Studies Department at the University of California, Santa Cruz.

JOHN BROWN CHILDS is of Massachuset/Brothertown-Oneida/Madagascan descent through his maternal family, the Burrs, and his paternal family, the Childs. He is professor of sociology at the University of California, Santa Cruz. He is author of "Transcommunality, from the Politics of Conversion to the Ethics of Respect: Learning from Indigenous Philosophies," *Social Justice* (Winter 1998), *Leadership, Conflict, and Cooperation in Afro-American Social Thought* (Philadelphia: Temple University Press, 1989), and *Transcommunality: From the Politics of Conversion to the Ethics Of Respect* (Philadelphia: Temple University Press, 2003). He is a member of the Native American Studies Research Cluster at the University of California, Santa Cruz. In 1997 he was recipient of the Fulbright "Thomas Jefferson Chair of Distinguished Teaching" at the University of Utrecht in the Netherlands.

J. KĒHAULANI KAUANUI (Native Hawaiian) is an associate professor of American studies and anthropology at Wesleyan University. She earned her Ph.D. in the program of history of consciousness at the University of California at Santa Cruz. Born and raised in California, she earned her BA in Women's Studies at UC Berkeley in 1992. In 1994–95 she was a Fulbright Fellow in Maori Studies at the University of Auckland in New Zealand. Kauanui has also been awarded a National Science Foundation Minority Predoctoral Fellowship, a Ford Minority Predoctoral Fellowship, a Smithsonian Graduate Fellowship, a Smithsonian Predoctoral Fellowship, a Rockefeller Archive Center Research Grant, and a University of California Pacific Rim Grant. Her work appears in *Amerasia Journal*, *Women's Studies International Forum*, *Social Text*, *Pacific Studies*, and *Contemporary Pacific*. Kauanui has also testified on behalf of Hawaiian communities outside Hawai'i before the Unrepresented Nations and Peoples Organization (1996) and before the President's Advisory Commission on Asian Americans and Pacific Islanders (2000).

DAN TAULAPAPA MCMULLIN is a Samoan American writer, painter, and filmmaker. His 2004 illustrated poetry chapbook, "A Drag Queen Named Pipi" (Honolulu: Tinfish Press), continued a line of work that began with the 1996 performance poem "The Bat" and other early works, which were awarded a 1997 Poets and Writers Award from The Loft. His film, *Sinalela*, received the Best Short Film Award at the 2002 Honolulu Gay and Lesbian Film Festival. He contributed political essays on colonization in American Samoa to *Resistance in Paradise*, winner of the 1999 Gustavus Myers Humanitarian Book Award. In 2005 his first children's book in the Samoan language, *'Olo 'u Igoa 'o Laloifi*, was published in Wellington. Currently he is completing a book of short stories, *The Only Paradise Is Paradise Lost*, and he is developing a film project, *Shark in the Woods*, with producer Merata Mita. In October 2005 Chase Gallery at Bates College presented his first solo exhibit of paintings.

ROBERT J. MILLER (Eastern Shawnee Tribe of Oklahoma) is associate professor at Lewis and Clark Law School in Portland, Oregon, and an appellate judge for the Confederated Tribes of the Grand Ronde Community of Oregon and the Northwest Intertribal Court System. He earned a J.D. in 1991 at Lewis and Clark Law School. He is a board member of the National Indian Child Welfare Association and Oregon Native American Business Entrepreneurial Network.

KILIPAKA KAWAIHONU NAHILI PAE ONTAI is a Kanaka Maoli, born and raised in the Palolo-Kaimuki 'Ahupua'a, on the Island of O'ahu. He serves as a member of the legislature of the Hawaiian Nation, Ka Lahui Hawai'i. He is the author of the Ka Lahui Hawai'i National Economic Plan, adopted by the national legislature, the Mokuna, at its twentieth legislative session. He is a descendant of a line of spiritual kahuna from the Island of Hawai'i. Kilipaka Ontai earned his master's degree from Washington University, St. Louis, and his B.A. from the University of Hawaii, Manoa. He is an urban redevelopment and economic consultant to numerous public and private agencies as well as an architect in private practice. He currently lectures as adjunct professor at the University of California, San Diego, and Springfield College, Springfield, Massachusetts.

MICHAEL P. PEREZ is a Chamorro of Guam born and raised in Southern California. He is currently an associate professor of sociology at California State University, Fullerton, and was an assistant professor at the University of Guam in 1997–98. He earned his Ph.D. in sociology from the University of California, Riverside, in 1997, upon conducting field work on Guam and completing his dissertation, *The Dialectic of Indigenous Identity in the Wake of Colonialism: The Case of Chamorros of Guam*. While at UC Riverside, he was awarded the Distinguished Scholars Fellowship and Dissertation-Year Fellowship. His scholarly interests include racial, ethnic, and indigenous relations, colonialism, identity politics, Pacific Studies, Chamorro identity, and criminalization. His work appears in *Racial and Ethnic Relations* (Salem Press), *Deviant Behavior: An Interdisciplinary Journal*, *Amerasia Journal*, and *Ethnic Studies Review*.

LEONIE PIHAMA is from the *iwi* (tribal groups) Te Atiawa and Ngati Mahanga and is a mother of three. She is a lecturer in Maori Education at the School of Education, University of Auckland, lecturing in the following areas: Kaupapa Maori theory, critical theory, gender and education, Maori women's issues, Maori film and television, and politics of representation. She is the director of the International Research Institute for Maori and Indigenous Education at the University of Auckland and a filmmaker with the Maori women's production company Moko Productions.

DÉBORAH BERMAN SANTANA is a native of Puerto Rico (Boricua) and her family's first high school graduate; Santana earned her Ph.D. in geography at the University of California, Berkeley. Her book *Kicking Off the Bootstraps: Environment, Development, and Community Power in Puerto Rico* (University of Arizona Press) won the CHOICE Award for outstanding academic books of 1997. Currently a professor in the Ethnic Studies Department of Mills College (Oakland CA), she teaches courses that explore the effects of racism and colonialism on economic, political, and environmental issues in Latin America and the Third World as well as for communities of color in the United States. She is a long-time community activist in Puerto Rico and the United States. Her recent publications reflect her interests in reviving indigenous perspectives on social and human-environment relations as an alternative to the destructive dominant paradigm. She also serves as adviser on military and environmental issues to the Committee for the Rescue and Development of Vieques.

Index

CPSIA information can be obtained at www.ICGtesting.com
Printed in the USA
BVOW04s0602240414

351525BV00004B/7/P

9 780803 262515